Laughter is the Best Medicine

Laughter is the Best Medicine

MY AUTOBIOGRAPHY

JIMMY TARBUCK

WITH IAN GITTINS

EBURY
SPOTLIGHT

EBURY SPOTLIGHT

UK | USA | Canada | Ireland | Australia
India | New Zealand | South Africa

Ebury Spotlight is part of the Penguin Random House group of companies
whose addresses can be found at global.penguinrandomhouse.com

Penguin Random House UK
One Embassy Gardens, 8 Viaduct Gardens, London SW11 7BW

penguin.co.uk
global.penguinrandomhouse.com

Penguin
Random House
UK

First published by Ebury Spotlight in 2025

1

Typeset by seagull.net

Printed and bound by CPI (UK) Ltd, Croydon CR0 4YY

The authorised representative in the EEA is Penguin Random House Ireland, Morrison
Chambers, 32 Nassau Street, Dublin D02 YH68.

A CIP catalogue record for this book is available from the British Library

ISBN 9781529970678

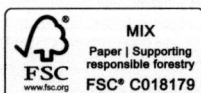

For Tom Jones
who introduced me to Elvis Presley

CONTENTS

The last of the dinosaurs

It wasn't that long ago that my son, James, suggested making a documentary about my life. I was up for that. He's a talented lad who runs a production company and, I mean, if someone is going to tell your story, and try to get to the heart of you and what you're all about, who could do it better than your own flesh and blood? 'OK,' I said.

But then James told me the title that he had in mind.

The Last of the Dinosaurs.

Well, I can't say I was that chuffed, at first. In fact, I thought something along the lines of *You cheeky bugger!* I didn't just think it – I said it! But then, when I'd calmed down a bit, stopped spluttering, and removed my boot from James's backside, I thought about it, and I realised:

You know what? He might just have a point.

Because I've been doing what I love for a very long time now. More than sixty years. And that thing is making people laugh. It's what I've wanted to do ever since I was a nipper in Liverpool: to get noticed, and to make people laugh. It's true what they say: laughter is the best medicine. I've always sworn by it.

Mind you, it got me in trouble as a kid. God knows how many times I got the cane in school for piping up with a one-liner in class just to get everyone going. Especially when I was being taught by Jesuit priests. They were a bit short on chuckles, that lot (which was why they kicked me out).

When I became known, in the early sixties, I suppose I was part of a new wave of British comedians and performers. We were what you might call family entertainers: comics who would walk onstage and have the crowd falling about, and who'd do it without effing and blinding.

Now, I'm not saying I never swear. You should hear me on the golf course when I miss a four-foot putt! But there's a time and a place for it and I don't think it's onstage. And I was fortunate enough to come up alongside, and become close mates with, a generation of entertainers who all felt the same.

I'm talking about Bruce Forsyth, who helped me when I got my first big break on telly. I'm on about the great Eric Morecambe and Tommy Cooper (ah, Tommy, who must be the most impersonated comic of all time!). I'm remembering good old Ronnie Corbett and Kenny 'Kipper' Lynch, two of my best mates in showbiz.

I'm going to talk a lot about all of those guys in this book. But you know what else they've got in common? Sadly, they're all no longer with us. I'm the only one of us left standing. So, maybe James is right after all. Maybe I *am* the last of the dinosaurs.

I made my name at the London Palladium, when I began hosting the biggest show on British TV when I was still a newcomer. Suddenly, I was on every telly in the country, every Sunday night, introducing superstars like Judy Garland, Liza Minnelli, Rudolf Nureyev, Roy Orbison … oh, and my old mucker from the Cavern Club, Cilla Black.

The Palladium show got me known and that took me places. It took me to America, where I, somehow, found myself onstage performing with Bob Hope, chatting to Elvis in Vegas, and chinwagging with Sinatra in Miami. Which, let's face it, was pretty mad for a gap-toothed tatty 'ead from Liverpool.

Sometimes, life comes full circle. In 2024, sixty years after I first hosted shows at the Palladium, I was back there. Barry Manilow, one of the biggest stars in the world, was doing two weeks there on his farewell tour, and asked old Tarby here to open for him.

Well, it was an honour and a pleasure. I loved it. All through my life, I've always been at my happiest onstage, firing out gags, getting my fix of the drug of laughter. Making people roar. Saying stuff to the crowd that you have to be a right cheeky sod to get away with. Stuff like this:

'Nice to see you, luv. Thanks for getting dolled up and coming out. How old are … no, I won't ask you that. You should never ask a lady her age.'

Pause.

'So, how much do you weigh?'

Mind you, sometimes the laugh is on me nowadays. I was back in Liverpool recently and walking down the street when I overheard two young women having this conversation:

'Look, over there! That's Jimmy Tarbuck!'

'Oo's 'e?'

'Liza's dad!'

I've had sixty years at the top of the comedy tree, and an amazing life. But I'm not getting any younger: as I write this, I'm eighty-five years old. I want to get it all down before I go – or before I go extinct, as James would probably say! So, sit yourself down, and let me tell you about a life spent in pursuit of the best medicine: laughter.

A life that began, as everybody knows, in Liverpool.

CHAPTER 1

Dan Dare is from Liverpool

It's surprising how many comedians are serious people. Sad, even. You laugh your head off at them onstage or on the telly, then you come to read their autobiography and find out they've led a really unhappy life. Their book reads like one of those – what do they call them? – misery memoirs.

Well, I'm afraid there'll be none of that in these pages. If that's what you're after, you'll have to look elsewhere. Like everybody, I've had my ups and downs in life, and I'll talk about both, but I've always tried to keep a smile on my face. I've always tried to look on the bright side. And it helped that I had a very happy childhood.

There was no misery in my childhood … but plenty of horse-racing. My grandad, Jim Tarbuck, was a big book-maker in Liverpool. He also sometimes appeared in stage shows as a Pierrot: a clown. He was in a show on the Isle of Man when he first met my nan, Alice. She was working as a waitress.

My dad, Joseph Frederick Tarbuck – but most people called him Fred – followed his father into the bookmaking business and worked alongside him at an office and betting shop on London Road in the city centre. And, funnily enough, it was the gee-gees that brought my mum and dad together.

My mum, Ada McLoughlin (but *she* always went as Fanny), was a chorus girl. She sang and danced in Tiller Girls-style line-ups in theatre and cabaret revues. One day, she and her mates in one of the shows decided to let their hair down and go and have a day out at the races at Aintree.

My old man used to work as a bookmaker at the race-courses and he took a bet off her. He was a bit of a charmer and he started chatting her up. 'Let's take a black hair from your head and wrap it around a white fiver,' he suggested. 'And then we'll put it on the favourite.'

My mum wasn't having that. 'I don't want to bet on the favourite,' she replied. 'I like Mr Blue.' So they put the bet on Mr Blue, who won at 10–1. And £50 was *serious* money in those days. My dad gave her the winnings, asked her out and they started courting.

Mum already had two kids when she met my dad. When she was very young, she had a son, Kenneth, by a man who was never mentioned. Then she'd married a guy named Hannagan and they'd had a daughter, Norma. That had ended in divorce and so Mum was living with her own mum and raising the two kids.

Mum came from a huge family. The McLoughlins were well known, and even a bit feared, in Liverpool. People were careful around them. They weren't a criminal family, not quite, but they knew how to look after themselves and people didn't mess with them. There were a few hard cases in the family.

But they were always great with me. I never met my grandad, who died young, but he was a mail driver in Northern Ireland when the mail was still pulled by horses. He'd moved to Liverpool when he met my Grandma McLoughlin, who was lovely. They had Mum and four other kids: my Auntie Mary, Auntie Nora, Uncle Jimmy and Uncle Joe.

My mum and dad, with Kenneth and Norma, set up home in Wavertree, which was – and still is – a nice suburb of Liverpool. By everyone's account, they were a happy family unit and it grew a big bigger when my mum got pregnant and had a little boy. Mum and Dad called him Freddie.

Poor Freddie was to have a tragic life. The little lad was only eighteen months old when he caught pneumonia and died. Mum and Dad were devastated. It broke Dad's heart: Freddie was his first-born. When I was a lad, we always marked Freddie's birthdays and the anniversaries of his death.

Yours truly came along on 6 February 1940. I was born in Sefton General Hospital, Liverpool, and christened James Joseph Tarbuck. I was a war baby, because the Second World War had kicked off by then, and I got named after a member of the family that I never met, one of the millions of victims of the war – Uncle Jim, my dad's brother.

Private Officer Jim Tarbuck was a Spitfire pilot who got shot down in an air battle over Malta. He was picked up out of the sea by an MTB, a motor torpedo boat, but died from his wounds. Dad loved his brother to bits and was devastated by his death. Uncle Jim was buried in Malta. Dad went to his grave a lot over the years.

* * *

Although I was a war baby, I was too young to remember a lot about the war. I dimly recall going in air-raid shelters like funny tin sheds. The Nazis bombed the centre of Liverpool and the docks, but our bit of town got off lightly. Dad was an air-raid warden, taking his turn up on the roofs, looking out for the Luftwaffe.

My brother, Kenneth, was eighteen years older than me and I didn't meet him until I was six because he'd signed up for the Army as soon as the war started. He was stationed in the Middle East with my uncle, my mum's brother, Joe McLoughlin. Joe did his best to look after him and sent my mum letters to tell her that Kenneth was OK.

One time, Joe wrote to my mum: 'Kenneth is fine. He's taking ammunition up to the front line.' When I re-read that letter, years later, it made me think to myself: *Bloody hell! Taking ammunition to the front line? That doesn't sound fine to me!*

Mum got a telegram from the Army in 1945. It looked like one of those that usually said: 'We're sorry to report that your son has been killed in battle.' She was so scared that she didn't dare open it. My dad had to take charge and tell her, 'Come on, we have to read it. See what it says.'

My mum opened it. It said: 'Your son is on his way back to Britain. His troop ship will dock in Liverpool at noon tomorrow.'

Mum was on the quayside waiting at 9am. When the ship pulled in, she saw Kenneth on the deck and waved to him. He waved back. Just imagine the relief, and joy, she must have felt.

When they got home and came in the door, Mum just said, 'Jimmy, this is your brother, Kenneth.' And there he was, twenty-four years old, in his Army uniform. I was wary at first and Kenneth and I never got super-close because of the age gap. It took me a while to get to know him. He was a quiet guy but he was a very nice feller.

Kenneth moved back in with us. He began work as a long-distance lorry driver. I never asked him about his time in the Army until one day, in my early teens, I just said, 'What was the war like, Kenneth?'

He looked at me: 'Do you really want to know?' he asked.

'Yes, please.' So, he sat down with me and told me about it.

'Look, it wasn't very nice,' he said. 'The camaraderie between the lads was really good. But you made friends with these great guys – and then you'd wake up in the morning and some of them just weren't there any more. They'd be gone.'

But he said that even war had its funny moments. Kenneth told me that one day, his battalion was taking ammunition to the front when German planes swooped in and began bombing them. The British troops jumped off the trucks and ran for it. They found caves and legged it in there to hide.

The soldiers were sitting in darkness. As the noise of the Messerschmitts receded, someone asked: 'Anybody got a light?' One of them lit a match … only to see the walls and floors of the cave crawling with massive spiders. Kenneth said that the squaddies screamed, and ran outside to take their chances with the German bombs.

* * *

I'm told that, as an infant, I was very happy. Well, I had every reason to be. I got a lot of love showered on me. I know a lot of it was what my brother, Freddie, would have got if he hadn't died. My mum was always hugging me. So was my dad, which was brilliant, really, because a lot of men of his generation didn't do that.

Like everybody, we had ration books for years after the war, but my parents always made sure we had food on the table. We didn't go short of much. Sometimes, if a guy from the docks had a bet with my dad and he couldn't pay, Dad might say, 'OK, give me a crate of oranges instead.' That sort of thing went on for years.

Dad was a kind, polite man and very well dressed. He wore beautiful suits. If a funeral went by in the street, he' d stop and raise his hat. Dad was what you'd call an alehouse comic: if he was out with pals for the night, he'd get up and tell a joke, or get a sing-song going. He loved making people laugh.

Dad was well connected in Liverpool. He went to school with Ted Ray, the comedian, and they kept in touch throughout his life. In later years, when I'd broken into showbiz, every time I bumped into Ted – a very good comic – he'd ask, 'How's Fred? Say hello to him for me.'

Another of Dad's best mates was Dixie Dean. Dixie was the world-famous footballer who scored sixty goals for

Everton in one season. That record will never be broken: not even by Erling Haaland! My dad was such a close pal of Dixie that he's even in a book that was written about him.

Dad also knocked around with a great boxer named Nel Tarleton. Nel was amazing – he only had one lung but he twice fought for the world featherweight championship, and he held the British featherweight title until he was forty. Dad used to go everywhere to watch him fight. To me, he was just Uncle Nel.

I was very close to my sister, Norma. Her friends would come round to our house and she'd let me play in the garden with them. Norma looked after me and fought my battles for me. When I was about six, we were in a local park, Calderstones Park. I fell in the lake and Norma waded in and pulled me out. It was just as well she did. I couldn't swim.

A happy home life gives you confidence as a kid. I was a cheery little chap. Starting school didn't faze me. I went to a kindergarten and then, when I was five, to Dovedale Primary School, round the corner from our house. It was fun. Drawing with crayons and running around the playground? No complaints from me there!

We moved house a short distance to Allerton Road and then, when I was about seven, to Queens Drive – basically the ring road around Liverpool – in an area called Mossley Hill. I was to live there for the rest of my time in Liverpool. That's the house I think about when I look back on growing up in the city.

Mossley Hill was a nice bit of town. We'd gone up in the world because we had a lounge. Mum and Dad put a piano in it, and one of Mum's friends, Mrs Cole, used to play it when she came round. She was really good. I always used to ask her to play 'The Laughing Policeman'.

We were just around the corner from Penny Lane, later made famous by the Beatles song. In fact, Brian Epstein, their manager, lived further up our street – not that I knew him as a kid. We got a dog, Kip. Kip was a bit of this and a bit of that, a mongrel, and I loved him. I walked him up and down Queens Drive every day.

Penny Lane had a great chip shop. In fact, there were four or five chippies near us. My favourite nights were the ones when Dad would get home from the office and say, 'Let's have fish and chips tonight, Fanny.' *Yes, please!* Our Norma would jump on her bike and go pedalling off to get them.

Norma was great. She looked out for me. I remember our mum going on a trip to Ireland and coming back with a pair of white ice skates for her. Norma loved skating and she just adored those skates.* She took me to the rink with her once in Old Swan, just out of Liverpool. I was useless. Just kept falling all over the place.

We had two Jewish sisters living next door. They were lovely people. My mum and dad went to one of their weddings. I felt so proud when I saw them all dressed up. There were six synagogues in Liverpool in those days, and loads of Catholic and Protestant churches (when the new Catholic cathedral was later built, in the 1960s, the locals quickly nicknamed it 'Paddy's wigwam').

---

* When Norma got those skates, I used to call her 'Sonja Henie', after the great Olympic skating gold medallist. That made her laugh.

We lived near a picture house, the Plaza, and I'd go to the kids' matinees on Saturday mornings. They were a right laugh. I'd see Buster Crabbe – the former Olympic swimmer – as Tarzan, and as Flash Gordon battling Ming the Merciless. It'd be madness in the cinema. Kids shouting and running about, high on sweets and fizzy pop.

One poor old doorman was supposed to look after us all. He had no chance! There was a fishpond right outside the pictures. I saw him get shoved in there a few times. After the films, we'd be up the nearby back entries, climbing fences and stealing apples from the trees in people's gardens.

I got caught nicking apples once, from a local allotment. The police turned up, marched me home and told my old man what I'd been up to. After the cops had gone, he gave me a belt round the ear. 'That's not for stealing apples,' he told me. 'It's for getting caught.' That was Dad for you.

Family holidays were brilliant. Sometimes we'd go to Blackpool to see the lights but mainly we went to the Isle of Man, because my Grandma McLoughlin was over there. The ferry from Liverpool to Douglas took five hours but was a thrill for a nipper. I remember how excited I felt the first time that we sailed over.

On that first visit, I couldn't believe my eyes when we got off the boat and I saw horses pulling trams down the street. *What?!* 'Mum! Dad! Norma! Come and look at this!' I thought I'd never seen anything so funny in my life. I was laughing my head off. What do they say? Simple things please simple minds.

My dad charmed the Isle of Man fishermen into taking us out on the boats with them. They'd be having an ale and he'd get them a small whisky chaser. They loved him for that. We'd go out on the boats and try to catch herring. They'd let us have a couple to take home for our tea.

We did a sad trip to the Isle of Man when Grandma McLoughlin died. Mum was really upset and Dad booked us all on a Dakota plane. Mum dressed us in black and we flew over for the funeral. It was only a half-hour flight, but what an adventure! Apart from servicemen, *nobody* flew in those days.

I'd get half a crown a week pocket money: two shillings and sixpence (12½p in decimal). Every week without fail, as soon as I'd got it, it'd go on sweets. There'd be nothing left over for toys, so I'd generally have to wait until my birthday or Christmas.

Christmas Day was great in our house. Very jolly. There'd be a few uncles, aunties and cousins hanging around. Dad would get a couple of bottles of Scotch out for the blokes, and gin for the ladies (no wonder our house was popular at Christmas). And we'd open the presents.

Dad bought me my first bike. And it was pretty flash. It wasn't a standard-issue BSA or Raleigh; a well-known local bicycle manufacturer, Jim Fothergill, made the light alloy frame and built me a lovely racing bike from scratch. It was my pride and joy. I used to go everywhere on it.*

* * *

---

* A few years later, Dad bought me an air rifle for Christmas. A few windows got broken in our area, and it wasn't hard for the neighbours to identify the culprit: 'It's Tarbuck! He's the only boy who's got a gun!'

By the time I was nine or so, I was well settled into Dovedale Primary School. I liked it. What kind of pupil was I? A mischievous little sod, always on the look-out for a chance to cheek the teacher and make my pals laugh. If I found a lesson interesting, I'd work hard. If I didn't, I wouldn't bother.

I spent a fair bit of time in detention, normally for shooting my mouth off. One day I played truant, and when I went in the next morning, the teacher said, 'Tarbuck, you should have been here yesterday.'

'Why, what happened?' I asked. I had to stay behind after school, but it was worth it for the roar that it got.

A couple of fellow pupils at Dovedale Primary were to become very well known – well, a bit more than that! They became two of the most famous people in the world. And that was because they happened to be in a band called The Beatles.

George Harrison was a couple of years below me and he was a very quiet feller. Well, he *did* always get called 'The Quiet One', didn't he? His dad was a bus driver. It's funny how The Beatles have a reputation as a working-class Liverpool band, but only two of them were properly working class: George and Ringo.

George didn't say a lot, but the other future Beatle at Dovedale Primary certainly did. And that was John Lennon.

I lived really near to John, so I'd bump into him all the time around our way. He famously lived with his auntie, Mimi, in a very nice semi-detached house on Menlove Avenue. I suppose it might have seemed an unusual arrangement to outsiders, but who cares? John was loved and, like me, had a pretty well-off, comfortable life.

I got on great with John. He was just a normal Liverpool lad. I remember acting daft with him and running around the playground playing football and shouting. He wasn't a sit-in-the-corner like George: if anything kicked off at school, John would be in the middle of it. As would I.

John sat two desks away from me in class. He used to take the piss out of me, which I liked. It made me laugh. He was a proper acerbic character, very sarcastic, and always ready with a quip. I remember one time the headmaster, 'Pop' Evans, came into our class during a maths lesson.*

'So, Lennon,' the head said, 'I hear that you're good at sums. Can you answer a question for me?'

'Yes, sir.'

'If I had five half-crowns in one trouser pocket, and three half-crowns in the other, what would I have?'

'You'd have Tarbuck's trousers on, sir!'

I think even the head laughed at that one.

I remember once hanging out with John on the Isle of Man. I was there on holiday with my family, and Dovedale Primary had organised a trip for some kids in the big school holiday. We were staying in a lovely hotel on Douglas prom but I asked my mum and dad if I could join up with my schoolmates.

I had a good time on the beach with my pals, but when I went to crash out with them that night, they were all sleeping on the floor in a school, on sacks full of straw. Then a teacher picked me to stuff some extra, empty sacks with straw. I thought, *Huh! Bugger this!* and pissed off back to the nice hotel.

---

* Or *doing sums*, as we used to call it.

In the evenings on that holiday, Mum and Dad would take Norma and me to the shows at the Villa Marina. We'd see a comic called Jimmy Charters. I watched him closely every night and what he was doing; the way he made people laugh fascinated me. I didn't understand the jokes. I just loved the laughter.

One evening, I went with my dad to a pub in Douglas for a game of bowls. Jimmy was having a drink in there. I went right up to him and told him one of his own jokes that he told onstage. Jimmy looked surprised, laughed, and said, 'Oi! Don't go stealing my gags, you young bugger!'

Other nights at the Villa Marina, I saw Joe Loss and his orchestra. They had a beautiful singer with them, Elizabeth Batey, and I got a crush on her. One night, Elizabeth saw me staring at her, doe-eyed. She was lovely. 'Where's your mum?' she asked. 'Does she work here?'

'No,' I said, blushing. 'I'm on holiday.'

Back in Liverpool, in March 1949, the whole of Dovedale School got taken to see the Queen – still Princess Elizabeth then – officially open part of Liverpool Anglican Cathedral. We saw her get driven past in her car. She was very young. Three years later, on my twelfth birthday, her father died and she became Queen while on a royal visit to Kenya.

* * *

It was around now that I began a passionate love affair. 'Bloody hell! A bit young, weren't you, Tarby?' you might say. But this was dead innocent. I've been in love with two sports for my entire life. One is golf – and you'll hear plenty about that later, believe you me. The other, and the one I fell for as a lad, is football.

You had two teams to choose from: Liverpool or Everton. My dad was a mad Evertonian, which was how he got to be such big mates with Dixie Dean. I chose the other path. My dad took me with some of his fellow Everton-supporting mates to see Everton play Liverpool. A striker called Billy Liddell smashed a goal in for Liverpool, and I jumped out of my seat.

'Yes! Get in!' I yelled.

My dad's mates looked at me askance. 'Bloody hell, Fred,' one of them said. 'The little bastard's a Red!'

I *was* a Red and it was all down to Billy Liddell. He was a Scotsman who'd been in the RAF in the war and he was a winger or centre-forward who used to bang in the goals week after week. He was a great player. Liverpool fans idolised him. When he retired, 40,000 people went to his testimonial at Anfield.

Dad started taking me to Liverpool matches. We'd get there early and he'd vanish into the supporters' club with his mates for a pint. He'd leave me in the door of the club with a bottle of lemonade and a packet of crisps. If he had a second pint, he'd bring me another bottle of lemonade.

When we got to Anfield, I'd often see Billy Liddell driving up to the ground and parking in his little Hillman Minx (I'm not sure you'd spot Mo Salah doing that nowadays!). It was a thrill, but I never once dared go up to Billy and ask him for his autograph. I was too much in awe of him.

My dad took me to London for the 1950 FA Cup Final between Liverpool and Arsenal. We went down on the train: I can still remember Mum saying, 'Look after him, Fred!' as we left the house. I couldn't have been more excited as we saw Wembley's Twin Towers, but the game didn't go well. Arsenal won 2–0.

I was gutted. In tears. I was trying to make sense of this tragedy on the train home. 'Why didn't Billy Liddell score, Dad?' I asked.

'One reason,' he told me. 'A feller on the Arsenal team called Alex Forbes kicked him early on and put him out of the game.'

Years and years later, I met Alex Forbes at some do or other. 'Can I ask you something?' I said.

'Well, I know what you're going to ask,' Alex replied. 'And, yes, I *did* kick him.'

I was football mad. I was lucky that our house at Queens Drive had a playing field right behind it. It had a running track for athletics meetings, a baseball pitch and – far more important – a football pitch. Every afternoon after school I'd be out there with my mates, playing till teatime. Getting our kicks in.

I was still a young lad but I was a *wanderer*. From an early age, my parents didn't mind me going off on my own, and I'd take off around Liverpool any time that I felt like it. One day, when I was about ten, I got on a bus and turned up at my Grandma Tarbuck's house, right on the other side of the city. She was very surprised to see me and phoned Dad at his office: 'Fred, your Jimmy's here!'

'Huh? How did he get there?' Dad asked.

'I've no idea,' Nan said. 'I'll go and ask him.' But when she came to find me, I'd taken off again. She got back on the phone: 'Fred! He's gone!'

'Ah, don't worry!' My dad laughed. 'He'll turn up.'

Another time, I went missing from school – which, as I'll explain, I used to do every now and then – and went into the city centre. I phoned home from a callbox. Dad answered. 'Where are you now?' he asked.

'I'm in town,' I said.

'Whereabouts?'

'By the fat lady.'

'The fat lady? What the hell's that?' he asked.

It was the statue of Queen Victoria.

Another of my solo wanderings took me to Sefton Park. There was – still is – a beautiful bronze statue of Peter Pan there. I took it upon myself to climb up it, slipped, fell off, landed on my head and cracked my skull open. I spent two days in hospital, which was really boring. I was relieved when the doctors let my mum take me home.

I had another spell in hospital when I had a lump cut out of my neck. It was something to do with my glands. I had it done in quite a plush hospital called Gateacre Grange. I wasn't scared because I didn't really know what was going on. And I liked that I got time off school while it healed.

* * *

My dad used to go to race meetings for his work and he started taking me with him. We'd just go to Aintree at first, but then he started taking me all around the country: Haydock Park, Epsom, Lingfield. We'd go at weekends and in my school holidays. I'd look forward to it because it was dead exciting.

Dad loved the racing business and he knew everybody: jockeys, trainers, the lot. He even knew all that tic-tac business, where bookies stood on a crate and flailed their arms about to communicate with other bookies and make sure their odds weren't too different. They looked to me like they were trying to guide an invisible aeroplane in to land.

I was a real go-getter at the racecourse. I must have been, because my dad was always saying, 'Go get us a sandwich, Jimmy.' Important work! The bookies would give me the odd quid, and I got to know a few of the jockeys. They'd sometimes give me a tip.

'How are you, young Tarbuck?' they'd ask me.

'Fine,' I'd reply.

And they'd give me a wink: 'You know, I *might* just win this next race.' And when they said that, they invariably did.

Because Dad used to drink in a couple of pubs down by the docks, he knew a few sailors. One of them used to sail to New York and he'd bring back American comics like *Superman* and *Batman* that Dad would buy off him and give to me. I thought they were great: yonks ahead of British comics like the *Beano* and the *Dandy*.

Then I used to get the *Eagle* when that came out. I loved reading about Dan Dare. I stood up in class at school one day and said, 'Sir, do you know that Dan Dare is from Liverpool?'

'Eh?' the teacher said. 'Why do you say that, Tarbuck?'

'When everyone sees him, they go, "Hello, Dare!"' The class roared at that one.

I loved comics and, on TV, I loved Laurel and Hardy. I thought they were hilarious and I was glued to their films whenever they were on. I'd impersonate them: '*That's another fine mess you've got me into!*' Then, one day when I was about eleven, I got home from school and Mum said three immortal words: 'Wash your knees!'

'Eh? What for?'

'Your dad's taking you out.'

I put my best shirt and shorts on and we set off. Dad wouldn't tell me where we were going. We fetched up at the Liverpool Empire, went in, and had seats on the end of a row. The theatre was packed. We sat and waited … then the lights went down, that famous theme music started up, and *there they were*, right in front of me. The fat one and the thin one. In their bowler hats.

'Dad!' I shouted. 'Dad! It's Laurel and Hardy!'

I couldn't control my excitement. I jumped up and ran down to the front of the theatre. I leaned on the orchestra pit wall and, as Oliver Hardy stared at me, I yelled, 'Hello!'

Hardy paused, with perfect comic timing, then replied: 'Hiya, kid! Are you enjoying it? Good!'

It was too much to take in. I ran back to my seat: 'Dad! He spoke to me!' I said. I could see that my dad had tears in his eyes.

'You look so happy, son!' he said. And, my God, I certainly was.

A couple of years later, Dad took me to see Bob Hope at the same theatre. It blew me away. I admired the way Bob strolled on with total style, looking like a million dollars, and talked to people in the audience as if he knew them: 'And how are *you* tonight, sir?' I loved just how stylish Bob was. The teenage me gazed at him and had one thought:

It must be great to do that.

* * *

At the end of junior school, like every other kid back then, I had to take the eleven-plus exam. Unlike some other kids, I failed it. If I'd passed, I would have gone to a public school, Liverpool College. Dad had gone there, but he didn't give me a hard time for not getting in. Mum and Dad weren't pushy like that.

If I'm honest, I was glad that I wasn't going to Liverpool College. The kids there had to wear straw boaters in the summer. We Dovedale kids used to snatch them off their heads and dent them. We were little buggers. But I soon realised that the place I was going to instead was even worse.

It was called St Francis Xavier School, or SFX, and the teachers were Jesuit priests. They were strict, and cruel, and I hated them. The priests threw religion at us non-stop and ruled by fear. You knew that if you did anything wrong in class, or stepped out of line in any way, you were for it.

We had to learn Latin at SFX. It did my bloody head in: *When am I ever going to use Latin in Liverpool?* All I remember about it now is *amo, amas, amat.* I couldn't get to grips with it, and I didn't want to. This meant that I'd frequently get sent off to the headmaster's office to be punished.

Actually, hang on, I *do* remember one more word of Latin: *ferula*. That means *cane*, and it was a whalebone stick encased in leather. The head and the priests used to beat the kids with it, on the hand or the arse, all the time. I hated SFX so much that I soon started skagging off, as we called it.

Mum and Dad didn't know. I'd put my uniform on and pick my satchel up in the morning, then go into town and mooch about. 'How was school?' Dad might ask when I got home that afternoon. 'Oh, fine,' I'd say. Sometimes, I'd hide my swimming trunks and a towel in my school bag and spend the day at Woolton Baths.

On one visit I swam a length and smacked my mouth into the end of the pool. It knocked one of my front teeth out. It hurt, and we went to the dentist, but the work to correct it would have been complicated. I wasn't bothered about missing a tooth so we left it as it was.*

One day it all went tits-up at Woolton Baths. I was in the pool when the whole of my school turned up for their swimming gala. *Yikes!* The priests were doing a head-count so I climbed out of the water and joined the end of the row of pupils lined up by the side. The teacher, Father Burns, walked down the line, marking off the names:

'Edwards. Johnson. Rogers. Smith. Tarbuck ...'

He stopped dead.

---

* And 'the gap-toothed comedian' was born!

'*Tarbuck?* You haven't been in school for four days! What are *you* doing here?'

'Er, swimming, sir?'

So that was another appointment with the *ferula* back at school. I'd had enough. The next time I was sent for a caning for not conjugating – whatever that bloody means – my Latin properly, I decided I wasn't going to take it any more.

A teacher called Mr McCann was holding the *ferula* on one side of a big desk and I was on the other. 'You again, Tarbuck?' he said. 'You're still not learning your Latin. Do you think you can make fools of us?' He started walking round to my side of the table. So I started walking round to his.

'Stand still, boy!'

'No!'

We did two laps of the desk, him waving the *ferula* menacingly at me. There were French windows open at the far end of the room so I ran off into the garden. McCann was an old guy so he couldn't catch me, but one of the really nasty priests collared me. He took me back in and they gave me a proper caning. Cut my back open.

When I went home that afternoon, they gave me a letter to take to my dad. I told him about being thrashed with the *ferula*.

'Did they hurt you?' he asked.

'Yeah.'

'Well, you're not going *there* any more, then,' he said. 'I've never liked those bloody priests.'

He opened the letter, and read it.

'Oh, they've expelled you, anyway!'*

* * *

So that was the end of SFX, thank God. Once they'd kicked me out, I went to Morrison Secondary Modern in Rose Lane, round the corner from our house in Queens Drive. This was loads better. The school had great swimming, football and basketball facilities, which made it alright in my book.

I didn't like the head, Mr Shepherd, a very cold man, but some of the teachers were OK. I was still a cheeky sod but it was the same story – I'd work if I found the topic interesting. My favourite lessons were English and history. I loved learning about adventurers like Sir Francis Drake, sailing off to the Americas.

I wasn't being taught by nutty Jesuit priests any more but I still got into trouble now and then. Back in those days, kids used fountain pens in school. One day, we were all supposed to be writing essays, but I was bored. Sitting near me, a lad named Williams was working hard, so I dipped a piece of blotting paper in my inkwell, bent my ruler back and flicked it at him.

Splat! Direct hit! Ink went all over his paper. Williams was furious and stuck his hand in the air. 'Sir! Sir!'

'Yes, boy?' asked the teacher.

---

* The weird thing was, SFX later asked me to play for their old boys' football team. I did, as well. And I was better than most of their players.

'Sir, Tarbuck did this!' He waved his messed-up essay in the air.

'Oh, really?' said the teacher. 'Tarbuck, go to the head-master's office and get the cane!' I did. When I got back to the class, the teacher gave me four whacks on the hand. *Ouch!* They were real beauties.

As I went back to my seat, the teacher said, 'Williams, now *you* come up here.'

'Eh? What for, sir?' the lad asked. 'Tarbuck did it!'

'Yes, but *you* told on him.' And Williams got four of the best on his hand as well. I have to say, that teacher went right up in my estimation after that.

I was in the cast of a school play. It was called *Wayside War* and, because it was an all-boys school, I got given a female part. Alicia Pemberton, my name was. I didn't mind: it was a good laugh. My sister, Norma, worked on the cosmetics counter at Bon Marché by now, so she did my make-up. I looked lovely, if I say so myself.

Come the night of the play, in front of the parents, I came walking on in my dress and a pair of falsies, carrying a riding crop. A teacher called Mr Cash, who used to do all the canings, was in the cast and had to say a line to me. When he did, I gave him a right good slap across the arse with the crop.

Mr Cash winced: 'Ow!'

'Now you know how much it hurts,' I told him.

My best friend at Morrison school was Henry Pearson. He was a great feller to be around, not least because I was still a little short-arse and he was a big lad. Whenever a fight kicked off in the playground, if I was getting a whacking, Henry would step in: 'Oi! That's enough!' He looked after me.

Henry would come to the playing field behind my house after school and play football. Or I'd go round his place and we'd use his dad's garage door as the goal. His dad was the local undertaker, so there were often funeral flowers lying around the driveway and in the house.

I loved visiting Henry because in the loft, over his dad's morgue, he had a beautiful train set. There were Hornby versions of special trains like the *Flying Scotsman*. We'd play up there for hours. One day, as I was leaving their house, his father stopped me.

'Jimmy, can we have the blue engine back, please?' he asked.

'Sorry, Mr Pearson,' I said, as I took it out of my pocket and handed it to him. I'd thought that I might borrow it. You know, just for a day or two.

Liverpool used to have a great joke shop called the Wizards Den, run by an old feller who looked like a wizard himself. I went in there and bought a pack of banger cigarettes. They looked just like normal fags but when you lit them, they exploded. I put a couple in one of my mum's old fag packets and took it around to Henry's house.

I offered his dad one: 'Do you smoke, Mr Pearson?'

'I do, Jimmy,' he replied. 'Thank you, son.' And he put them in his pocket.

Well, Henry's dad was meeting a man the next day who was coming in from Rhyl to talk about a funeral. He gave this feller one of the cigarettes and put the other one in his own mouth. He lit them. *BOOM!* They both blew up. They nearly shat themselves.

The funny thing was that Mr Pearson never bollocked me for it. Henry told me later that his dad had come home from the meeting and told his family what had happened. They'd all fallen about. And Mr Pearson had said, 'I'll tell you what – that boy Tarbuck is going to go places …'*

I was also big mates with a pair of Jewish twins called Cohen. When I was about fourteen, they took me down to a sports and social club called Harold House. It was strictly for Jewish people (not that people ever asked what religion you were, in those days), so the twins told me, 'Just tell them that your mother is Jewish.'

'OK,' I said.

When we got to Harold House, the Cohens told the guy on the door, 'This is our friend, Jimmy Tarbuck.'

'Are you Jewish?' he asked me.

'My mother is.'

'That's fine. You can come in.'

I started going to Harold House in the evenings and at weekends. It was great. I played football and basketball for the club. They also had an ex-pro fighter who gave boxing lessons. I had a few, but I stopped because I wasn't very good. The guy would let you hit him but then he'd hit you back, *harder*. He knew how to punch. I didn't.

---

* I've kept in touch with Henry Pearson for my entire life. He followed his dad into the family funeral business. Nowadays, he's retired and lives on the Wirral.

They had dances at Harold House as well (discos hadn't been invented yet!). I liked those a lot because, at fourteen, I was getting interested in girls. I started chatting them up: I didn't know, or care, that they were Jewish girls. But some other people minded more than I did.

A guy named Ted Sconey used to have a shop selling tools beneath my dad's office. He went up to have a word. 'Fred, your Jimmy is getting among the girls at Harold House,' he said. 'They like him because he can dance.'

'Oh, that's nice,' Dad said.

'No, it *isn't!*' Ted said.

My father came home and told me, 'If I were you, I'd be careful at Harold House.' And, shortly after that, the guy who ran the club called me into his office.

'You said your mother is Jewish?' he asked me.

'Yeah.'

'What's her maiden name?'

'McLoughlin.'

'I have *never* heard of a Jew called McLoughlin!' he told me. 'You're still welcome here, Tarbuck, but *stay away from the girls!*'

* * *

School was still rolling along. One lad was a bit of a genius with anything mechanical. He found a crappy old motorbike in the school science lab and told us he'd be able to get it going. I don't think any of us believed it, but he was messing about and tinkering with it for yonks, and he did it. He fixed it.

We got hold of a can of petrol from somewhere, pushed the knackered old bike into the playground and took turns to go bombing around the yard on it. Christ knows how we thought we'd get away with it. Of course, we didn't. The teachers ran out to see what the hell the noise was, and all of us culprits got caned in front of the whole school.

We wanted revenge. The teacher who caned us used to ride a motorbike to school so, a few days later, we stuffed a potato up its exhaust pipe and hung around at home time to see what happened. He nearly ruptured himself trying to kickstart his bike and, when he did, the spud shot out with a BANG! *Result!*

Just down the road from us was the Morrison School for Girls. When we lads learned that the older girls played netball after school on Thursdays, we were down there like a shot to watch them, in their short skirts and blue knickers. That was a definite highlight of the week. Teenage-boy heaven!

The school took us to the Lake District camping. Mr Deadman, the sports teacher, told us to swim across Lake Windermere. These were the days before anyone cared about health and safety: can you *imagine* any school getting its kids to do that nowadays? If we made it out alive, we got a certificate.

We had big tents and slept eight to ten kids in each one. We went to bed one night, and a lad said, 'That Deadman is a right bastard.'

We heard the tent zip get pulled down. A man's head poked in. 'Yes, I am!' Mr Deadman said. 'Now, good night!' I still remember the panic when we heard his voice.

At the end of the fourth year, I took my exams. I did OK in a couple, such as history and maths, and not so well in others. Should I stay on for fifth form? I never got the chance. The headmaster, Mr Shepherd, disliked me as much as I disliked him. And he made it clear to me that I had to leave.*

In my leaving report, Shepherd wrote: 'Tarbuck courts easy popularity with the jukebox set.' Not exactly a glowing endorsement. It was the summer of 1955. I was fifteen years old, and my education was over.

Right, then. Now what do I do?

---

* Years later, when I got successful, Mr Shepherd tried to claim that he'd encouraged me at school. What a load of bloody rubbish!

CHAPTER 2

Cold tea on my willy

You know what? It's probably quicker to say what I *didn't* do!

As a lad, I was a typical Scouser in that I was always after ways to earn a bit of cash. I had a part-time job delivering meat for a local butcher. They gave me a bike and sent me off around Liverpool dropping off customers' pork chops and sausages. Well, can I be honest with you? It was too much like hard work. I lasted five minutes.

Bugger me! I thought. *There's got to be easier ways of earning a few bob than this!*

My first full-time job after leaving school was in a car-repair place called Mossley Hill Garage, just down the road from our house. I saw their ad for a trainee mechanic in the *Liverpool Echo*, went for an interview, and got the job. They didn't ask if I knew anything about car engines. That was just as well, because I didn't.

I had no real idea what I was doing. I could just about take a wheel off a car and change a tyre, but that was it. The other mechanics used to try to keep their overalls clean: I'd rub grease into mine to try to fool the boss that I'd been working. They kicked me out after a few weeks. I didn't blame them.

Then I got a job in a nearby laundry called Lune Laundry. My job was going out with a driver to pick up dirty washing from the posh houses on the outskirts of Liverpool, like where Mr Epstein lived. Then we'd go back and drop off the clean laundry afterwards. It was pretty easy and the drivers were a good laugh. But it had its risks.

I'd been at Lune Laundry a couple of weeks when one of the fellers working there told me, 'Jimmy, go up to the women's room and get us a pot of tea. We've run out.'

'OK,' I said, and went to the ladies' tea room, where the female employees took their breaks. I knocked on the door.

'Come in!'

Well, those ladies were expecting me. It was a trap. As soon as I got in the room, a big woman blocked the door behind me and three or four of them grabbed hold of me. They pulled my trousers and pants down … and tipped a pot of cold tea over my willy.

'Oi! Just you wait!' I yelled. 'I'm telling my mum about this!'

They all laughed: '*Aah!* He's going to tell his mummy!'

It was an initiation that all the new lads at the laundry got put through. And apart from getting cold tea poured on my willy, that job wasn't too bad. I stayed there for longer than I did the garage job, partly because I couldn't wait for the next apprentice to start, so I could send him up to the ladies' room for a pot of tea.

Once I'd had enough of the laundry, I got a job at a big Liverpool dairy called Reece's. This meant setting my alarm for stupid o'clock to go in and help get the milk ready for the early-morning milk rounds. Then I'd go out on the floats to help with the deliveries. This job was *never* going to last.

It didn't. One morning I was in the depot, loading the milk into the crates. A couple of fellers had been ducking down and skiving, and the foreman turned up to give them a bollocking. 'Where have you two been hiding all morning?' he asked them. 'If you don't pull your fingers out, I'm giving you the sack.'

Well, one of the blokes wasn't having this. 'Stick your job up your arse!' he told him.

I loved the defiance of this. I thought it was great, and I burst out laughing. The foreman was livid. 'Don't you talk to me like that …' he began. He didn't get any further. They were a pair of big blokes, and they grabbed him and carried him to a cake delivery van. He was struggling but he couldn't get away.

There was a low shelf inside the cake delivery van. The two guys chucked the foreman in there and slammed it firmly shut. 'There you go!' they said, and left him trapped in there. I thought it was hysterical. Reece's didn't agree: they sacked the guys who'd done it *and* the fellers who'd laughed at it. So I was out of a job again …

* * *

Around this time, skiffle was getting big in Britain. I liked a few of the songs, but I wasn't too big a fan. But for something to do, and to try to make a bit of dosh, I formed a skiffle band with a few mates. We called ourselves The Blackjacks.

It was the normal set-up: a couple of kids on guitars, someone on a tea-chest bass, and I played the washboard* and sang. I wasn't very good at either of them, but I quite liked being in the band because it gave me the chance to do something that I've *always* been good at: showing off.

We did a handful of shows at local working men's clubs, getting paid a couple of quid a pop, playing stuff like Lonnie Donegan's 'Rock Island Line' and Chas McDevitt's 'Freight Train'. But we'd have rows about who would sing which songs and I got bored of it pretty quickly. The Blackjacks were short-lived.

One day I was in a coffee bar on Allerton Road with a couple of mates. A lad that I only knew slightly came in. He said he'd just washed his dad's car and was taking it for a drive to dry it off. 'Why don't you all get in and come with me?' he said.

We climbed in and this kid set off at a right lick. He was a typical teenage lad, driving much too fast and not really knowing what he was doing. We came to a roundabout and he lost control of the vehicle and smashed into the edge of it. The car rolled over and over, just like they do in the movies.

I was sitting by one of the back doors. It flew open and I found myself deposited on the road. This is Tarbuck's luck: I didn't have a bruise on me. Not even a scratch. A feller who had seen us crash ran over to help and I just asked him, 'Is my

---

* What's the trick to playing the washboard? Borrow your mum's thimbles.

jacket ripped at the back?' That was all I cared about. Nobody was too hurt.

Christmas came around and, with a good mate called Tex Williams, I got a seasonal job sorting the mail. Early in the morning, we'd be going through all the cards and letters and getting them ready for the postmen. We had to load the mail onto the steam trains, so there was smoke everywhere. I'd go home black from the soot.

I worked in a television shop for a bit. This was in the winter, and one morning it had snowed all night. The snow must have been six inches thick. It was hanging right over the edge of the shop's roof. 'We won't sell much today!' the manager said, and told me to rearrange the tellies in the shop window.

I was working away when a feller stopped outside the shop. He tapped on the window and pointed at one of the TVs. 'How much is that …?' he began to mouth. He got no further, because a load of snow fell off our roof and knocked him flat on his arse. It was like watching a cartoon show.

It looked hilarious and I howled with laughter. The guy was furious. He picked himself up and came storming into the shop, still covered in snow. 'Are you OK, sir?' the boss asked. 'Can I help you?'

'This little bastard just roared laughing at me!' the customer complained.

'Well, it was bloody funny!' I said.

And that was the end of *that* job.

Who cares? Next!

I got a summer job as a gardener, looking after the grounds of a school in Mossley Hill. I didn't have particularly green fingers but at least I ate healthy, because there were loads of apple and pear trees. But, like the others, the job didn't last very long ... and didn't end very well.

There was an open-air swimming pool at the school. One night after work, I met a few pals in a pub called the Rose of Mossley and told them about it. Well, one bevvy led to another, and at closing time we all piled up to the school, climbed over the gate, and went for a midnight swim.

You'll never guess what? There were some young female trainee teachers staying in digs at the school. They heard all the noise, came out to investigate, and found us splashing around in the water. 'Get out of there, now!' one of them told us.

'We can't. We've got no clothes on!'

'Never mind that! Get out!'

We gave them a mouthful. They gave us a mouthful back and said they were calling the police. When we climbed out they laughed at us, because the cold water had made us ... not the men we were. A bit shrivelled. Anyway, they told the school about us, and I was out of work again. This seemed to be a bit of a trend.

* * *

I didn't earn much money from any of these jobs but what I did earn, I spent dead quick. Sometimes, if my dad had had a good week at work, he might give me a ten-bob note. And like any lad in their mid-teens, I spent most of my dosh on the very important business of trying to meet girls.

I was never a big boozer but I'd go with a few mates to a pub by the Mersey, near to the Adelphi Hotel, called The Big House. It was a good laugh, and a great night out, unless a ruck broke out. And they often did. Why? Just youth. Testosterone. Half the time, they'd start just because someone looked at someone else a bit funny.

But a better way of meeting girls was to go on what they used to call the router cruises. On Saturday nights in Liverpool, a ship called the *Royal Iris* would become a floating dance hall. You'd pay your seven-and-six and spend the evening cruising up and down the Mersey, dancing and desperately trying to chat up girls.

The big problem with these nights was that there'd invariably be a fight. There'd be lads in from north Liverpool, and some from The Dingle in the south of the city, and a big ruck would break out. I used to get on the boat with a mate called Davy Fitzgibbon and a few others. Davy was a terrific fighter and he was fearless. He'd fight a bull if he had to.

One Saturday night there was a really bad brawl. Davy knocked a feller clean out but I could hear sirens and see flashing blue lights on the quayside as the *Iris* sailed back in. I ran up to the top deck and shouted down to him: 'Davy! Davy! Get up here, now!'

He came sprinting up: 'Eh? What are we doing?'

'Follow me!' I said. I knew where the loading area was for loading goods onto the boat. It had a gangplank that wasn't open to the public, so when the boat docked, Davy and I scrambled down there and scarpered.

Everybody else we were there with got arrested. When we met them the next day, they asked: 'Where did you go? What happened?'

'What do you think?' replied Davy. 'This crafty bastard, Tarbuck, got us off the boat. He knows everything!' But, like I say, a night on the *Royal Iris* was only a success if you pulled a girl.

On the boat and in the dance halls, we were dancing to rock and roll because this was the time it started coming over from America. I loved it. I'd listen to Radio Luxembourg on Sunday nights – when I could make it out, through the bloody crackly reception – and hear Elvis and Little Richard and Chuck Berry. And I'd think: *This is wonderful!*

I saw the first ever American rock and roller to come to Britain at the start of 1957 when I went to Bill Haley and his Comets at the Liverpool Odeon. *Talk about exciting!* They were all in checked suits, and the saxophonist and the double-bass player were rolling about on the floor while they were playing. They were terrific.

Like all the lads, I got properly into rock and roll. I even started trying to comb my hair into a quiff – no easy job, that – and dress the part in jackets with velvet lapels, Teddy-boy drainpipe trousers and suede shoes. Well, when I could find any of that clobber in the local church hall jumble sales, that was.

A new music club opened up in a cellar in Mathew Street in the middle of Liverpool. It was called the Cavern Club, but it wasn't of much interest to me at first. The owner, a guy called Alan Sytner, was a big jazz buff and wanted it to be a cool jazz club like he'd seen in the Latin Quarter in Paris.

The Cavern had jazz concerts in the evening. Sytner didn't allow rock and roll in the place but he'd grudgingly put on skiffle gigs at lunchtime. He famously bollocked John Lennon in 1957 when Lennon's skiffle band, The Quarrymen, were doing a show and started playing Elvis's 'Don't Be Cruel'.

All this going out didn't come cheap. I needed to be earning some money again. A guy called Howard, who lived next door to us, worked in a hair salon in town called Andre Bernard, and our Norma asked if he could get me a job. They took me on as a trainee ladies' hairdresser (you've got to give me this – when I was young, I'd try anything!).

Andre Bernard was a snazzy London salon so it was big local news when they opened their branch in Liverpool. I worked there with Lewis Collins, who went on to be a big TV star in *The Professionals*. I don't remember him very well. Paul McCartney's brother, Mike, later worked in the salon as well.

I quite liked it at Andre Bernard. I started off making the tea and sweeping all the hair up from the floor. Then Bernard, one of the owners (I suppose he was lucky his name wasn't Bernard Bernard), started showing me how to cut hair. Well, he didn't take any risks: he trained me on cutting the hair at the back of the head, where the customers couldn't see it if it went wrong.

'Pull it down, twist it around, and cut it,' he'd instruct me. 'Twist it around your finger and get a clip on it.' I got the hang of it, but I wasn't very good at cutting hair. Average at best. But, with the personality I've got, I liked talking to the customers. And the best thing about working in a ladies' salon? It was a good place to meet girls.

* * *

While I was doing all this stuff, though, I couldn't help feeling that I wanted something more. I wanted … *to get noticed*. I didn't yet know for what, exactly, but I knew that I wanted to make a name for myself. And, for a while, I thought that the best way to do that might be through football.

I was still mad about footie. Dad was still taking me to stand on the Kop to watch most Liverpool games and I loved playing the sport myself. Any chance I got to have a game, I'd grab it. I'd played for my schools, and in works teams, and at weekends I played for two different pub teams.

One was based at a boozer called the Dunkeld Arms on West Derby Road. Our goalie was a big lad nicknamed Chunky Ellis. If an opposing striker got clean through on goal against Chunky, his speciality was flattening them. We weren't a bad team at all and we won a couple of local cups.

What kind of a player was I? Look, I'll be honest with you. I was a goal-hanger. I didn't do a whole lot of running up and down or tracking back. I hung about up front, played one-twos, and I loved to get a shot off. I'd shoot from anywhere. 'If you don't shoot, you don't score!' That was my motto.

I also felt a little drawn towards the stage – I'd enjoyed being in my school play, even playing a woman – and I enrolled for weekend classes at a local acting school, Elliott Clarke. I liked it, and I was good at doing accents: American, Irish, Welsh, the lot. But I only stayed for about three weeks. It was getting in the way of my football.

I dreamed of playing football professionally. Dreamed of playing for Liverpool. I tried to get a trial for the club but they didn't give me one because, the truth was, I wasn't good enough.* But I was about to meet a few of their future great players.

My dad used to work in his bookmaking business with a man called Pa Melia. His son was a lad called Jimmy, who was three years older than me and who was playing for Liverpool's boys' team. One weekend, Dad told me they were playing a match on the pitches at Penny Lane, right by our house. So, I went along to watch.

Jimmy was a great player, a clever midfielder. We got talking after the match. 'Hello, son, did you enjoy the game?' he asked me.

'Yeah,' I said. 'My dad said I should come and watch you.'

'Oh, really? Who's your dad?'

'Fred Tarbuck.'

'Fred's your dad? He gives me a shilling a goal. He's getting fed up with me!'

I became matey with Jimmy very quickly. Through him, I met Bobby Campbell. Bobby lived next door to Jimmy in the

---

* I still do a routine about this in my stage show. 'I had a letter from the FA. They said I had f-a chance of being a footballer.'

Scotland Road area and was about to sign professional terms with Liverpool. And then the two of them introduced me to a guy called Johnny Morrissey, who had just broken into the Liverpool youth team.

Those three were to become huge football stars. Jimmy played for England, Bobby was to manage Fulham and Chelsea, and Johnny achieved the rare feat of playing for both Liverpool and Everton. But back then, we were just four teenage scallies who started knocking round together. We became big mates.

I hadn't known them that long when, one day in the summer of 1958, when I'd just turned eighteen, the three of them told me, 'Eh, Jimmy! We're going on holiday next week! Do you want to come?'

'Where you going?' I asked.

'Butlin's at Pwllheli.'

'Sounds great,' I said. 'I'll ask me dad.'

Dad said yes, so we were on. The four of us were sharing a chalet: I think it was £22 for the week. And we had the time of our young lives.

Johnny Morrissey's dad had just bought him a Ford Zephyr, so we all headed off to Wales in it hoping for two things: to have a good laugh, and to meet girls. We achieved them both. That was when the penny dropped for me: not only do boys go out looking for girls, but girls go out looking for boys. Who'd have thought it, eh? Well, it's a good system … and it worked that week.

But into every life a little rain must fall. It was a British summer holiday, so, of course, we had a day or two when it pissed it down. One morning, it was torrential. We were sitting around bored in our chalet when an announcement came over the camp Tannoy:

'Radio Butlin here. Because of the bad weather, all of today's outdoor activities have been cancelled. But we will be holding a talent contest for all campers in the Gaiety Theatre at 3pm.'

Well, Jimmy, Bobby, Johnny and I had nothing better to do so we all went down to watch. The theatre was full: there were probably about six hundred people in there. We got four seats at the end of a row and settled down to enjoy the entertainment. It wasn't easy. Because it was bloody awful.

A couple of entrants were halfway decent but most of them were terrible. The worst was a guy who got up and started mangling Johnnie Ray and Frankie Laine songs. It sounded like he was strangling a cat. The four of us burst out laughing, and started heckling the poor bloke:

'Rubbish!'

'Get off!'

Now, the Butlin's Redcoat who was hosting the show didn't like this. He ran onstage and started telling us off. 'Look, this is unfair!' he said. 'If any of you can do better, let's see you get up here!' And Bobby Campbell shoved me out of my seat and into the aisle.

'This one can!' he shouted. 'He's funny!'

'No, I'm not!' I protested.

A Redcoat came marching down the aisle, grabbed hold of me and pushed me up on the stage. I had no say in the matter, nor any clue what I was going to say. I looked out at a sea of expectant faces. My mates were grinning. I opened my mouth and told a joke. I can't for the life of me remember what it was, but it was greeted with stony silence.

'Huh! Don't laugh, then!' I said.

That was met with a roar of laughter. *Ah-ha!* Now *that* was more like it! And I just carried on talking. It was all off the top of my head. I hadn't got a thing prepared – *how could I have? I didn't know I was going to do it!* – but I just kept going. I started talking to random members of the audience:

'How are *you* doing, sir? Are you having a good time? I've seen you hanging around by the chalets, checking out the girls ...'

I had no idea what I was saying but I kept on saying it. People were getting right into it and howling with laughter. I was doing my favourite things – being daft, showing off and getting noticed – and I absolutely loved it. I don't even know how long I was up there but when I sat back down, with everyone still clapping, it was *such* a buzz. Such a thrill.

And, sod me, you'll never guess what? I only went and won the contest!

The Redcoat announced me as the winner. I got three quid – a lot in those days! – and a week's free holiday at the camp at the end of the season for the talent-contest finals. So, I went back down to Pwllheli later, this time on my own. I even thought of a few gags in advance, rather than busking the whole thing.

And I had a bit of luck. I was halfway through my act in the Gaiety Theatre when all the lights went out. 'This is Radio Butlin!' I said into the mic. 'Has anyone got two bob for the meter?' A gale of laughter came back at me out of the darkness. *Yes!* I was on my way. I won that final, too.*

It got me into the regional final in Blackpool a week or two later. *Now you're talking!* I was dead excited about this. Butlin's put me in a smart hotel right on the promenade. The final was in one of the town's theatres. I was on a roll by now, I was getting more confident, and I won that too.

This meant an invitation down to the national final in the West End of London. This felt proper big-time. Tommy Trinder was the host although, if I'm honest, I didn't think he was anything special. He was certainly no Max Miller. And I gave it my best shot … but it wasn't quite good enough.

I didn't mind losing because the talent contest had shown me exactly what I wanted to do with my life. *I wanted to be a comic.* And I can't have been *too* rotten in that final because, at the end, a smart older gent called George Ganjou came up to me and introduced himself. He said that he was a theatrical agent.

'I'm putting together a rock and roll tour,' George told me. 'Would you like to compere it?'

Well, I had no bloody idea what he was talking about. 'Compare it to what?' I asked.

'*Compere* it,' he explained. 'It means introduce the acts. I'll give you forty pounds a week.'

---

* On that second trip to Pwllheli, I made a friend for life. His name is Ken Hatton and he was the Butlin's camp barber: his speciality was the Perry Como cut. Nearly seventy years on, Ken's still one of my best mates. He's been all around the world with me.

Forty pounds a week!

'Oh, yeah, I can do that!' I said.

And that was how it all started.

CHAPTER 3

Tarbuck, England schoolboys

The gig that George Ganjou had offered me was a good 'un. I was to be the compere – now that I knew what the word meant – of a British rock and roll package tour called the Larry Parnes Extravaganza. It starred Marty Wilde (who was just getting famous on a new TV music show, *Oh Boy!*), Vince Eager and the John Barry Seven.

The tour was to visit towns like Clacton, Portsmouth and Southport, doing two shows every night. My job was to get up between the acts, talk to the audience and tell a few gags as the bands got set up to come on, and then introduce them when they were ready. It sounded pretty easy, and so right up my street.

Larry Parnes was … dodgy. If I'm honest, he was not a nice man. He was only in his late twenties but he was already a successful showbiz impresario, managing nearly all of the young acts in the first British wave of rock and roll. He was very money-minded. I remember the papers used to call him Parnes, Shillings and Pence.

You had to be careful around Larry Parnes. He was a gay feller who was out, which was unusual for those days. Nothing wrong with that, but he had wandering hands. He made advances to everyone. You certainly didn't want to go to his flat, or his hotel room, to go over any business. Let's get straight to the point here: he was a right pervert.

The tour kicked off on 20 September 1958 at the Savoy Cinema in Burnt Oak in north London and it was absolutely fantastic. How could it not be? I was eighteen years old and I was onstage introducing rock and roll stars to two thousand or so screaming girls every night. Let me tell you, I had the time of my young life.

Marty Wilde was a giant of a man, six foot four inches tall, but he was a lovely, quiet, gentle bloke. I could have a good chat and a laugh with him backstage. Then he would get up onstage and start his set with 'Rave On', which had just been a hit that year for Buddy Holly, and the whole place would go berserk.*

I'd normally stand in the wings while the acts were play-ing, but every now and then I'd venture out into the crowd to watch them. Sometimes, girls would clock me from having seen me on the stage and come to say hello. In fact, they'd

---

* Like me, Marty Wilde is in his mid-eighties but still going. He's still playing gigs today. When I see him, I ask him, 'Jesus Christ, Marty, how long are you going to go on singing "A Teenager in Love"?' That always makes him laugh.

be all over me. Look, I'm not going to deny that was a bit of a bonus!

Nearly two weeks into the tour, we had a date just down the road from Liverpool at the Essoldo in Birkenhead. Before the show, there came a knock at the stage door. When I opened it, there was a good-looking lad with a quiff standing there, with a guitar around his neck that was nearly as big as he was. He looked dead nervous.

'Excuse me, sir …' he began.

Sir! I'd never been called that before! I was only a kid myself!

'Yes?'

'My name's Ronnie. I sent a tape in to Mr Parnes and he told me to come here and see him.'

'Right. Wait here,' I said. I went to tell Larry Parnes that Ronnie was here to see him. He was sitting with Marty Wilde in his dressing room. 'Oh, yeah,' he said. 'His tape wasn't bad. Show him in.' So I went back and fetched the lad.

'Come on, then. Show us what you can do,' Parnes told the youngster.

Ronnie played us all a couple of songs. I think he'd written them himself. He was shit-scared but you could tell he was really good. Parnes was nodding along. 'Yeah, OK,' he told him. 'I'll put you on tonight. Jimmy, introduce this lad as the first act in the show.'

'Alright,' I agreed. I asked the lad: 'What's your name?'

'Ronnie Wycherley.'

'Oh, don't call him *that*!' Parnes laughed. 'Call him Billy Fury.'

And, there and then, that was how Billy Fury was born. He didn't have any stage clothes on, or anything. He was only an eighteen-year-old Scouser (like me), and dead shy (unlike me), and he looked petrified, but he went onstage and he was electric. He brought the place down. After that, he was on the tour. And the rest is history.

* * *

My taste for being onstage was really whetted by that tour. Once it was over, and I was back in Liverpool, I started trying to get gigs as a stand-up comic. I'd go around all of the local pubs, social clubs and working men's clubs, offering to get up on the stage and do a few jokes. A lot of them said no. But some said yes.

I started playing a pub called the Blue Ball (sounds painful!) just outside the city centre. I'd do fifteen minutes and they'd give me thirty shillings (£1.50). The Blue Ball was pretty rough and ready and there'd often be girls in there who were getting married because they were in the family way. I'd have a right laugh with them (well, *I'd* be laughing, anyway).

I'd get up and say, 'Alright, luv, how are you? You're getting married, are you? You must be pregnant!' And everybody would roar, including the girl I was talking to. The whole pub would be in stitches … but, sometimes, it went wrong.

One night, I asked a woman, 'What's your name, darling? Alice? Lovely to meet you. Are you pregnant?'

And the girl went bloody mental at me: 'How dare you! Who do you think you are?' The more everyone roared, the angrier she got. After I retreated off the stage, the landlord collared me.

'Well, that's nice, isn't it?' he moaned. 'Thanks for winding up all my customers! You're going to ruin my business, you are. Here's your thirty bob. Now, piss off!'

My mum and dad would sometimes come to watch me and support me. If I was going down well, I'd look out into the audience and see my dad, sitting with his pint at a table, beaming with pride. Mum looked a bit more as if she didn't know quite what to make of it all.

A few mates might come along as well. Once I'd got paid, we'd all go around the corner to The Grafton dance hall. It cost ten bob admission. I'd pay to get in and my mates – Davy Fitzgibbon and some others – would hang about outside by the side door. I'd open the door and they'd run in before the security men could cop hold of them.

'Quick!' we'd yell. 'Scatter!' And then we'd be in there for the night.

The Grafton was a great laugh. As well as playing records, they had an ace band, led by Mary Hamer. Now and then, they held talent contests, where you got up and sang or mimed to records. I'd enter sometimes, just for a laugh. But, obviously, the main point of going to The Grafton was to pull girls.

One week I liked the look of a lass and started chatting her up. We were getting on dead well so I asked her, 'Would you like a coffee?'

'Ooh, I'd love one!' she replied.

'Great, you go and grab a table, and I'll get two coffees!' I said. Well, I bought the drinks, and when I carried them over to the table area, bugger me if I hadn't forgotten what she looked like. There were just all these girls, sitting down, looking at me curiously.

'Er, which of you asked me for a coffee?' I asked. That was the end of *that* romance.

The goal was to try to walk a girl home at the end of the night and get a snog, or, if you were lucky, a bit more. Mind you, that all depended on where she lived. There were bits of Liverpool that you didn't escort a girl home to, if you knew what was good for you.

Like where? Well, Huyton, for one. You'd be walking the young lady home, minding your own business, and a couple of fellers would come up: 'Oi, where are you going? Where are you from? They're our girls round here – she's *ours*! Clear off!' Or words to that effect. But I still remember going to The Grafton as happy days.

As well as trying to get comedy gigs, I was still mad about the footie. Liverpool weren't a great team at the time, they were in the old Second Division, but I'd go to the games as often as I could: reserves, as well as first team. Secretly, I still hadn't totally given up on my dream of playing for them.

Bobby Campbell had just broken into the first team. He'd help me get into the matches for free. On the terrace at Anfield, there used to be the boys' pen. Liverpool's youth players could watch the games from in there for nothing, and Bobby would walk me round to the entrance.

There'd be an old guy on the door. 'Alright, Bobby, who've we got here?' he'd ask.

'Jimmy Tarbuck, from the youth team,' Bobby would say. 'You know him! He plays for the England boys' team.'

'Oh, yeah? Well done, Jimmy! Come in, lad!'

Well, at first I'd just use that trick for the reserve games, but soon I got cocky and started doing it for first-team matches.

'Who are you?' the security would ask.

'Tarbuck, England schoolboys.'

It went on for a few weeks, until one day Phil Taylor, the first-team manager, happened to be walking past the pen. He saw me and stopped dead.

'Oi! You!' he said. 'Are you the one that's going about telling everyone you're an England youth international? Who the bloody hell are you, anyway?'

'I'm Jimmy Tarbuck,' I answered, adding, hopefully, 'I'm a friend of Bobby Campbell's.'

'Oh, *are* you now?' said Taylor. 'Well, like all the other young lads coming in here today, you can go to the turnstile and pay your one-and-six. Now, piss off!'

So, that was the end of that scam. The worst thing was that word about it got around. For weeks, every time I bumped into a mate, they'd start taking the piss: 'You alright, are you, Jimmy? You still playing for England?' It took me a while to live it down.

Bobby Campbell used to tell me that National Service would be the making of me. He'd just done his, and he'd say, 'Wait till they get you in the Army. *They'll* sort you out.' He couldn't believe it when the government abolished it and I missed out on having to do it by literally a few weeks. 'You jammy bugger, Tarbuck!' he said. 'Typical!'

There again, if I'd had to join the Army, all I'd have been bothered about would have been trying to play for their football team. And I'd have done it, too.

* * *

While I was starting to play the pubs and working men's clubs around Liverpool, I was still working at Andre Bernard. Why? I needed the money. The salon bosses knew that I was trying to break into stand-up and they didn't mind. In fact, Bernard would sometimes give me a lift to gigs. He was a real supporter of mine.

Right at the start of 1959, I had to take a load of time off from the salon because I got offered the chance to compere another rock and roll tour. And this time the headliner was an even bigger star than Marty Wilde. His name was Cliff Richard.

Cliff was huge news. He was only eighteen, the same as me, but at the end of the previous year he'd had a big hit with his first single, 'Move It'. It was a great rock and roll song and people started calling him the 'English Elvis'. Well, this was music to Cliff's ears, because he absolutely *loved* Elvis.

He looked a bit like him, with the quiff, and he wore similar gear: a pink jacket, tie and socks, with black shirt and trousers. And he'd got all the moves onstage. He'd come on, start gyrating and thrusting his pelvis, and the girls would go crazy. The mums hated Cliff Richard because they thought he was a sex object.

Yet offstage, Cliff was anything but a wild rock and roller. He was a nice, polite, well-spoken lad. A lovely feller. He freely admitted to me that everything he'd done so far was based on copying Elvis. He told me, plenty of times: 'If there'd been no Elvis Presley, there'd be no Cliff Richard.'

His band were the Drifters: they hadn't yet changed their name to the Shadows. I liked the two Geordie guys, Hank Marvin and Bruce Welch. Hank was very funny. Bruce was quieter. I got on great with Jet Harris (until he had too many beers inside him). But Tony Meehan, the drummer, was a pain in the arse. Always late for everything.

We travelled separately to some of the shows. If I got there first, I'd volunteer to do Cliff's soundcheck for him. I loved doing that. The technicians would be going 'Two! Two!' and all that palaver, and I'd get on the mic and belt out a couple of numbers. I used to sing Elvis's 'I Want to be Free': '... *like a bird in the tree* ...'

But mostly we all travelled together on an old Bedford coach hired from a feller called Joe Lee. Joe was also the driver. It was a right shitty old bus – cold, draughty and slow – and it regularly broke down. Cliff was one of the biggest stars in Britain but there he'd be, with the rest of us, pushing that bloody coach down the road to try to get it started.

Not that long ago, I went to a tribute dinner for Cliff. We were reminiscing over that tour, and he asked me, 'What's your strongest memory, Jim?'

'That's easy,' I answered. 'Joe Lee's coach.'

And Cliff's eyes clouded over with the recollection. 'Dear God,' he said. 'Joe Lee ...'

Bruce Welch was also there with us. 'I don't remember that bus,' he told me.

'Well, you *should* do,' I replied. 'It was the first time you got laid!'

Bruce scowled at me. 'You've got a bloody nerve!' he said. 'Only you'd dare to say that ...'

Those shows were amazing, though. Cliff Richard and the Drifters were a proper rock and roll band then. It was before they'd started doing gentler stuff like 'Living Doll'. I'd go out and tell a few gags before they went on. They billed me as 'the comical compere'. I should have written on the posters, '... if you're lucky'.

When I got the nod that the band were ready, I'd say, 'And now, here's what you've all been waiting for!' The screams would take the roof off. They'd deafen you. If those girls could have got to Cliff, they'd have ripped his clothes off. They were very attractive girls – and there were a lot of them. Enough to go round.

At the end of the night, we'd never have anywhere booked to stay, so we'd tear around the streets looking for a B&B with a light on. We'd be stood haggling on the doorstep: 'How much for a room for the night?'

'Three quid.'

'Can you do fifty bob? And give us egg and bacon in the morning?' We'd often all end up kipping on Joe Lee's coach.

The support act at some shows was Wee Willie Harris. They called him the wild man of rock, and *bloody hell! You could say that again!* He was only a tiny guy, five foot two in his socks, but he'd go onstage, hurl himself around and beat hell out of a piano. He used to dye his hair pink and wear polka-dot bow ties.

I liked Willie's manager, Les Bristow, and I got on great with Willie, whose real name was Charlie. He was mad offstage as well. One day, we went to see a Hammer horror film. The cinema was trying to terrify its customers. They'd put a coffin in the corner, under the screen, and had someone in the balcony dropping rice on people to shock them.

Charlie and I were sitting in our seats when two girls came in slightly late, straight from work. They looked scared as they arrived and were hugging each other as they walked down the aisle, staring at the screen. They took two seats right on the end of a row. Charlie whispered to me, 'I'm gonna have some fun with them!'

'Eh? What do you mean?' I asked.

Charlie slipped out of his seat, got on all fours and crawled down the aisle. When he got level with the girls, he jumped up and roared at them: 'Aaargh!' Well, they were *terrified*! They started screaming and didn't stop. The cinema had to pause the film, and chucked me and Charlie out. *And* they wouldn't give us our money back.

It was worth it, though.

I hit it off with Wee Willie Harris's mum. When I was down in London, I'd stay with the two of them in their prefab. Their spare bed was comfy and warm: I loved snuggling down in it. Or I'd bunk on a couch in Cliff's flat in Marylebone. Those rock and roll tours were great days. We were all young. Everything felt possible.

* * *

Back in Liverpool, things were looking up at the Cavern Club. Alan Sytner had sold the gaff to a feller named Ray McFall, who didn't have the same objections to rock and roll. The club started putting bands like The Searchers on at lunchtimes. It was a good place to chat to girls, because they'd come down to have a dance in their lunch hours.

And that was where I met Pauline Carfoot.

Pauline was from The Dingle. I'd actually seen her once before, walking her bloody great Alsatian dog with two mates at the fair in Sefton Park. I hadn't spoken to her then. But I noticed her in the Cavern for two reasons: she was very pretty and, most of all, she was a great dancer.

Pauline was a terrific jiver. Everyone liked to dance with her, including Lennon. I wasn't too bad, either. I couldn't be arsed with the twist and the mashed potato, and all that stuff, but I loved jiving: picking up the girls and twirling them around. And when I asked Pauline for a dance, we were good together.

She was quite wary of me at first. She told me later that she'd heard I had a bit of a reputation. (Eh? I've no idea what she was talking about!) But we got on well. She told me that she was working in the advertising department of a clothing company, and hoping to study graphics at college. And, after a few weeks, we started dating.

Pauline didn't live too far from me so we'd get on the bus and go off into town together. We'd go to coffee bars – because they played music – to the pictures and to the Cavern. My parents liked her, I got on with hers, and everything was great. It made a nice change to be in a couple.

At the same time, I was still doing my stand-up in the pubs and WMCs. And I was very ambitious. I wanted to do more, and to get better. *I wanted to be a star.* Any time a big-name comic like Arthur Askey or Jimmy Jewel was playing at the Empire, or the Pavilion, or the Shakespeare, I'd sneak in a side door to see them.

I'd get paid a few bob for a show or, if I was lucky, a fiver. Someone or other told me that the clubs in Manchester paid more than Liverpool ones, because they were bigger, so I headed off on the train to try to get some gigs there. I did a few social clubs, and played at the Southern Sporting Club, a big venue at the time.

What was my act like? Something old; something new; something borrowed; something blue. Cheeky quips. Bantering with the audience. I always dressed up smart, in a suit and tie. I loved Bob Hope, and I'd read an interview where he'd said, 'Give 'em two minutes to look at the suit.' So, I did. I didn't go on like a scruff-bag.

I was paying my dues. There were tough nights, and tough crowds, but they didn't faze me. I wouldn't let them. I saw comics get so nervous that they'd vomit before they went on, but I never let it get to me in that way. How did I do it? Well, even as a youngster, I guess I was a confident feller.

I didn't mind hecklers, either. Why? The odds were on my side. They were just one voice in a crowd and I was up on the stage, wielding a microphone. So, I'd take them on. I went on once and a feller straight away yelled, 'Gerroff!'

'OK!' I said. 'Open your mouth and I'll take a short cut!' *That* got a roar.

I played a new Manchester venue that had just opened: the Embassy Club on the Rochdale Road. It was run by Bernard Manning. He paid me a fiver.* I liked Bernard – he was an alright feller, not an arsehole like some, and he was also a very good comedian. He had great timing.

Mind you, some of Bernard's material was debatable, to say the least. He'd use fatal words that you just shouldn't say, like the N-word. I told him not to do it: it was wrong, and he'd get people on his back. He just said, 'Fuck 'em!' But we comics probably all said things back then we wouldn't say now. The world changed. Bernard didn't.

Then, in the summer of 1959, I went even further afield. I was still in touch with Wee Willie Harris's manager, Les Bristow, and he helped me get a gig down the bill at the Metropolitan Theatre on the Edgware Road in London. It was a very prestigious venue – and they booked me for a few weeks.

Yes! This is it! I thought. It felt like a really big deal.

The week before I played the Met, Les told me, 'I'm going to show you the best comedian in England.' And he took me down to London to meet the great Max Miller, who had just done a run at the Met. I was dead excited by this. Max was a wonderful comic, and I'd always loved him on the telly.

I was introduced to Max backstage at the Palace Theatre. He looked me up and down. 'Son, you're a bit young, ain't ya?' he asked, in his famous Cockney accent. 'You're just a baby!'

---

* About twenty years ago, I read an interview with Bernard. He said, 'Well, I paid Jimmy Tarbuck a fiver – and I'd pay him the same today, because he's still doing the same act!' Cheeky bastard! R.I.P.

I wasn't sure *what* to say to that. 'Yes, Mr Miller.'

'Well, listen 'ere, son,' he went on. 'When you get onstage, don't be blue. It wouldn't suit you. Don't be blue.'

I nodded, while at the same time thinking, *Bugger me!* Max was just about the rudest comic going! Half of his act was double entendres. But then he granted me some more advice.

'Make sure you learn your act,' he continued. 'And take your time. *Take. Your. Time.* It's not a race. Don't rush it.' And that tip has stayed with me ever since.

I stayed to watch Max at the Palace that night. He came out and started doing his spiel, and then suddenly stopped dead. A young woman in the front row was breast-feeding her baby. You didn't see that out in public so much in those days, and Max couldn't stop himself gawping.

The woman stared up at him. 'What you looking at?' she demanded. She moved the baby away so she was just sitting there with one boob hanging out. 'Do you want some?' she asked Max. 'Are you hungry?' And the whole place fell about. Not even Max Miller had a comeback for that.

My dates at the Met started. As well as doing my own gags, I was also compering the show – at nineteen years old. And I thought I was holding my own. Of course, there was the occasional tough crowd, complete with hecklers. One night, I'd hardly said a word before a voice from up in the gods yelled, 'Gerroff!'

'Give the kid a chance!' someone else shouted. And the heckler came back: 'I'll give him eighteen months.'

But that wasn't typical. Most nights were good. I was trying to *take. my. time.* and I was going down pretty well. The headline act on the bill was a large lady, a Welsh singer and comic called Tessie O'Shea, who went as 'Two-Ton Tessie.' I didn't meet Tessie, or have anything to do with her, until the day that I was summoned to meet her in the theatre manager's office.

It didn't go well.

'I've watched your act and I'm afraid that I don't like your material,' she told me. 'I don't want you on the bill. We'll pay you off in full but you're no longer required.'*

Well, *this* was a setback. I hadn't seen it coming at all. I was totally knocked backwards. I collected my things from backstage and left the theatre for the final time. I wandered down the Edgware Road and found a red phone box to call Pauline at her parents'.

'I've got some bad news,' I said. 'I've been sacked from the Met.' And I told her all about Two-Ton Tessie binning me off. Pauline listened … and then she spoke.

'And I've got some news for *you*,' she said. 'I'm pregnant.'

Jesus Christ! Talk about a double whammy! I was still only nineteen. Pauline was just eighteen. We hadn't been together more than a few weeks, and we certainly hadn't been trying to start a family. Although, come to think of it, we hadn't exactly been taking any precautions *not* to start one, either.

But I knew exactly what to say. 'Don't worry,' I told her, down the phone. 'I'll marry you.'

---

* Years later, when I was famous, I bumped into Tessie O'Shea at Elstree Studios. She walked towards me, beaming. 'Jimmy! I've always wanted to meet you,' she said. 'But you did!' I answered. 'At the Met, Edgware Road, when you fired me. Which wasn't very nice, was it?' Tessie's face fell, and she walked off. We never met again.

'You'll have to tell my mum and dad,' Pauline said.

'Yeah. Leave it to me.'

As soon as I got back up to Liverpool, I went round Pauline's house. Her dad, Barney, was sitting in their front room with his braces over his shirt, as usual. 'Hello, son,' he said.

'Can I have a word with you please, Mr Carfoot?' I asked.

He looked at me. And the expression he said to me has stayed with me ever since: 'Appertaining to what?'

Appertaining to what? What the bloody hell does THAT mean?

'Appertaining to … that Pauline is pregnant,' I said.

Barney looked shocked. So did Pauline's mum, Frances. Neither of them had known. But Frances told me, 'We can look after her, Jimmy. You don't have to marry her.'

Pauline's brother, Terry, who was a soldier, was also in the room. 'Yes, he bloody does!' he said.

Pauline and I got married about four weeks later, on 9 September 1959, at Our Lady of Mount Carmel Roman Catholic church in Toxteth. She wore a lovely green dress. My best man was Bobby Campbell. As we stood at the altar, Bobby was grinning and whispering in Pauline's ear: 'You don't have to marry him! Marry me, instead!'

It was quite a small do, just family and a few friends such as my mates from Liverpool FC that I'd gone to Butlin's with. We had the reception in a room at a beautiful, historic local hotel called Childwall Abbey. It was a really happy day. But when it was over, we didn't go on honeymoon.

Why not? Because we just couldn't afford it.

CHAPTER 4

Sell it to The Everly Brothers

We couldn't afford to buy anywhere to live, either. Once we'd got married, Pauline moved into my mum and dad's with me as we waited for the baby to be born. And I went on cutting the backs of customers' hair at Andre Bernard by day and doing stand-up by night, knowing we'd soon have three mouths to feed.

Right at the start of 1960, Larry Parnes gave me another Marty Wilde tour to compere. It was a bit of a weird one: Sunday nights only, mostly in London but also with shows in Nottingham and Carlisle. Joe Brown was on the bill. I'd never met Joe before but he was a nice feller and a very good guitar player.*

Then Les Bristow got in touch with me again. He was taking Wee Willie Harris to do a show in Paris. Billy Fury

---

* I bought my first dog off Joe: a labrador called Louis. Well, I say I *bought* Louis: I 'forgot' to pay for him. For years afterwards, whenever I saw Joe, he'd say: 'Where's the money for that bloody dog, Tarbuck?'

was also going over to play with him, because he'd just had his first hit with 'Maybe Tomorrow'. Les asked me if I would compere the show.

'But I can't speak French!' I said.

'So what?' Les snorted. 'You can say *Monsieur* Billy Fury, and *Monsieur* Willie Harris, can't you?' So, that settled it. I was off to France.

It was the first time I'd been abroad (the Isle of Man doesn't count!) and it was thrilling. We all went on a bus down to Dover and then the ferry to Calais. I loved how everything felt different in Paris: the streets, the buildings, the cars, the food and, of course, the language. Not that I could speak a word of it. *Merde!*

Back home, I was still chasing comedy gigs in Liverpool as hard as I could. Which led to a somewhat unfortunate incident.

The posh London comic and actor Terry-Thomas, who always went as an upper-class cad in movies, came to play a show at the Liverpool Odeon. I did what I often did: went down to the theatre and asked at the stage door if I might be able to go on and do five minutes down the bill.

The doorman went off and fetched Terry-Thomas. He took me to his dressing room and asked me what kind of show I did.

'I tell jokes,' I told him.

'Ah, I see,' he drawled. 'Well, wait here, and I'll see what I can do.'

Terry-Thomas strolled off … and never came back. He left me waiting on my own in his dressing room for over an hour. Once or twice, I wandered out to the wings to try to talk to him, but he didn't want to know. He ignored me. It was rude, and I can't stand rudeness.

I went back to his dressing room. I was about to give up and go home when I spotted a snazzy-looking cigarette holder lying on a table. *I'm having that!* I thought, and stuck it in my pocket. It was stupid, really. I mean, I didn't even smoke. But I wasn't thinking straight. I was just pissed off with him.

I had no use for the cigarette holder so I gave it to a mate. My problems started when he tried to flog it. Terry-Thomas had gone to the police, who tracked my mate down and nicked him. When they asked him where he'd got it, he only went and bloody told them. I got arrested and charged with theft.

I had to go to court. Terry-Thomas said the fag holder was worth £600, which I still think was a load of bollocks. He had a bit of a set-to with my defending solicitor over that. I had to plead guilty (well, because I was) and got put on probation for two years. What can I say? We all make mistakes in life, and that was one of mine. I had to learn from it.

It wasn't my finest moment … but, weirdly, in some people's eyes, it made me a hero. And, being Liverpool, everyone took the piss. The next week, I was playing football for a pub team and, before the game, everyone was asking, 'Have you got a light, Tarby?' When I scored, I celebrated by miming smoking a fag.

My only worry was that it might have embarrassed my family but they didn't seem all that bothered. My dad just told me to put it behind me and 'get busy, lad'. And I immediately got very busy indeed … because I became a dad.

Pauline gave birth to our first child, a daughter, on 6 April 1960. I was doing a club show, but as soon as I got offstage, I raced down the hospital. It was me that chose the name: Cheryl. There was no particular reason or family history to it, I just liked it. It suited her as a baby, and it still does today.

I'd just turned twenty, so it was young to become a dad, but it didn't change me at all. I loved Cheryl, of course I did, but my focus was still on doing what I did best: getting up onstage. I was still working days and nights, which could have been tough on Pauline. Luckily, we were living with my folks, so my mum could help out with the baby a bit.

Which was just as well. Because I was about to be away working for quite a while.

* * *

In the summer of 1960, I went back to the first place I had got up onstage and told jokes: the place that had kicked it all off for me. I went to work a summer season at Butlin's in Pwllheli. But I wasn't up onstage this time. Not at first, anyway. Because they hired me as a kitchen porter.

This was livelier than it might sound. I started off washing up and pushing trollies around but the guy who ran the kitchen took a shine to me and gave me supervisory duties. This suited me because I could tell *other* people to do the work: 'Oi! Get a move on!' I'd say. 'There's people out there waiting for their dinners!'

One day, I caught one of the kitchen workers, who was a right pain in the arse, skiving and having a crafty ciggie. 'Come on, lad!' I told him. 'Get those dishes sorted out.'

He stared at me, riled. 'I'll do it when I've had my fag,' he said.

'No, you'll do it *now*,' I said. 'Because then we can go off duty.'

Well, the feller took a swing at me. I saw it coming and managed to duck out of the way. I picked up a brush that was next to me and hit him over the head with it: *smack!* He went down like a sack of spuds. When he got up, the kitchen manager fired him.

I got matey with the guys who worked in the bar. One day, I *borrowed* – well, nicked – fifty chicken legs from the kitchen, and they took fifty bottles of beer from the bar. That night, we staff all met up and had a bloody great barbecue and party on the beach. Let me tell you, it was a right laugh.

The next morning, the kitchen manager took me to one side.

'Jimmy, you'll never guess what happened last night,' he said. 'Some bastards had a big do on the beach. There's chicken legs and beer bottles everywhere. We've got to find out who it was!'

'Leave it to me,' I said. But, oddly enough, I didn't solve that mystery for him. Funny, that.

After I'd been in the kitchen for a few weeks, the Butlin's staff who could sing or dance a bit put on a show for the campers. They asked me to compere it. It was a lot of fun, and I enjoyed bantering with the audience: 'Oh, hello, luv? Is that your hubby with you? Did you always want to marry an older man?'

I got a lot of laughs, and Butlin's said to me, 'Why don't you start introducing the main shows and be the camp compere? You're a lot better than the feller we've got doing it now.' They made me a Redcoat and suddenly I was hosting all of the performances. And I absolutely loved it.

We had some good acts on. The main band that season was a group that I knew from Liverpool called Rory Storm and the Hurricanes. Ringo Starr was their drummer. I hung out a lot with Ringo in Pwllheli. He was a good guy and a great laugh, dead sarcastic, and it was obvious that he was a fantastic drummer.

I introduced their gigs in the Rock 'n' Calypso Ballroom. Ringo would do a 'Starr-time' solo singing slot during the shows. Rory Storm was a nice guy, as well. The weird thing about Rory was that he had a really bad stutter when he talked. If he tried to tell a joke, it might go on for days. But his stammer vanished as soon as he started singing.

I used to escort the acts from the dressing room to the stage and park them in the wings as I introduced them. A singer called Michael Holliday came through, who'd just had a number one with 'Starry Eyed'. Arthur English was a nice old feller as well. His act was doing a Cockney 'spiv' character.

Mind you, not all of the comedians were half as funny as Arthur. I've got to admit, we had some distinctly second-division comics on the bill that year. I'd introduce them, then go and stand on the side of the stage, watch their act and think, *Bloody hell! I'm a lot better than this rubbish!*

While I was down in Wales, I asked for a trial with the local non-league football team, Pwllheli FC, and played a few matches at inside-right for them. I'd never say no to a game of footie, and they slipped me a few bob per game, which was all the better. Their player-manager was a guy called Orig Williams, and what a character *he* was.

Orig was a massive bruiser of a guy. He was a proper dirty player who used to boast that he was sent off more than any other player in the Welsh league. By Christ, he was hard. I saw just *how* hard the week that an opponent clattered me then gave me a sneaky kick in the ribs. I was bent double and winded. Orig saw it.

'Go and stand on the wing, lad,' he said. We had a corner, and I was watching the ball come in when I heard an '*Ow* – *oof!*' I looked over to see the bloke who'd just belted me laid out, unconscious, at our player-manager's feet. 'That bastard won't be kicking anyone else, will be?' Orig murmured to me as he wandered past.*

Pauline brought Cheryl down to Pwllheli a couple of times to see me. I had a great time at Butlin's, but at the end of the season it was nice to get back to Liverpool and spend time with my wife and baby daughter. And, just after I got back, Pauline and I went to the flicks to see a new Alfred Hitchcock film, *Psycho*.

Let me be honest here. This wasn't the best date that Pauline and I ever went on because the pictures was almost sold out so we couldn't get tickets to sit together. I sat in the

---

* After he retired from football, Orig Williams became a professional wrestler. He grew a handlebar moustache and fought in Europe, Asia, the Middle East and America under the name 'El Bandito'. A true one-off.

front row and Pauline was about three rows behind me. The other problem was that the film was bloody terrifying.

When the famous scene came where Anthony Perkins hacks Janet Leigh to bits in the shower, a woman sitting next to me screamed – 'Aaagh!' – and jumped on top of me. That made me scream as well: 'Gerroff!' I looked behind me and Pauline was pissing herself laughing. But that film proper put the shits up me.

I was getting known as a comic and compere so I got offered more stuff. I did a short tour of US Army bases, mostly in Norfolk, telling a few gags and introducing the acts. I liked being able to get import American rock-and-roll records and chewing gum at the PX stores on the bases.

I *didn't* like that the audiences at the shows were virtually segregated. The Black soldiers sat on one side and the white guys on the other. It was daft. When I hung out with the US servicemen, of whatever colour, they all liked talking about the same things: music, sport and women. I had some lovely evenings with them.

* * *

Back in Liverpool, something was happening that was impossible to miss. And that was that The Beatles were suddenly becoming an absolutely brilliant band.

They had gone off to Hamburg in August 1960. Oddly enough, it was a booking that had originally been offered to Rory Storm and the Hurricanes, but they couldn't do it as they were at Butlin's with me. I remember some folk mithering about The Beatles, going: 'Eh? They're a Liverpool band! They're ours! What've they got to go to Germany for?'

They had done about ten weeks of shows in Hamburg, playing for eight hours every day in clubs like the Kaiserkeller and the Top Ten Club. They didn't have that many songs yet so they just played them over and over, along with covers of stuff like 'Johnny B. Goode'.* And playing non-stop like that had made them bloody good.

We all only realised *how* good when they played a lunchtime show at the Cavern when they came back. They'd always been an OK band, but when they plugged their gear in, said, 'One-two-three-four!' and started firing out their riffs, our gobs were hanging open: *What the hell is this?* Because they were phenomenal.

They still weren't quite the band they were to become. Despite his name, Pete Best was a weak drummer, and Stuart Sutcliffe couldn't really play the bass. He used to just pose around the stage. But John, Paul and George sounded incredible. We all knew we were listening to something special.

Cilla Black had started working in the cloakroom at the Cavern. Or Cilla White, as she still was then. (It's a funny story, how she changed her name. When she played her first gig, a local journalist, Bill Harry, called her 'Cilla Black' by mistake, so she thought she'd better stick with it. She always told me that she preferred her real name.)

---

* I remember Lennon saying to me once, 'They shouldn't call it rock 'n' roll. They should call it Chuck Berry.'

Cilla was a force of nature in the cloakroom. A livewire. I still say it onstage today: 'You'd give Cilla your coat and, if you were lucky, you might get it back!' She had a word, and a joke, for everyone. You'd have a proper hoot with her. And Cilla's big thing was getting up onstage to sing with the bands.

Everybody who played, she'd ask them if she could do a song with them. It wasn't just The Beatles. She'd get up with Rory Storm, and with Kingsize Taylor and the Dominoes. You name it, she'd sing it: anything from rock and roll, to Sinatra, to Doris Day. She had a great voice, and an even better personality.

Cilla was madly in love with Cliff Richard. She used to idolise him. Once, when Cliff played in Liverpool, a rumour got around that he was staying the night at my house. It was bollocks, but Cilla turned up outside Queens Drive, yelling up at the window. I'll tell you, it was bloody lucky for Cliff that he wasn't there!

Cilla's best friend until the day she died was a woman named Pat. She used to go as Little Pat, because she was only knee-high to a grasshopper. I first met Pat down the Cavern. I was chatting to a mate, and Pat came up to me and said, 'Oo are you talking to, Tatty 'ead?' That nickname stuck to me … forever.

Work-wise, I got booked to do my first Scottish gigs in Arbroath, up on the east coast south of Aberdeen. I was on an old-fashioned variety bill at a smashing theatre venue called the Webster Memorial Hall. I remember there was a musical group, dancers, and a Scottish chap who was very good on the accordion.

Pauline and Cheryl came up with me. We stayed in a B&B. Arbroath is famous for its smokies, a bit like kippers. They're nice ... if you have them once a week. Well, our boarding house fed us bloody smokies every day, breakfast, lunch and dinner. We got totally kippered out.

After one show, a feller came up to me. He was in the junior team at the local Scottish League club, Arbroath FC. 'I hear ye're no a bad player?' he asked.

'I'm OK,' I said. 'My left leg's for standing on, but I'm quite good with my right.'

'D'ye fancy a game for us?'

Of course I did! I was in.

The Arbroath youth team had got through to the semi-finals of a local junior cup. They put me in the team at inside-right. 'But you can't use your real name,' they said, 'or they'll know you're a ringer. We'll call you Jock McGregor.'

'OK.'

It was a good game. I think we won 3–1. Halfway through the second half, I played the ball through for our centre-forward and he scored (they'd call it an assist nowadays, but no one said that back then). He wheeled around and ran to me. 'Aye! Nice one, Jimmy, mon!' he yelled.

'Er, don't you mean Jock?' I whispered.

They told me I wouldn't be able to play in the final. There'd be pen-pictures of all the players in the programme and I'd get found out. 'No worries!' I said. They won the cup and that night, while I was onstage at the Webster, the team turned up and walked down the middle aisle with the trophy. It was brilliant. We went on the piss to celebrate.*

That summer of 1961, I went back to Butlin's, this time in Brighton. It was in a hotel, not a holiday camp. And I wasn't going anywhere near the kitchens this time. I was hired as a Redcoat. And it was fantastic.

Being a Redcoat suited me. Fitted my personality. I loved walking around the hotel, jollying along the holidaymakers. I might stop a retired couple and say to the lady: 'You must be here for the Miss Brighton contest!'

And she'd laugh and say, 'Ooh, you cheeky pup!' It's funny: at Butlin's, once you put a red coat on, you were a star.

I'd be organising all kinds of competitions: talent contests, beauty pageants, knobbly knees, glamorous grandmother. I'd get elderly ladies, who hadn't done any sport since school, playing netball. I'd have a good laugh with them, and poke gentle fun, but it was all done affectionately. It was never cruel.

There was one Redcoat job that I didn't like. That was calling the bingo. It was so bloody boring, but it was part of the job. So, I started doing it wrong on purpose. Instead of shouting out 'Three and one: thirty-one!' I'd say 'Three and one: four!' My plan worked. Some campers complained and I got taken off the bingo.

---

* A few years later, when I'd got famous and did my first stand-up tour of big venues, I told the promoter I wanted to play Arbroath. He looked at me like I was mad: 'Why? It's in the middle of nowhere!' 'Just book me into the Webster Memorial Hall,' I said. We called the show 'Welcome Home'. It was grand.

I enjoyed going in the swimming pool with the holidaymakers. I remember I got a mate from Liverpool, Ray Feldman, a job as a pool lifeguard. *That* was a joke: Ray could barely swim! He'd just sit by the pool sunbathing with his cap pulled down over his face. The managers used to moan about him. I didn't blame them.

The Redcoats played football against a team of campers once a week. Those matches could get a bit fierce. I was still clinging to my dream of being a professional footballer, and asked for a trial with Brighton & Hove Albion. I got a few games for the youth team, and the reserves, but I wasn't good enough for the first team.

That was made pretty clear to me. One day the reserve team had a Southern Cup game against Eastbourne. The manager, a Mr Curtis, went round the dressing room, telling players, 'plenty of quick one-twos' and 'keep going down the line'. When he got to me, all he said was, 'Nothing tricky from you, right?'

Well, no matter. I was about to have a very special encounter when Liverpool came to town to play Brighton. It was with a legend called Bill Shankly.

My mate Jimmy Melia was in the first team by then. He got me a ticket for the game and I went to meet him in their hotel beforehand. He introduced me to their new manager: 'Mr Shankly, this is a lad from Liverpool.'

Shankly narrowed his eyes and looked me up and down. 'So, what are ye doing down here, son?'

'I'm working at Butlin's as a comedian, sir.'

Shankly had moved from Huddersfield Town to take

over at Liverpool at the end of 1959. He didn't like what he found when he arrived. The team was still languishing in Division Two and the players were pretty ordinary. No money had been spent on the ground for years. Anfield was falling to bits. It was a shithole.*

Shankly had set about grabbing the club by the scruff of the neck and sorting it out. He'd put almost the whole team on the transfer list, and signed two fantastic new players in Ron Yeats, a colossus of a centre-half, and Ian St John, a brilliant midfielder who came down from Scotland. Within a year of us meeting, Liverpool had got promoted.

When I met Shankly in Brighton, I didn't yet know what a football genius he was, but he cut an impressive figure. He was dapper and well dressed and, while he was clearly a hard man, he was also friendly. He was charismatic: when he spoke, you listened. I was to get to know Bill Shankly very well over the years.

And, really, I had a wonderful time at Butlin's in Brighton. I was learning my trade: learning to talk to people and make them laugh: 'Ooh, watch that husband of yours, luv. He's a rascal!' I was lucky in that the campers liked me. Because, even today, if anybody asks me the secret to being a comic, I always tell them this:

'It's an easy answer. People have got to like you. If they don't like you, they can't laugh at you. And if they happen to love you, well, you're home and dry.'

* * *

---

* Dare I say much like Old Trafford nowadays, boom boom?

When I finished in Brighton and went back home, I carried on working the northern club circuit. I was doing OK by now. I was probably making about £20 per week, which was a lot of money back then. The Pavilion in Liverpool booked me for a week for £25 and I felt proper flush.

I entered a talent contest in New Brighton. It was for amateurs only: if you'd worked professionally, you weren't allowed to enter. So I did it under an assumed name. I told the organisers I was called Andy King. I got up and told a few gags – *bang, bang, boom!* – and I won it. The first prize was £50. Nice!

As I walked back from collecting my prize on the stage, a feller in the crowd collared me. 'Hang on!' he said. 'Didn't I see you at Butlin's? You're not Andy King. Your name's Jimmy Tarbuck!'

'*Shush!*' I said. He didn't snitch me out, and the venue booked me to do a week. I used a few other stage names, occasionally. Buggered if I can remember now what they were.

Around now, I actually *did* go professional. Andre Bernard had been great to me, and given me weeks off at a time when I needed it, but I felt like I'd cut my last back of the neck. And, if I'm honest, I hadn't made the progress in the job that they'd hoped I would. I was a crap ladies' hairdresser.

Once, I was chatting away to an old dear as I trimmed the back of her head … until I cut right through her deaf aid. *Oops!* Another time, Pauline came in, and I made such a bad mess of her hair that a senior stylist had to salvage it. *That* didn't go down well. It felt like time to fully commit to comedy and give it my best shot.

My stage work was still up and down (showbiz is like that, at the bottom!) so I did a third stint at Butlin's in the summer of 1962. I went back to Pwllheli as a Redcoat. I remember Johnny Ball was there as well. If I'm honest, I thought he was a bloody awful comedian. A lot of his jokes were too familiar from other comics' material.

I was very good at being a Redcoat by now and I had the holidaymakers roaring as I compered the shows … but not everyone was impressed. One day, the national director of entertainment for Butlin's, one Colonel Basil Brown, visited Pwllheli and watched me perform. I think the good colonel was baffled by my Scouse accent.

After the show, he delivered his verdict: 'That young man could be a good comedian, if he spoke the Queen's English.'* He reported back to Butlin's and, for some reason, they tried to move me to their hotel in Cliftonville, down by Margate. I was perfectly happy where I was, and a bit offended by this, so I left.

Back in Liverpool, I bumped into John Lennon. And he had a lot of news. I knew that Stu Sutcliffe had sadly died, but John told me The Beatles had fired Pete Best on drums and brought in Ringo (a masterstroke). They'd got a new manager, Brian Epstein, who'd fixed them up with a record deal with Parlophone. And they'd just written a song called 'Love Me Do'.

'Do you want to hear it?' he asked me.

'Yeah, great!'

---

* There again, I'm still trying to do that today.

So John took me back to his Auntie Mimi's house, got his guitar out, and sang me 'Love Me Do'. And I came out with an absolute classic.

'That's cracking, is that!' I told him. 'You ought to sell it to The Everly Brothers. It's perfect for them.'

John looked at me like I was a lunatic. He never let me forget that comment. For years afterwards, every time I ran into him and asked what he was up to, he'd say, 'Oh, I'm still writing songs for The Everly Brothers!' And he'd piss himself laughing.

I was still going further afield for my gigs, and early in 1963 I went to Leeds to play their City Varieties Theatre. It's a beautiful playhouse, which is still going, and at the time it was used by the BBC to film *The Good Old Days*, their long-running old-time music-hall show hosted by Leonard Sachs. I remember they paid me £30.

Not everything at the City Varieties was quite so salubrious as *The Good Old Days*. I walked in the venue to be told by the manager that the compere hadn't shown up so, as well as doing my set, I'd have to do some hosting. Starting straight away. 'Get out there and introduce the first act,' he said. 'It's the stripper.'

I was flummoxed. 'You what?' I gulped. 'I can't do that. What do I say?'

'Just get out there and say something nice about her. Go on!'

There was a woman waiting in the wings who appeared to be wearing suspenders under a short jacket. I walked past

her onto the stage and looked out at a bunch of eager, expectant dirty old men.

'Ladies and gentlemen,' I said. 'Settle down. We have a
young lady for you now who is a wonderful singer. Sadly, she's
lost her voice tonight, so she's going to show you her tits instead.'

Well, there was uproar! The audience fell about.
Everybody loved that joke … except the stripper. As I walked
offstage and she walked on, she smacked me in the mouth.
Ouch! But, of course, I then stood in the wings and watched
her act. I mean, I was just being professional, right?

I must have done OK in Leeds because a guy who was in
the audience got in touch with me. He was a showbiz agent
called Terry Miller and he said he wanted to manage me. I
went down to his office in London for a meeting with him.
Terry was a quiet, shrewd guy. 'How much do you earn a
week?' he asked me.

I wanted to impress him so I decided to inflate the figure
a bit. *Quite* a bit, in fact. 'Sixty pounds,' I said.

'OK,' said Terry, 'I want you to sign a one-year contract
with me. And if you're not earning two hundred pounds a
week by Christmas, I'll rip the contract up.'

'That'll do me,' I replied. 'You've got a deal.'

And, almost straight away, I got a big break. There used
to be an ITV programme called *Comedy Bandbox* that was
only broadcast in the North West. It was for both established
and new stand-ups. I used to watch it most weeks: I'd seen
Arthur Askey, Ted Ray, Jimmy Clitheroe, Dick Emery, Mike
and Bernie Winters and tons of others on it.

I'd called ATV, who made the show, a few times, asking them to put me on. Now that Terry was managing me, he started doing the same. And, at the start of October 1963, he called with me with some great news. We'd worn *Comedy Bandbox* down. They'd agreed to give me a go.

This was exciting! Going on the telly! It felt like a big step up. The show was recorded in front of a studio audience in Manchester. I knew I'd only have about three minutes so I was determined to make them count. I rehearsed hard – well, for me – and when I got there, I was nervous but not overawed.

It's weird. I vividly remember being on the show but I can't recall a single thing I said. All I remember is that I met Les Dawson on the same show (the start of a strong friendship) ... and that I went down well. I came offstage feeling proud, and felt even prouder when I watched it back on TV that Saturday night with Pauline, Mum and Dad.

Although *Comedy Bandbox* was only broadcast in the North West, Val Parnell, who was a big cheese at ATV, always got a recording of the show to watch in his office in London on Monday mornings. And, two days after my episode went out, I got the phone call from Terry Miller that was to change my life.

'Jimmy, I've just heard from Val Parnell's office,' he said. 'He wants you on *Sunday Night at the London Palladium* this Sunday.'

CHAPTER 5

What's trumps? Crusts. Buttered.

I nearly dropped the phone. I couldn't believe what I was hearing. My first thought was that Terry Miller must have made a mistake. 'Eh? Are you joking?' I asked him. But Terry wasn't joking.

He explained what had happened. Val Parnell was the head honcho of *Sunday Night at the London Palladium*. The show was Val's baby and he was a light-entertainment-world god. His right-hand man, Alec Fyne, who helped him to book the acts, had played him the recording of me on *Comedy Bandbox*. And Val had said, 'He's good. Put him on next Sunday.'

'Are you sure?' asked Alec.

'Yes,' said Val.

It couldn't have come as a bigger shock. *Sunday Night at the London Palladium* was the peak of British entertainment television. It went out live nationwide, across the ITV network, every Sunday night, and everyone watched it. I say, *everyone*. Up to twenty million people tuned in each week.

I mean, *bloody hell!* They wanted *me*? I was in awe of the show, and I was in awe of the Palladium. When I was in London, on tour with Cliff Richard, I'd been to a show there. I'd seen Max Bygraves. Max was good, but it was the theatre that had really blown me away. It was stunningly beautiful. It's still my favourite venue today.

I felt disbelief at the news and, as that faded, I felt sheer joy. *Me! At the Palladium! Me! On telly!* But there was one complicating factor. They wanted me to go on the show on Sunday, 27 October. This meant rehearsing all day … but, the night before, I was already booked on a variety bill up North, at Manchester City Social Club. And I hated pulling shows.

So, I didn't. I did the gig in Manchester. I remember that also on the bill were a pair of up-and-coming northern comics called Cannon and Ball.* I was headlining so, as soon as I got offstage, I got in my Volvo with Pauline and a mate from Liverpool, Ray Feldman (yep, the non-swimmer Butlin's lifeguard), and we drove to London.

Bear in mind, that wasn't as straightforward a route as it is today. In 1963, the M6 and the M1 were both still works in progress, so we had to weave our way down the country via various A roads. Ray and I took turns to drive through the night. And, all the way, I had butterflies in my stomach. I'll never forget that journey.

---

* They told me later that they'd been gobsmacked. They played a Manchester social club with me … then, the next night, turned on the telly and saw me at the Palladium.

In the early hours, we pulled up outside Terry Miller's apartment in a block of flats next to the Lord's cricket ground in St John's Wood, north London. I didn't want to disturb him, so we slept in the motor in the car park. In the morning, Terry knocked on the window with a cup of tea and woke us up.

We headed off to the Palladium rehearsals ... and I was bloody awful. Atrocious. I had hardly had any sleep and I was eaten up with nerves. I was mangling my words. Couldn't get them out. I'd totally forgotten Max Miller's advice: *Take. Your. Time.* I was gabbling, and fluffing. It couldn't have gone any worse.

A break came. I went outside and leaned against a wall in despair.* When I went back in, I wasn't surprised when someone told me that Val Parnell wanted a word. As I was led to the great man's office, I thought, *Fair enough. He's realised he made a mistake. He's kicking me off the bill.* But when I was shown in, Mr Parnell was all smiles and affability.

'What are you nervous for, young man?' he asked me. 'It's me that ought to be nervous – I'm the one that booked you! And I booked you because you're very good. Now, go out there and show them what you can do.'

Before showtime, the producers came to my dressing room to give me the dos and don'ts. It was a live show, they stressed. They were giving me seven minutes. I had to do my act and get off. No matter how it went, I wasn't to come back on and take a bow. It would throw the timings out – and timings were crucial.

---

* I still have a photo of me doing that.

Huh! I thought. *You saw my rehearsal! I shouldn't worry about me having to come back to take a bow ...*

The show's headliners were Billy J. Kramer and the Dakotas, and also on were Xavier Cugat and Abbe Lane, an American bandleader-and-singer couple playing sultry Latin music. The compere was Bruce Forsyth. 'Ladies and gentlemen, please welcome a young man from Liverpool!' he said, as I hovered in the wings. 'Mr Jimmy Tarbuck!'

As I walked out, I was sure the audience would be able to hear my heart thudding in my chest. And, you know what? It started just the same as my first talent contest at Butlin's. I told my opening joke and it only got a few titters. 'Huh! Don't laugh, then!' I said. *That* got a roar. And, more than that, it got them on my side.

Looking back, I guess the crowd could tell that I was a nervy young lad trying his best. I think they liked my energy, and my enthusiasm. Because when I went into the main bit of my act, they absolutely loved it.

'I was in a bar and this feller asked me if I wanted to play cards,' I said. 'I told him "OK" and he got out a sliced loaf of bread. I thought, "Crumbs!"'

There was a howl of laughter from the audience. Encouraged, I went on.

'"What's trumps?" I asked the feller. And he said: "Crusts. Buttered."'

It was just a piece of daftness, really. But, sometimes, daftness is what people like. What they want. Everyone was in stitches. They laughed so much that I ended up being on for

A truly treasured memory: a signed photo from seeing Laurel and Hardy at the Liverpool Empire.

In one of my school football teams. Can you spot me?

'Dad! I thought you'd brought the oars!' 'I thought you had!' On the lake in Sefton Park.

With Marty Wilde and the fabulous Billy Fury on the Larry Parnes Extravaganza, 1958.

'Get those dishes done!' In the kitchen at Butlin's in Pwllheli.

Pauline and I get hitched, 9 September 1959. It's lasted rather well.

The home of The Beatles... and Tarby! Performing at The Cavern, 1963.

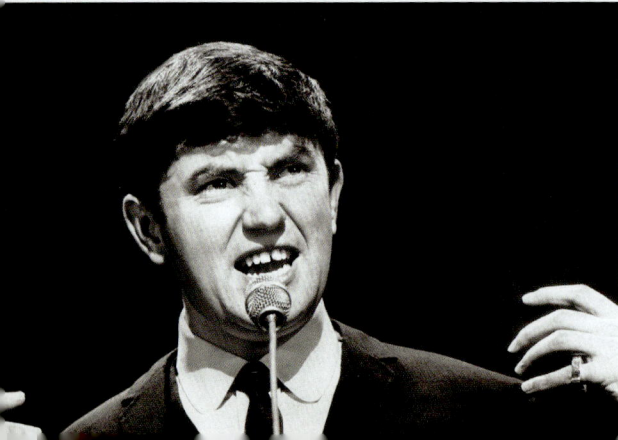

The night of my life: my debut at the London Palladium, 27 October 1963.

'Come back 'ere!' Pegging it down the pier during my 1964 Blackpool summer season.

Scouse in the house: with Cilla before the 1964 Royal Variety Performance.

With Pauline, Cheryl and baby Liza in Great Yarmouth, 1965.

'I got the job!' Leaving the Yarmouth grocery shop where I learned I was to host *Sunday Night at the London Palladium*.

'Yes, it's me!' Being announced as the new host at the Palladium, 1965.

Cutting a rug with Hollywood star and hoofer George Raft, 1965.

With Norman Vaughan and the great, great Harry Secombe.

Hanging out by Tarby's Wall in *It's Tarbuck*, 1964.

Duetting with Cliff – and trying to forget Joe Lee's bus – on *Sunday Night at the London Palladium*, 1965.

'How will we get back to Coventry?' 'We'll worry about that later!' At the 1965 FA Cup Final with Frankie Vaughan.

With two of my all-time British comic heroes, Eric Morecambe and Ernie Wise.

On the Palladium stage with the small but perfectly formed Ronnie Corbett, 1966.

'Always give them two minutes to look at the suit': the peerless Bob Hope.

'This is Your Lie', ho ho! Helping Eamonn Andrews to line up a putt.

Pauline and I welcome our lad, James, to the world in Watford hospital, 1968.

'There's only one Man in Miami...' Pauline and I with the great Frank Sinatra (plus Ben Novack, owner of the Fontainebleau Hotel), 1969.

Meeting Muhammed Ali.

Giving Henry Cooper a few tips.

GAUMONT, DONCASTER
Manager M. S. MOORSE
5.00 | SUNDAY, 27th SEPTEMBER | 7.30
LARRY PARNES presents
THE RESIDENT STAR OF
IN PERSON
"BOY MEETS GIRLS"
BRITAIN'S YOUNGEST ALL-ROUND ENTERTAINER
THE FABULOUS
MARTY
WILDE
& HIS NEW WILDCATS
Philips Hit Recorder of DONNA & TEENAGER IN LOVE
THE SENSATIONAL VISCOUNTS
THE DYNAMIC WEE WILLIE HARRIS
No. 1 TEENAGE COMPERE JIMMY TARBUCK
THE ROCKETS
THE BACHELORS
PRICES: 7/6 6/6 5/6 4/6 All Bookable, Phone: 3864
To the Manager, Box Office, Gaumont, Doncaster
STRIKE OUT WORDS NOT REQUIRED

WINTER GARDENS
MARGATE
Gala Opening TUESDAY, 8th JULY at 8p.m.
AND THEREAFTER FOR THE SEASON NIGHTLY at 8p.m.
RICHARD STONE presents
JIMMY TARBUCK
in
TARBUCK AND FRIENDS
A Ross Taylor production
with
choreography by DENISE SHAUNE
BASIL BRUSH
JOYANNE DELANCEY
Audrey & Roger MISTIN
THE VOYAGERS
BETTY SMITH AND HER ORCHESTRA
DENISE SHAUNE DANCERS
RONNIE HILTON
Children Accompanied by an Adult Half Price to all Parts at Monday Performances Only

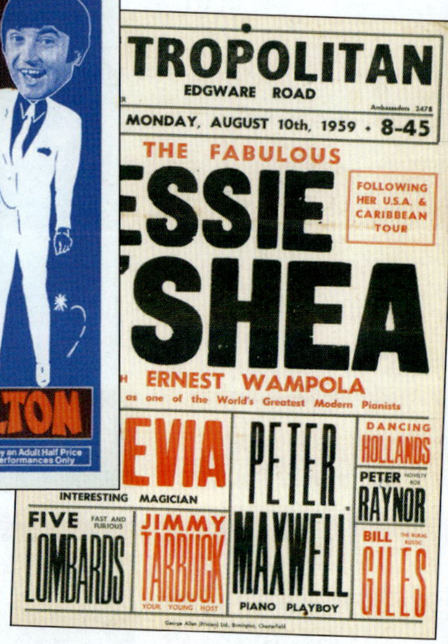
TROPOLITAN
EDGWARE ROAD
MONDAY, AUGUST 10th, 1959 · 8-45
THE FABULOUS
ESSIE
'SHEA
FOLLOWING HER U.S.A. & CARIBBEAN TOUR
ERNEST WAMPOLA
as one of the World's Greatest Modern Pianists
EVIA
INTERESTING MAGICIAN
PETER MAXWELL
PIANO PLAYBOY
DANCING HOLLANDS
PETER RAYNOR
BILL GILES
FIVE LOMBARDS
FAST AND FURIOUS
JIMMY TARBUCK
YOUR YOUNG HOST

THE ROYAL VARIETY PERFORMANCE 1964
AT THE LONDON PALLADIU

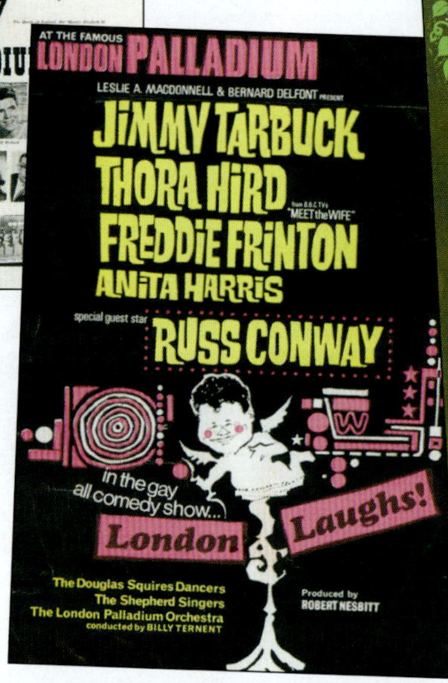
AT THE FAMOUS
LONDON PALLADIUM
LESLIE A. MACDONNELL & BERNARD DELFONT PRESENT
JIMMY TARBUCK
THORA HIRD
"MEET the WIFE"
FREDDIE FRINTON
ANITA HARRIS
special guest star
RUSS CONWAY
in the gay all comedy show...
London Laughs!
The Douglas Squires Dancers
The Shepherd Singers
The London Palladium Orchestra
conducted by BILLY TERNENT
Produced by ROBERT NESBITT

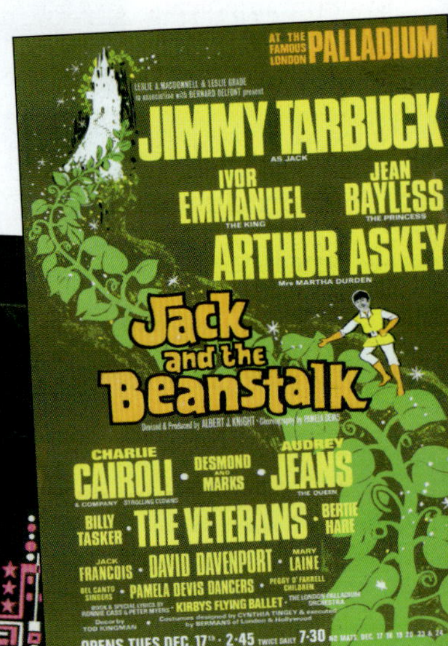
AT THE FAMOUS LONDON PALLADIUM
JIMMY TARBUCK
AS JACK
IVOR EMMANUEL
THE KING
JEAN BAYLESS
THE PRINCESS
ARTHUR ASKEY
Mrs MARTHA DURDEN
Jack and the Beanstalk
CHARLIE CAIROLI
DESMOND AND MARKS
AUDREY JEANS
THE QUEEN
BILLY TASKER
THE VETERANS
BERTIE HARE
JACK FRANCOIS
DAVID DAVENPORT
MARY LAINE
PAMELA DEVIS DANCERS
KIRBYS FLYING BALLET
OPENS TUES DEC. 17th · 2·45 TWICE DAILY 7·30

nine minutes rather than seven. I finished off with eight bars of singing – *boom!* – and as I walked off, they rose from their seats. I got a standing ovation.

I went straight to my dressing room. The applause was still going on. A producer came running to fetch me. 'Quick! Come back on and take a bow!' he said.

'I can't,' I answered. 'I've been told not to.'

'Well, you'll have to, because they won't stop clapping. Come on!'

When I walked back onstage, there was a deafening roar. Bruce Forsyth was waiting for me. I took a bow. 'Well done, young man!' Bruce told me.

'Thank you, Mr Forsyth.'

Bruce mugged at the audience. 'Ooh, isn't that nice?' He grinned. 'He just called me Mr Forsyth!'

It all felt like a dream. I bowed again and went off. Because I'd overrun my slot, Xavier Cugat and Abbe Lane were going to have to cut a song from their act. *Oops!* A producer suggested that I go to their dressing room and apologise. I knocked on their door and Abbe Lane opened it.

Abbe was a stunning woman. She was very beautiful and her dress appeared to have been painted on. She smiled and squeezed my cheek. 'Ah, the young boy,' she said. 'I didn't understand everything you said, but you are very cute ...' And I fell in love, for a few minutes.

I floated away from the London Palladium that night. Terry Miller took me to a beautiful restaurant at the Hilton hotel with his partner, Charlie Tucker, who was Julie Andrews's manager. '*You* are going to be a very big star,' they both told me. And the next morning, I woke up to find that I was all over the newspapers:

YOUNG LIVERPOOL COMIC
STORMS PALLADIUM SHOW!

I will never forget 27 October 1963. It was the night that changed everything for me. The night of my life.

* * *

One reason that I'd got invited onto *Sunday Night at the London Palladium*, of course, was that Liverpool was super-trendy at the time. The week I was on, Gerry and the Pacemakers were number one with 'You'll Never Walk Alone' – their third chart-topper of the year. And The Beatles had just exploded.

The lads had three number ones in a row in 1963. They'd been on the Palladium show two weeks before me, and they were about to do the famous Royal Variety Performance where Lennon told the punters in the cheap seats to clap and the rest to 'rattle their jewellery'. And, by the by, they were opening doors for me.

Because I always went on in a high-buttoned suit and tie, like them, and I had a similar moptop of hair, one or two journalists took to calling me 'the fifth Beatle.'* And, I'll tell you what, I never once tried to put a stop to that. Because it

---

* Although I'd sometimes joke that I was more like the fourth Beverley Sister.

did me no harm at all. Suddenly, my accent was an advantage, not a hindrance.

It was around now that I met Brian Epstein properly for the first time. What was he like? Very pleasant, very charming and very posh. I thought he was OK. He could see that I was starting to get big and he offered to manage me. I was flattered, but I declined as I already had a manager.

Right after the Palladium, I was back in the northern theatres and working men's clubs. I had dates pre-booked so I honoured them. It was hard to miss that the clubs were fuller than usual, and people seemed keener to see me. And then, as I went into 1964 … it all exploded for me, too.

I was back on *Sunday Night at the London Palladium* in January, with the opera singer Charles Craig and pop stars The Kaye Sisters (who weren't really sisters). It was different this time: I didn't kip in my car the night before, I was higher up the bill, and some people had actually heard of me. It went as well as the first time. It was great.

In February, I compered a rock and roll tour with Gerry and the Pacemakers. I knew the guys already from Liverpool. Gerry Marsden used to live in the next street to Pauline: he was a good lad. There was one date on the tour that he couldn't appear at, for some reason. So, Cilla filled in for him.

Also on that tour was an American soul giant, Ben E. King. He was a lovely bloke and, *my God*, what a voice. I could listen to him all night. I felt like I was in the presence of soul music royalty, but Ben had no airs or graces. He mucked in backstage with everyone else.

Oh, speaking of unbelievable voices … I made a third trip to the Palladium and was on with Ethel Merman, the American star of stage musicals. Blimey, Ethel belted it out! She could have shattered every window in the West End. But she went down a storm and was gracious and lovely to me.

Suddenly, now the Palladium show was making me well known, I didn't have to badger theatre managers for gigs. They were coming to me. My manager, Terry Miller, set about fulfilling his promise to make me a big star … and sent me to Coventry. Specifically, to the Coventry Theatre, for their two-month 'Spring Show'.

It was a proper old-fashioned variety bill. There was no danger of young Tarby getting big-headed: on the posters, I was billed beneath Pinky and Perky. Who? Well, you may ask! They were a pair of puppets: two oinking, singing, dancing piggies with their own BBC children's show. Kids loved them.

Also on the bill was Jimmy Clitheroe, the northern comic. Jimmy was a smashing feller who built his act around how tiny he was. Not that he had much choice: he was four foot two. Yep, *four foot two*. He put a cap on every time he drove his car because he got so fed up with the police stopping him, thinking he was a child who'd nicked it.

The headliner in Coventry was Dickie Henderson. Now, Dickie was a gent. He was quite a posh chap – an ex-Army officer – and a big star from telly shows like Arthur Askey's *Before Your Very Eyes* and his own *Dickie Henderson Half Hour*. But he was a lovely feller and very nice to newcomers like me (which wasn't true of everyone).

One day, Dickie asked me a question: 'Do you play golf?'
'I have done,' I said.

This was true. *Just about*. When I was fourteen, I'd gone
to the Allerton municipal golf course in Liverpool with a pal
from school, Roger Heath. It was two-and-six for a round and
two-bob deposit for the clubs and balls. We hadn't got a clue
what we were doing. We hacked and bashed our way around
the course, then buggered off home.

By contrast, Dickie had been playing for years and was
an excellent golfer. He took me for a few rounds. He politely
wiped the floor with me, of course, but he was a patient and
helpful coach, showing me how to stop swinging and missing
on every tee. It was Dickie that got me interested in the sport
(oh, he's got a lot to answer for ...)

I was starting to make proper money. A year earlier, I was
still getting twenty quid a week from WMCs. Terry Miller had
told me he'd have me earning £200 per week in a year, but I
hadn't really believed him. I thought he was just saying it to
draw me in. But then, guess what? He only went and did it.

That was what I was to be paid for a 1964 summer season
in Blackpool. I had to pinch myself. *£200 per week!* I was
going to do three months in the big theatre on the North Pier
in Blackpool, in a variety show headlined by the well-known
comedy brothers Mike and Bernie Winters.

Let me tell you, Blackpool summer seasons were big
in those days. Anybody who was anybody did them. In
1964 alone, there was Frank Ifield and Kathy Kirby at the
ABC, Joe Brown and Johnny Kidd and the Pirates on the

South Pier, and Dick Emery and The Dave Clark Five at the Winter Gardens.

And now there was me.

Mike and Bernie Winters were also hosting the *Blackpool Night Out* ITV show. They were OK with me. Mike was very well educated, at public schools. Bernie ... wasn't. He was as you saw him on telly: a big, gormless, gleeful smile and loads of fun. I found Bernie a bit easier to engage with, of the two. But I got on well with both of them.

I rented a house in Blackpool. Pauline and Cheryl joined me for the summer. When I wasn't playing golf in the day, Pauline and I would take Cheryl on the trams, and on the donkeys on the beach. We showed her the illuminations. It took me back to my own parents taking me to see the lights as a kid.

Pauline had brought our labrador, Louis, with her as well. One afternoon, Pauline took Cheryl to a show and I went for a drive down the seafront. I was in a convertible and it was a lovely sunny day, so I had the roof down. Louis, the daft lump, was lying by me in the front passenger seat, fast asleep.

We got stuck in traffic behind a horse-drawn carriage. It had four ladies in it, all done up and having their treat. Louis woke up, saw the horses, and went nuts. He was barking his head off. The horses reared up, the carriage almost tilted over, and the driver and the women gave me a mouthful. I made a sharp exit, on the wrong side of the road. *Bloody dog!*

Mind you, Pauline wasn't riding donkeys, or even horse-drawn carriages, in Blackpool ... because she was expecting again. It was the same story as the first time: it wasn't planned, nor was it *not* planned. But we were happy. Cheryl was four by now and it felt like a good time to have another kid.

One day, Terry Miller turned up at the theatre out of the blue. He'd driven up all the way from London to see me. *Huh?* I wondered. *What's so important that he can't tell me in a phone call?* Well, I soon found out. Terry handed me a letter: 'I think you'd better read this.'

I opened it, and the first line leapt out at me:

'Her Majesty Queen Elizabeth II requests the pleasure of your appearance at a Royal Command Performance on …'

Well! I had to sit down. A lot of things had happened to me lately: things that I'd always wanted to happen. Going on the telly. Playing big theatres. Doing a Blackpool summer season. But … *appearing in front of the Queen?* Here was something I'd never dared contemplate. The idea had never even occurred to me.

It meant a lot. It meant everything. I loved the Queen. Not everybody in Liverpool did, but I was a fervent royalist. My dad was: his brother, my Uncle Jimmy, had died fighting for his country in the war. Dad would stand and salute the national anthem on the telly, and his passion had passed on to me.

A Royal Variety Performance. *What an honour.* It was to be at my new second home, the London Palladium, on 2 November 1964. And I knew one thing already: it would be very, very special.

* * *

Looking back, this was an incredible time for me. Life kept coming up with surprises. As I was still absorbing the fact that I was going to be telling my silly jokes to the Queen, Terry Miller gave me yet more surprising news. I was getting offered my own telly show.

We hadn't even asked for one. The offer had come, out of the blue, from Lew Grade, the managing director of ATV. He must have seen that I'd been doing well at the Palladium and was pretty hot at the time, because he decided that I should front my own comedy sketch show. What could I say to that? How about, '*Yes, please!*'

It was a lot to take in … but first, I had to focus on the Royal Variety Performance. Make sure I did myself justice. Because I was to be in very elevated company.

Gracie Fields was on. Gracie lived in Capri by now, but she had been a huge star since well before I was born. And there were some more big female singers: Brenda Lee, Kathy Kirby and Millicent Martin, who were all to come on, via the Palladium's famous revolving stage, sitting in cool sports cars.

Cliff Richard was to be on, as was Cilla, who by now was managed by Brian Epstein and had broken big in 1964 with two number ones in 'Anyone Who Had a Heart' and 'You're My World'. There was a big-name American comic, Bob Newhart, and some British comedians who were like gods to me: Morecambe and Wise, and Tommy Cooper.

No pressure, then, Tarby!

Cilla was crazily nervous. She said she was scared of falling over when she curtsied to the royal box. I must admit,

I got the Charlie Drakes – the shakes – as well. I mean, I'd only ever seen the Queen on a postage stamp! *And* I was sharing a dressing room with Tommy, Eric and Ernie! But they were dead nice to me.

I was second on in the second half of the show, after some ballet from a Russian dance company. I was standing in the wings, breathing heavily, going over and over my routine in my mind, when two performers appeared either side of me.

It was Tommy Cooper. And Eric Morecambe.

'You alright, son?' asked Tommy. 'I'll tell you what: you've got something. Don't think too hard what it is. Just go out there and do it. You're in front of the Queen. Make sure you enjoy it, OK?'

Wow! I didn't know what to say. 'Thank you, Mr Cooper.'

'He's right,' said Eric. 'I've seen you before. You *have* got something. You're going to be great.' And then Eric repeated the sound advice that Max Miller had given me: 'Just. Take. Your. Time.'

And, after those two comedy giants had spoken to me, I felt better.

The big moment came. The host, David Jacobs, introduced me, and I walked out. I saw a sea of faces. I couldn't help having a quick glance up at the Royal Box. *Yep, there she was! Her Majesty!* And then I opened my mouth.

'Good evening, my name is Jimmy Tarbuck,' I said. 'I'd better tell you this, as I'm the only one tonight that you've never heard of …'

There was a wave of laughter from the audience. You know what? There's a great thing about the Palladium. This may not make sense to you but, because of the brilliant shape the theatre is, when people laugh, the laughter hits the back of the stalls and rolls back to you. That was happening to me right now. And I was on my way.

If I'm honest, I can't remember much that I said. I think I might have quipped: 'I've got two nephews, Seven and Eleven. Odd names!' But I could tell that I was going down well. *I took my time.* The laughter kept rolling back from the stalls. I skipped offstage relieved and happy.

Tommy Cooper stole the show. Tommy had you in stitches as soon as he appeared, with his pretending-to-be-baffled face and his daft fez. 'I'm delighted to be in the show,' he said. 'I couldn't afford to be in the audience.' He finished off with one of his magic tricks that looked like a disaster but, somehow, worked. He brought the house down.

After the show, we all got to stand in line to meet the Queen. I was between Brenda Lee – pint-sized, but what a singer! – and Tommy Cooper. Her Majesty worked her way down the line, Prince Philip right behind her. When she got to me, she looked me up and down.

'You're very young to be doing this,' she said, in those world-famous, cut-glass tones. (I suppose you'd call it the Queen's English?) How old are you?'

'Twenty-four, ma'am.'

'Oh. Well done tonight.'

'Thank you, ma'am.'

She moved on to Tommy Cooper, who still had his fez on. Before she could say anything, Tommy spoke to her.

'Can I ask you a personal question, ma'am?'

We all stared at him. *Eh? What's he doing? He'll get us sent to the bloody Tower!* The Queen looked a tad nonplussed. 'Er, yes,' she said.

'Do you like football?' Tommy asked.

'Not particularly,' she replied.

'Good. Can I have your FA Cup final tickets, then?'

The Queen burst out laughing, Prince Philip roared his head off, and the whole line fell about. And that was Tommy Cooper for you. Wonderful.

What a night. The next day, I floated back up to Liverpool on cloud nine. My family had all watched it on the telly, of course. When I got home, they wanted to know everything. Even a couple of the neighbours had come round our house to hear all about it.

'What did the Queen say to you then, lad?' my dad asked.

'I'll tell you what, Dad,' I replied. 'She's very well informed.'

'Eh? How's that?'

'Well, she said, "Ah – Jimmy Tarbuck. Is your father still a bookmaker on the London Road?"'

My dad gasped. 'She never?' he said. Before he realised that everyone else was laughing at him. 'Oh, bugger off, you!' he told me. 'You're mad, you are!' Which was fair enough, really.

The big events in my life kept on coming. Three weeks after I'd done my turn at the Royal Variety Performance, Pauline gave birth to our second kid, on 21 November 1964.

It was another daughter, a lovely little baby who was a bundle of life and energy from the get-go. It was great for Cheryl, who loved having a sister. We called the new arrival Liza.

You know what? You might even have heard of her …

CHAPTER 6

A Meccano death trap

My life had changed beyond all recognition. I was suddenly a star. It was impossible for me to walk down the street without being stopped for a chat or an autograph. Did I mind this attention? Did I heck as like! One thing about me is that I'll talk to anyone. Plus, fame was what I'd always wanted. I could hardly start complaining about it now I had it.

Mind you, I could rely on my family to keep my feet on the ground. I remember once a gang of girls stopped me in Allerton Road and asked me for my autograph. I was in the middle of them, signing away, when my mum suddenly appeared. She pushed through the crowd and handed me a lunch box.

'Your dad's forgotten his sandwiches,' she told me. 'Drop these off at the office for him, will you?' And, of course, I did.

And around now was when I realised that it was time for one of the biggest changes of all. Time to move to London.

Was it a wrench? Yes, and no. I was Liverpool to my core, and I loved the city I'd grown up in and spent my entire life in. I didn't particularly want to leave it. At the same time, I knew I had no choice. All the big work that I wanted to do was in London: the Palladium shows, and all the big TV programmes, including my own new one.

Pauline knew this too so she, Cheryl, baby Liza and I upped sticks and rented a flat in a lovely building called The White House in central London, handy for Euston station. We loved it there from day one. And, like every young hopeful who moves to London to try to make his name, I found it exciting. *Let's see if the streets are paved with gold, then.*

I remember, very soon after moving to London, going to see an Australian stand-up I'd heard about called Barry Humphries. He played this glammed-up female 'housewife superstar' called Edna Everage and his show ended with him/her hurling gladioli into the crowd. I'd never seen anything like it. I thought it was terrific.

It was time to start work on my ITV show. It was to be called *It's Tarbuck* and it was to be a mix of stand-up and sketches. I suppose it was a bit intimidating in a way, to suddenly be making a telly show with my name in the title, but that wasn't really how I reacted to it. I just felt like it was great to be recognised.

I was to have two main co-stars in *It's Tarbuck*. One was a diminutive actor and comic called Ronnie Corbett. I'd seen Ronnie before on the kids' TV show *Crackerjack* and in one or two movies. The other was Amanda Barrie, who'd just played Cleopatra in *Carry On Cleo* (and later starred in *Coronation Street* for donkey's years as Alma Sedgewick).

I loved Ronnie from the off. He was an ex-officer in the RAF and was very correct and meticulous in everything he did, but he was also very funny, with brilliant comic timing. At the same time as we were filming the show, he was doing cabaret with Danny La Rue. I used to go to see it a couple of times a week.

Ronnie invited me down for dinner at his home near Crystal Palace in south London with his lovely fiancée, Anne. And I started making gags about how short he was … but not *too* many. He could take a joke, as well as make one, but he'd had so many about his stature that he could tire of them. You had to know when to make them, and when not to.

Why do friendships happen? It's impossible to analyse. *They just do.* Ronnie and I hit it off from day one and grew incredibly close. He was to become one of my best friends – and golfing partners* – in showbiz for the next fifty years. There again, this closeness as we made *It's Tarbuck* could occasionally be a problem.

I remember doing a sketch set in a Japanese massage parlour. I was a customer on a massage table and Ronnie was the manager. He came up and asked me, 'Is everything OK, sir?' And I grabbed him by the balls. The cameras couldn't see it but I was squeezing his knackers all the way through the sketch. Poor Ronnie's eyes were watering.

I was trying not to laugh and Ronnie was trying not to cry. After we'd done the sketch, Lew Grade, our executive

---

* The only problem was that when you played nine holes with Ronnie, he'd fall in six of them. Boom boom!

producer, called us in for a word. He gently reprimanded us: 'Can you two please try to ensure, in future, that your comedy is for the benefit of our viewers, not for each other?'

And what was Amanda Barrie like to work with? Well … let's just say again that Ronnie Corbett was fantastic.

There were other regular co-stars. Bob Todd and Henry McGee, who both went on to *The Benny Hill Show*, were brilliant straight men (although Bob didn't turn up for filming once or twice). We also had a musical guest every week. Brenda Lee came on, whom I'd met at the Royal Variety Performance, as did the great, great Dionne Warwick.

We acted out some of the sketches in front of what we called 'Tarby's Wall'. It was just a prop of a brick wall with all sorts of graffiti written on it: 'Kilroy Was Here'; 'Liverpool FC rule'; 'Happy New Year'. Again, it was just a bit of daftness, really, but it was fun thinking up what to scrawl on there, and people seemed to like it.

It's Tarbuck was fun to make. It did me a lot of good in terms of telling people who I was and what I was all about. Then, ironically, after moving my family and my life down to London, my next job took me back to Liverpool. Why? Because I was to do a Christmas panto at the Liverpool Empire.

It's impossible to overstate how important pantos were for we entertainers in those days. *Everyone* did them: comics, big-name actors, singers, the lot. My first one was to be *Puss in Boots* and my co-star, the main draw at the top of the poster, was Frankie Vaughan.

Frankie was a fellow Scouser who'd made it very, very big. He was an old-school crooner who'd had hits with songs like 'The Garden of Eden' and 'Tower of Strength', and he got nicknamed Mr Moonlight after his signature tune: 'Give Me the Moonlight, Give Me the Girl'. He was a great stage performer, always twirling his cane in his hands.

Frankie was a huge star but a delightful man to work with. He made a fuss of me and encouraged me. He gave me some very useful advice. He said, 'Never walk onstage with your head down. Walk on with confidence: everyone's pleased to see you!' I took heed of that and, thereafter, always bounced onstage at the start of my act.

Now, pantos can be magic, and it's fun to do all the 'Oh, yes it is!' … 'Oh, no it isn't!' palaver with the kids, but – and I think I can say this now – by Christ, they can be boring to be in. Week after week of 'He's behind you!' twice a day wears you down. Frankie felt the same, so we took any chance we could to liven things up.

You won't be surprised to learn that *Puss in Boots* had a cat in it. It was played by a little guy called Ken in a pussy costume. All of his lines were in rhyme: '*I have got a tale to tell* …' they usually began. It was bloody irritating for us, hearing this crap at show after show, so pity poor Ken, having to say it.

Anyway, at one matinee, Frankie and I hatched a plot. The stage set included a well. Ken came on, and before he could say his first line, Frankie and I delivered a new rhyme of our own:

We have got a tale to tell,
We'll throw pussy down the well!

And we grabbed hold of the little feller and chucked him in the well. He vanished for a second, then his moggy head popped up. Well, the audience were howling. I think that it livened things up for them, as well.

After the show, the director collared Frankie and me. 'Frankie, I'm surprised at you!' he complained. 'You're the ultimate professional. It's not the kind of behaviour that I expect from you!' I think the fact he never said it to me made it clear that it was *exactly* the kind of behaviour that he expected from me.

I had a night off from the panto and John Lennon invited me to see The Beatles. They were doing a three-week run at the Hammersmith Odeon called 'Another Beatles Christmas Show'. They were acting in sketches then playing a live set, so off I went down to London. We had a good catch-up in the dressing room before the show.

Well, you would not *believe* the screaming their girl fans were doing at the show! It was beyond deafening. It nearly took my bloody ears off. For their live set, Lennon parked me in the wings at his side of the stage. Even there, I couldn't hear the music: just a white wall of noise from the fans.

The Beatles couldn't hear themselves play, either. During one number, Lennon glanced over at me and grinned. He mouthed some words to me: '*I'm. Not. Singing!*' There was no point, so he was just miming.* When the song finished, sarky as ever, he stepped up to the mic to introduce the next one.

---

* Of course, this was why The Beatles soon gave up doing live gigs – they got so fed up with playing shows that nobody could hear.

'This one's called "Love Me Do",' he said. 'It's a song that we should have sold to The Everly Brothers ...'

You had to watch Lennon in those days. I remember going to a house party in London with him. I went to the toilet, came back, had a sip of my drink, and suddenly found myself yakking nineteen-to-the-dozen. The bugger had only gone and spiked my drink with speed. I hardly got a wink of sleep for the next four nights.

That was a one-off for me because I never touched drugs. People were smoking joints all over the place in the sixties but it never interested me. I could see how much damage it did to a few of them. There is only one drug that I've ever been hooked on, and that's laughter. I'll tell you this: it was the best medicine back then and it still is today.

* * *

In the spring of 1965, I was back on *Sunday Night at the London Palladium* again. And I was to meet the feller who is my surviving best friend in show business: Tom Jones.

Tom had got his debut single out, 'It's Not Unusual'. It had been climbing up the Top 40 and was at number two. And as I stood in the wings at the Palladium and watched Tom's rehearsal, it was obvious to me that it was going to go one higher than that. Because Tom's performance was electric.

He was even better when it came to the live show. His energy was extraordinary as he gyrated his hips, growled and raced around the stage. The women hadn't started ripping their knickers off and chucking them at him yet but, from the looks of a lot of them in the audience, they'd have liked to!

Sure enough, 'It's Not Unusual' jumped to the top of the chart the next week. I always joke with Tom, and tell him: 'People only tuned in to the show to watch me. It's me that helped you get to number one!' He humours me: 'Sure, Jimmy.' But the truth is, Tom didn't need any help. He was a ready-made superstar.

Amid everything else going on for me, my love for Liverpool FC was as strong as ever. Being in the Liverpool panto had meant I could go to Anfield, and even when I was at home in London, I still got to as many games as possible. Because this was an amazing time to be a Liverpool fan.

Bill Shankly had completely turned the club around. After bringing in Yeats and St John, he'd got us promoted back to the First Division, where we belonged, in 1962. Then we won the league in '64. It felt, to me, as if my rise in showbiz was going hand-in-hand with Liverpool's ascent as a football power. It was exciting and I loved it.

Shanks had a wise theory that the best teams always have a strong spine: a fantastic goalkeeper, centre-half, central midfielder and forward. He had brilliant players like the goalie, Tommy Lawrence (a hefty feller who got nicknamed 'The Flying Pig'), Tommy Smith, Ian Callaghan and Roger Hunt. I mean, *what* a team it was.

When I went to matches, I was the only person that Shankly would allow in the dressing room before the games. I used to joke with the players. I'd ask Shanks, 'Are you playing me today, boss? Am I getting a game?' and they'd all roar. I think he liked having me in there, pre-match, because it helped the team to relax and not get too tense.

In 1965, I was back in Coventry to do the Spring Show for a second year, this time with Frankie Vaughan, Des O'Connor and Jack Douglas. But Liverpool had got to the FA Cup final against Don Revie's Leeds United. There was no way I was going to miss it. I went down to Wembley, and Frankie, a fellow diehard Reds fan, came with me.

Before the game, I went to the Liverpool dressing room and poked my head around the door. 'Is it OK if I bring a friend in, boss?' I asked Shankly.

Shanks scowled at me. 'Ah don't think so, son,' he growled. 'Who is it?'

'Frankie Vaughan.'

'Frankie!' Shankly was suddenly all smiles. 'Come in, lad!' Frankie was dressed as smart as Shanks was: a proper couple of swells. We chatted to the team. Frankie was pinching himself. 'Jim, we're in the Liverpool dressing room, on Cup final day,' he kept saying. 'I can't believe this is happening!'

The day was magic. Liverpool won 2–1 and Ian St John, the Saint, my closest mate of all the players, scored the winner in extra time. *Yes!* But Frankie and I had to get back to the Coventry Theatre for that evening's show, so I'd hired a helicopter in advance to fly us back up there.

After the match, we got led down the road to a nearby helipad. And I'm telling you, that helicopter looked like a tin bucket. It looked like a Meccano death trap. The scruffy pilot grinned at me. 'Alright, Tarby, la'?' he said. 'I used to be at school with you. Remember me?'

I looked at him closely. I *did* remember him: he was a proper Scally and wide boy whom I'd had nothing to do with at Rose Lane. And seeing him confirmed what I'd decided as soon as I'd set eyes on the chopper. 'We are not getting in *that*!' I said. 'Forget it! We'll get a taxi instead.'

Frankie and I ran into the street and hailed a black cab. 'Take us to Coventry,' I said, as we climbed in the back. The driver looked as if he was about to have a seizure. 'I can't get all the way there!' he said. 'We *have* to get there,' I told him. 'Look, I'll make it worth your while.' He still didn't fancy it, but we set off for the Midlands.

Well, the cabbie was right. Bugger me if his taxi didn't break down halfway there! The engine just fell out onto the road. Frankie and I had to jump out and thumb a lift to Coventry. *That* was one surprised driver. By the time we pulled up outside the theatre, we were more than an hour late. *Uh-oh!*

The theatre owner, a guy named Sam Newsome, was waiting outside. He was *fuming*. A couple of comic mates on the bill, Hope and Keen, were onstage covering for me. I had a Liverpool rosette on that was nearly as big as my jacket, and I swerved past Sam and sprinted straight onto the stage. The place erupted.

It was a great show. Afterwards, of course, Sam gave Frankie and me a bollocking. Well, sort of. He told Frankie, 'I can't believe *you*, of all people, did this.' I was getting *déjà vu* here! It was the same story as the Liverpool panto: he wasn't a bit surprised at *me* doing it. But I was honest with him.

'Look, Sam, I'm sorry,' I said. 'It won't happen again. But: *Liverpool have won the FA Cup*. Of course I bloody had to be there …'

Oh, talking about football … by now, I'd sadly just about given up on my childhood hopes of being a professional footballer, and playing for Liverpool. I still loved playing, though, so when I got invited to join a celebrity football team called the Showbiz XI, I jumped at the chance.

The Showbiz XI played matches to raise money for charity. It was packed with famous names such as Sean Connery, Tommy Steele, Des O'Connor and Tony Newley. Some of them became close mates of mine and will feature very heavily in this book. And I was lucky enough to meet the guy who became my biggest friend in show business.

I just clicked with Kenny Lynch straight away. Why? Again, it's hard to say, except that he made me laugh. That's the key with me. Lynchy had such great stories. He was the youngest of fourteen kids; he'd been a boxing champion in the Army; he'd had hit singles and been on The Beatles' first tour. And he was hilarious.

Kenny was a real lad. He liked a joint, he loved the ladies, and the ladies certainly loved him. I nicknamed him 'Kipper' after Kipper Lynch, a famous jockey, and, over the years, I must have worked with him more than anybody in showbiz. He was like a brother to me; there was never a dull moment with Kenny.

What a feller he was.

* * *

Around this time I parted ways with Terry Miller as my manager and agent. Terry had done OK for me but he was moving to the States. He wanted to carry on managing me from over there but that made no sense to me. So, I hired a guy named Peter Prichard, who the year before had got The Beatles onto *The Ed Sullivan Show* in America.

Peter got me a summer season for 1965. The way this generally worked was your agent would gather all the offers that you'd been made, and ask you which seaside town you fancied spending the summer in. And I headed to Great Yarmouth to play the theatre on the Wellington Pier.

I was there with my old mates Mike and Bernie Winters, and Matt Monro. They used to call Matt 'The Man with the Golden Voice' and, bloody hell, you could see why. Even Sinatra loved his singing, and there is no bigger compliment than that. He was a likable feller, too.

Yarmouth was OK. Pauline and I rented a house and spent a fun summer there with the girls. Cheryl was old enough by now to appreciate being able to go to the beach every day. And I indulged myself in my rapidly growing golf fixation.

I went to a local course called the Gorleston Golf Club every day. The club pro was a friendly guy named George Willard: I took the big step of buying my first set of clubs off him. And George suggested I might like to play a few rounds with … his fourteen-year-old daughter, Anne.

Hear me out. It wasn't as odd as it sounds. Anne Willard had just won the British girls' golf championship. She was a sweet, lovely kid but she was also a seriously brilliant golfer.

The first time we went round the course at Gorleston, Anne gave me a stroke per hole. And she slaughtered me.

I'm not exaggerating. It wasn't even close. Anne's swing was poetry in motion and she was an eagle-eyed putter. All I could do was hack around in her wake. She started giving me a two-stroke advantage on par-five holes. She could afford to. I still couldn't bloody get anywhere near her.

Now, I'd like to report that I took these daily humiliations on the fairways in a calm and stoical manner … but I didn't. I was seething. Some days I'd throw my clubs in the boot at the end of the round and go back to Pauline and the girls in a right bate. *How can I keep getting annihilated by a teenage girl?**

At least I won one match at Gorleston Golf Club. Norman Vaughan was also doing a summer season in Great Yarmouth. One afternoon we took each other on. We called our game The Show Business Rabbits Cup. It was, as well: I can still remember that I went round in 124 and beat Norman by one shot.

* * *

Something else happened in Great Yarmouth that was rather more important than me playing golf very badly. Peter Prichard got me a load of shows in London at the Talk of the Town. This was a glamorous venue right on Leicester Square that loads of big stars had played. It was seriously prestigious.

---

* There was no shame in a novice like me losing to Anne Willard. Under her married name, Anne Smith, she had a fine golf career, including playing in the Curtis Cup.

Peter also told me that I was in the running to replace Norman Vaughan as the host of *Sunday Night at the London Palladium.*

Bloody hell! This really did knock me backwards. I'd been up on cloud nine even to get to appear on that show. I'd been on four or five times by now and every time had been a joy. Playing the Palladium never felt anything other than very, very special. But the thought of *presenting* the show ... well, this rarely happens, but I was lost for words.

Peter Prichard warned me that it wasn't certain. He told me there were other stars, big names, in the running. But he thought he'd know the decision by the end of the week. He asked me to give him a call at 4pm on that Friday afternoon.

That was a very long week in Great Yarmouth. I did my shows at the Wellington, did a few laps of the golf course, and I had only one thought in my head: *Am I going to get it? Is it going to happen?* I must have bored Pauline stupid banging on about it ... except she was as excited as me. She knew what a big deal it was.

The funny thing was that the cottage we were renting didn't have a telephone. You had to go to the local grocery shop to use the public phone. So, that Friday I went down to the corner shop and stood among the teabags and cat food to call Peter Prichard.

'Hello, Jimmy,' he said. 'You've got it.'

Oh. My. God. I couldn't have been more excited. I felt like running round the shop. I felt like shouting it from the rooftops. Like announcing it live that night from the theatre stage …

'But there's one thing,' added Peter. 'They're not announcing it for a few weeks. You can't tell anyone until then.'

Bugger! I can tell you, that was the hardest secret I ever had to keep. But at least it was a brilliant secret to have.

The summer season in Great Yarmouth came to an end. I went back home to London to get ready for my Talk of the Town shows, and patiently wait for ATV to announce my big news. And, while I was waiting, I got another intriguing offer.

A feller called Andrew Loog Oldham got in touch. He was a big name in the rock and roll world: he'd been a publicist for The Beatles, and for Bob Dylan on his first visit to Britain, and now he was managing The Rolling Stones. He'd just set up his own record label, Immediate Records … and he wanted me to record for it.

Blimey! The surprises just kept coming! Loog Oldham was a persuasive character. He was four years younger than me, but he was very confident, very successful and very flamboyant. He liked grand company, and flounced about in designer jackets, fitted shirts and cravats. He was a right poseur, but I liked him.

I also liked his offer, because I enjoyed singing. I'd belt out a song onstage; I'd even done a one-off gig at the Cavern. I knew that I could carry a tune. I couldn't 'go upstairs' – you know, hit any high notes – but I was OK as a crooner. So, I said what I said to all the new offers that came my way in those days: 'Bring it on! Let's give it a go!'

Loog Oldham had it all planned out. He knew the song he wanted me to record. It was written by Mick Jagger and Keith Richards, no less, and it was called 'Wastin' Time'.* When he played it to me, I liked it: it sounded quite slow for the Stones, an almost sad song, about a love that was going nowhere: '*We're wastin' time, inside your mind ...*'

I liked The Rolling Stones. I was obviously in The Beatles camp, but I didn't buy into the Beatles vs Stones rivalry: I thought it was just bullshit made up by the newspapers to sell copies. I reckon both groups felt the same. The Stones were a great band and they had some cracking tunes.

I met them a few times over the years. Brian Jones, the one who died in the swimming pool, was a lovely feller. Charlie Watts was friendly, as were Keith Richards, Bill Wyman and, later, Ronnie Wood. But I always found Mick Jagger rude. He'd look down his nose as if he was doing you a favour by talking to you. I thought he was right up himself.

Andrew Loog Oldham took me into a studio in London with some session musicians and we did a song called 'Someday' and 'Wastin' Time'. He produced them himself and stuck them out. How did they do? Well, let's just say that *Top of the Pops* weren't beating down my door. I didn't give The Beatles any sleepless nights.

I wasn't bothered. I'd enjoyed doing it but I had no illusions that I was a pop star. It wasn't my game. Plus I had more

---

* The Rolling Stones were to record this track themselves, ten years later, as 'We're Wastin' Time'.

important stuff to focus on. Lew Grade and ATV had made the announcement. It was all over the newspapers. Thank God, my big secret was finally out.

It was time to start presenting *Sunday Night at the London Palladium*.

CHAPTER 7

She needs no introduction from me

The papers made a big thing of me getting the Palladium show. The main theme was that they were surprised at the job being given to someone so young. They weren't the only ones – so was I! But I knew just what an incredible break it was for me and I was dead determined to show everyone what I could do.

I was following in some very big footsteps. Tommy Trinder had been the show's original host, back in the mid-fifties. Tommy was a proper old music-hall variety star, with his catchphrases like 'You lucky people!' By all accounts, he'd viewed the Palladium show as a job for life, and was miffed when it was taken off him.

But he'd been replaced by a master: Bruce Forsyth. And Bruce had grabbed the show with both hands and been terrific. He was warmer than Tommy, likable, and just so funny and witty. He could handle everything the show could throw at him. Whenever anything went wrong, he'd wink at the audience and tell them, 'I'm in charge!'

I admired Bruce and was lucky enough to have become mates with him. Not long after he'd introduced my first appearance at the Palladium, I'd bumped into him in the street in London. We'd chatted and Bruce had said the magic words: 'Do you fancy a game of golf?' We'd played a few rounds since then and become firm friends.

Sunday Night at the London Palladium had also been regularly presented by Norman Vaughan in recent years. Now, no disrespect to Norman, who was a lovely guy, but I didn't think he was a great host. He got the Charlie Drakes. He always seemed terrified of the show. I hoped, and thought, I could do a better job than him.

My first show was to be 26 September 1965 and, in between appearing at the Talk of the Town, I spent time down the Palladium. The producers held meetings every Wednesday where they'd finalise who'd be on that Sunday's show. I went to my first one and talked to the scriptwriters to come up with topical gags for my intros.

There was a full dress rehearsal every Sunday afternoon before the evening show. The first one emphasised to me – as if I didn't know already – what a big show the Palladium was. They ran through the whole show, from start to finish. It was a huge, glamorous production, right down to the Tiller Girls' sequins. ATV threw a lot of money at it.

When I took over the show, Lew Grade changed its name to *The New London Palladium Show* and dropped 'Beat the

Clock', a mini game show for two couples from the audience. I thought this was a shame: Bruce always made it hilarious, and I fancied a go at it.* At least they kept the famous revolving stage that the artists all stood on at the end of the show. I was thrilled to get on there.

On the big night of my hosting debut, I was to make a spectacular entrance. The producers had hung a paper screen onstage with Tarby's Wall from *It's Tarbuck* painted on it, complete with graffiti: 'Beatles are best', 'Wot no beer?' and 'Liverpool 5'. Instead of walking through the curtains when the show opened, I was to burst through this wall.

'Five minutes, Jimmy,' a producer told me in my dressing room. I stood up in front of the mirror to check my tie was straight and my flies were done up. And I walked through and stood in place behind the screen. *This is it!* I could hear the expectant murmurs of the audience in their seats. *Gulp!*

I listened to the voices in my ear:

'Fifty seconds, Jimmy.'

'Thirty seconds.'

'Twenty seconds.'

'Ten … nine … eight … seven … six … five … four … three … two … one … GO!'

It's time! The Jack Parnell Orchestra (led by Val Parnell's nephew) struck up and I burst through the paper wall, a ball of nerves and energy in my dapper three-piece suit. I launched straight into a song:

---

* A few years later, of course, Bruce took the 'Beat the Clock' format and turned it into *The Generation Game* for the BBC. And what a success that was.

Hey, look me over, lend me an ear,
I'm on your tellies, chuffed that I am here,
So don't switch me off yet, give me a chance,
I'll sing you a song, I'll tell you a gag,
   and I might even dance ...

'Oh, well! I'm 'ere!' I said at the end, and went into my opening monologue. I told the audience how proud I was to be on the stage of the greatest, and most famous, theatre in the world. 'Tessie O'Shea has stood here,' I said. 'Hattie Jacques. Some of the biggest drawers in the business ...'*

I had to introduce a proper mixed bill on my first show. Peter, Paul and Mary, the folk singers from America, were on. There was Sarah Miles, the actress, opera singer Susan Lane, Canadian singer Edmund Hockridge, and some Liverpool mates of mine, The Searchers. That was the Sunday Palladium show: something for everyone.

We had one or two surprises in the audience. Dave Mackay, the footballer, was there (God, Dave was a hardman! I played against him in a couple of charity matches). He stood up and gave the crowd a wave. So did Mike and Bernie Winters, who had come to support me. And Frankie Vaughan was sitting near the front.

I told Frankie to stand up, and the crowd went mad. They loved him. 'Frankie, why not come up here and talk to us?' I said. When he did, I went a step further: 'You can't come up here without doing a song for us,' I told him.

---

* Take that, Tessie!

The crowd probably assumed this had all been rehearsed, but it hadn't. It was all on impulse. Frankie laughed. 'Go on then, Tatty 'ead!' he said (not his normal nickname for me: he usually called me 'Sweet Lips' because, to my shame, I swore so much). And we duetted on 'Side by Side'. It brought the house down. What a great moment.

The headliners on that first show were Peter Cook and Dudley Moore. They did their 'Pete and Dud' characters and sang their comic hit, 'Goodby-eee!' If I'm honest with you, I didn't find them hilarious like I did Morecambe and Wise, but they were nice guys. They over-ran, and the TV broadcast had to cut off before the revolving stage at the end.

It was over. Nothing had gone horribly wrong. I felt a huge sense of relief, and elation. And as if I might just get the hang of this job, if I kept at it. And, over the following weeks, I gradually got used to being the presenter of the most popular and prestigious light-entertainment show in Britain.

* * *

Frankie Howerd headlined my second Palladium show. Frankie was a very good, very funny comic who'd first started performing in the Army during the war. He had some great routines, including one with a female piano player who got everything wrong. I think there was an edge, a sadness, to Frankie, but he was always lovely with me.

As I got used to presenting the show, I got into the habit of touring the dressing rooms before the performance to say hello to the acts and try to put them at their ease. I'd have a laugh and a joke with them, and ask if there was anything they particularly wanted me to say when I introduced them.

My next show had two huge headliners in Mike Yarwood and Shirley Bassey. Shirley was a great lady with a fantastic voice and was loads of fun. She was very attractive and you could have a hoot with her. She'd sometimes speak to me in her dressing room. What would she say? 'Get out!'

Mike Yarwood was a different kettle of fish. I knew Mike because he used to be on the club circuit in Manchester at the same time as me. He was a fantastic impressionist and a huge star by now: he was never off the BBC. But he was one of the most anxious men I ever worked with. Before shows, he'd be a bag of nerves.

When I got famous, Mike started impersonating me. He got me off well, and I liked it. He'd talk dead fast, in a Scouse accent, waggling his head from side to side and waving his arms in the air. After every joke he told as me, Mike would grin, nod, and go 'Oh-oh!' or 'Boom boom!'

I couldn't argue with that. If I ever see early footage of me performing, I can't believe how fast I spoke, how much I used to nod (people began calling me 'Noddy') and how I'd flail my arms about. Nerves, I guess. I started wearing waistcoats, so I could hook my thumbs into the pockets to help me keep my arms still.

When I got hired for the Palladium show, Lew Grade had given me Marty Feldman and Barry Took as chief scriptwriters. They were the hottest comedy writers going from TV series such as *Bootsie and Snudge* and radio shows like *Round the Horne*. But it didn't work out. They didn't suit me and I didn't suit them.

We didn't connect. The comedy they wrote was too arch and clever-clever for me. I was onstage selling my personality and their gags weren't right for my personality. So, we went our separate ways after three shows and Lew Grade hired a pair of northern comedy writers, Tommy Vaughan and Ron McDonnell. They were far more on my wavelength.

Dusty Springfield was the headliner on an early show. I was pleased because I was a fan. Dusty was another who got nervous before shows, though. I popped my head in her dressing room and she was looking stressed and going over her song lyrics. I just told her, 'You know what? I'll leave you to it. Good luck.'

Michael Bentine came on. He was a nice man, very posh – he'd been to Eton – and mad as a March hare. All of the Goons were. I was a fan, and an admirer, of Peter Sellers because he was so clever but, when I met him, he was pretty nutty as well. And very intense. You wouldn't want to upset Peter.

There again, those two both seemed completely rational next to Spike Milligan. What was Spike like? It depended where the moon was. You never had a clue what he'd say next. I'm not sure Spike did, either. If you ask me, Harry Secombe was the only sane one out of the lot of them.

Also on an early Palladium show was … a mouse. A mouse called Topo Gigio. It was an Italian puppet act and it was superb: the kids loved it. But one of the puppeteers messed up: he thought he was due at the theatre an hour later and he missed the show. The rest of them still carried it off.

Cliff Richard came on. Fame hadn't changed him a bit: he was just the same as he was when we were pushing Joe Lee's bloody coach down the road. The producers said they wanted us to perform together, so we sang and danced our way through an old show tune, 'Standing on the Corner'.

I could dance a bit but it wasn't my strong suit. I wasn't a proper showbiz all-rounder like Bruce, or Roy Castle; Roy could sing, tap-dance, tell gags, the lot. But the greatest performer of that ilk that I ever saw was Sammy Davis Jr. Sammy was extraordinary. He could probably play the toilet.

I worked with a few different producers at the Palladium. David Bell probably the most. He was very good. There was also Albert Locke, who was old-school but very efficient. Albert liked to do the warm-ups before the show. I'd tell him, 'Oi! Gerroff! I'm doing this!' Because telling a few gags helped get me in the rhythm.

I'd knock a few out: 'I just saw a feller outside lying in the gutter. I asked him: "Are you alright, sir?" And he said, "Yes, I just found a parking space so I sent the wife home to get the car."' Or I'd come on and say, 'Hello! Have we got a show for you tonight!' Then I'd shout into the wings: '*Have* we got a show for them tonight?' That one got a roar.

I got a thing going with Jack Parnell, the orchestra leader. I'd come onstage and ask him, 'You alright there, Jack?' I'd point at the audience and nod to him: 'OK, it's you and me against this lot!' The crowd would laugh, but Lew Grade was never keen on me doing all that. He told me to focus on the audience, not my mates in the band.

Sometimes, if there was a lull in rehearsals for a technical issue, I'd walk around the corner to Carnaby Street. I'd go in all the boutiques looking for smart clothes. They'd sometimes give them to me for nothing, hoping that I'd wear them on TV. I never got into wearing all the hippie clobber, mind you. It just wasn't my thing.

Mostly, I wore beautiful suits from Savile Row. I remember Dougie Hayward, the famous tailor, made me blazers in every colour you could imagine. I wore a different one every week. ATV paid for them. I took them all home with me. Someone from ATV asked me what had happened to them. I said, 'Oh, some feller came in and took 'em all away …'

I'd always be on an adrenaline high after the show. I might have a drink in the Palladium bar with one of the artists but normally I'd go for a meal at Alvaro's on the Kings Road, owned by a pal of mine, Alvaro Maccioni. He'd keep a table for me every Sunday night. Alvaro later opened a place called La Famiglia on the same road.*

George Raft came to the Palladium. George was a heavyweight New York actor and Hollywood star who'd made great gangster movies with Spencer Tracy, James Cagney and Humphrey Bogart. And we cooked up a fantastic entrance for him.

At the start of the show, a huge American car drove onto the stage. A bunch of guys all dressed like mobsters jumped

---

* Alvaro has passed, God bless him, but I still go to La Famiglia if I'm up in town. His daughter, Marietta, runs it now. If you go there, try the seafood pasta.

out, others ran onstage, and a huge fight kicked off. One of the gangsters grabbed a machine gun from the car and machine-gunned all the others, who slumped to the ground as if dead.

I bounced onstage to introduce the show and pretended to be amazed at the carnage around me. 'All we need now is for George Raft to get out of the car!' I said. At which point, George did exactly that. The place went crazy, and we did some comic banter. I pretended I thought he was James Cagney, then Edward G. Robinson.

George was a seriously tough guy in real life. He'd used to be a boxer and, I have read, had a few tasty mob connections of his own. But what very few people knew was that he had also been a dancer. He did a dance routine at the Palladium that was amazing for a guy of sixty-four.

George was living in London at the time. He'd been invited over to be the front man at the Colony Club, one of the big casinos that were opening in the West End. They'd have lavish cocktail bars, high-end restaurants and some serious big-money gambling. After I got to know George, I'd sometimes eat there with him after a Palladium show.

Those casino clubs had the best food, fine wines, and a very … interesting clientele, from showbiz stars to gangsters. You met all sorts in there. One week, I mentioned to George that my parents were in London visiting me. 'Hey, you got to bring those guys in here,' he replied. 'What's your father's name? What does he do?'

'Fred. He's a bookmaker.'

'A gambling man – fantastic! Bring him in and introduce him to me.'

I went back the next night with my mum and dad. Dad was starstruck at the prospect of meeting a movie star like George Raft, and George didn't disappoint. As soon as he saw us walk in, he came over to us and shook my dad's hand.

'Hey, Freddie!' he greeted him. 'How are you?'

'Great, George.' Dad beamed

'It's good to see you again!' said George.

'It's good to see you again,' replied Dad. And I thought, *Bugger me, Dad! The only place you've ever seen him is on your telly!*

I'd sometimes go in the casino and play a bit of roulette. I was never a massive gambler, but one night I got a bit carried away and suddenly I found myself a few hundred pounds down: maybe even a grand. Cyril Levan, who owned the Colony Club, wandered over to me.

'What the hell are you doing, Jimmy?' he asked.

'Just having a little bet, Cyril,' I replied.

'Well, I don't *want* you gambling,' he told me. 'I want you sitting in the restaurant, where people can see you, to draw customers in. I don't need your money in here.' And as it happened, the ball fell in the right place on the next roulette spin. I redeemed my losses and called it quits. And Cyril Levan became a very close friend.

* * *

I introduced so many people at the Palladium whom I was honoured to meet. One week, we had a comic who never said a single word and who had me weeping with laughter. It was Jacques Tati, the great French silent comedian. He did all these fantastic mime skits, such as a one-eyed footie goalkeeper. The place fell about.

Sid James came on. Because he always played Cockneys, people didn't realise he was South African. Sid was so sharp: you could bounce off him. We did a tap-dance routine together. Adam Faith had a great face, could sing and was a good actor. If he'd been six foot tall, rather than five foot four, he'd have been an international superstar.

One week, I had the honour of introducing the greatest ballet dancer who ever lived: Rudolf Nureyev. He was dancing with Dame Antoinette Sibley, who was absolutely charming. Before the show, I went to their dressing room to introduce myself. I knocked on the door and Nureyev let me in.

'Ah, our young host,' he said, in his strong Russian accent. 'Now, what are you going to say about me?'

'Um, I'm afraid I don't know a lot about ballet,' I admitted.

'Young man,' said Nureyev, gravely, 'neither do I!' That made me roar. I liked the pair of them, and their grace was unbelievable.

Another week, I was excited that Petula Clark was headlining the show. If I'm honest, I had the hots for Pet. Whenever I met her, she was always funny and lovely and friendly. I was looking forward to introducing her at the end of the show. It would be the highlight of my evening.

The show was going really well and towards the end the producer, David Bell, came up to me in the wings. He was holding a bottle of Champagne and a glass. 'Terrific, Jimmy!' he congratulated me. 'Fancy a little drink? You've earned it!' I wouldn't normally tipple while I was working, but I made an exception.

'Yeah, go on, then!'

Big mistake. I knocked back the champers, walked onstage at the climax of the show to introduce the gorgeous Petula Clark ... and my mind went completely blank. Well, not quite completely. I knew I was introducing a woman. But bugger me if I could remember her name!

'Ladies and gentlemen!' I said. 'Now, in the greatest theatre in the world, we have one of the biggest stars going. Er ... she is someone truly special.' I was playing for time, to give myself a chance to remember. '*I* know who she is, *you* know who she is ...'

The pianist in Jack Parnell's Orchestra saw I was struggling. He played the first few bars of Petula's biggest hit, 'Downtown'. *Nope.* The penny still didn't drop. '*He* knows who she is!' I said. But her name still wouldn't come to me. I had to give up. 'And she needs no introduction from me!' I concluded, lamely, making a swift exit as Petula swept onstage.

David Bell collared me backstage. 'What the hell was that?' he asked. 'How could you forget her name?'

'It's your fault – you gave me the bloody Champagne!' I replied.

David was still haranguing me ten minutes later as Petula finished her set, walked offstage ... and came straight up to me. *Uh-oh!*

'Jimmy, thank you for that lovely introduction!' Pet said, pecking me on the cheek. 'It's the nicest one I've ever had.' At least *that* shut David Bell up. But it was the last time that I ever had a drink while I was presenting the show.

After the show, there'd be fans and autograph hunters waiting by the stage door. They'd mob me as if I was a pop star. They'd grab me or try to get a snog. It may sound great, and it *was*, really, but some weeks it could all get a bit much. I started leaving via the front entrance to try to avoid the fuss.

Pauline met me after some shows. She didn't like the women hanging around. 'Why do you talk to them?' she'd ask.

'Oh, they're harmless – they're just fans!' I'd say.

One week, Pauline picked me up in our car. As I opened the door, a much older woman, who, to be frank, wasn't the most attractive lady I'd ever seen, came running up.

'Oh, Jimmy!' she said. 'Can I just have one kiss?'

Before I could answer, she grabbed my head and rammed our faces together. *Aaargh!* I don't think she had a tooth in her mouth and her breath was … pungent. As I got in the car, discreetly wiping my mouth, Pauline was laughing her head off.

'Don't worry, Jimmy,' she said. 'I don't mind *that* one!'

* * *

I made some great friends at the Palladium who remained pals all through my life. One of the closest was Des O'Connor. I'd first met Des in Liverpool when I was a teenager. He'd done a show with Lonnie Donegan and I'd waited at the stage door afterwards to ask for an autograph. Des had obliged, of course.

I became friendly with Des when we did a Spring Show in Coventry, and we cemented that friendship during his Palladium appearances. Des was what I call a toff: a true gentleman who was always gracious and who had time for everyone (come to think of it, maybe that's why he ended up getting married four times!).

Des was a huge name and a great performer, but I think he was undervalued as a singer. That was partly because he never took himself too seriously, unlike a lot of people in our business. He never minded when Morecambe and Wise took the piss out of him on their show. Actually, I think it did Des a lot of good. It made people like him even more.

I introduced so many acts at the Palladium that it would have been impossible to love all of them. One or two didn't do it for me. I never really got on with Charlie Drake. It was hard to say why, except that he had an attitude. He seemed to think that he was a bigger comic than Charlie Chaplin. Which really wasn't the case.

Richard Hearne was a nice enough guy, I suppose, but his Mr Pastry character left me cold, both onstage and in the movies. And I can't pretend that I was ever in stitches at Freddie 'Parrot Face' Davies. I guess his shtick was aimed at kids, which is fair enough, but I thought he was a pretty ordinary club comic.

Because the Palladium was a live show, sometimes things went wrong. I'd occasionally mess up a gag (on the occasions that I forgot to *Take. My. Time!*). I remember, one week, doing a routine pretending to have come from a life of poverty. 'The dustman didn't used to deliver at our house, he used to collect,' I said.

Oops! That doesn't sound right! 'I mean, he didn't used to collect, he used to deliver!' I quickly corrected myself. I couldn't get away with pretending it hadn't happened, so I mimed taking my teeth out and putting them back in. That meant the audience laughed with me, not at me.

But the biggest, most persistent problem on the Palladium show was acts over-running their time slot (which, let's face it, I knew a little bit about myself). It was a regular issue. David Bell had to stay bang on top of things as the evening progressed, sometimes asking singers to cut a song or comics to shorten their act.

One week, we had a sketch planned where I had to dress up like a musketeer. I was in the wings in a frilly frock coat and cape, with boots up to my knees. At the last second, David cut the sketch for time reasons. There was no time to change, so I had to march on in my silly costume to introduce the headliner.

I got no chance to explain why I was dressed up like bloody D'Artagnan. The audience must have thought I'd gone nuts. I felt a proper Charlie. I came off with the right needle, and was still fuming a while later when I phoned my parents, as I often did after a show on a Sunday night.

My mum picked up. 'Oh, hello, Jimmy love,' she said. 'Yes, we saw the show. It was lovely and you were great.' But in the background, I heard my dad say to her, 'Ask him if he was drunk.'

'What's that?' I asked. 'Mum, can you put Dad on?' She passed him the phone.

'I heard that!' I told him. 'What do you mean, was I drunk?'

'Well, what did you dress up like that for, you silly bugger?' he inquired.

'I love you too, Dad,' I said, as I put the phone down.

Not that my dad was my harshest critic. I obviously read the newspaper reviews of me hosting the Palladium show. It's human nature; it's impossible not to. Most of the critics were complimentary and said that I was a young lad doing a tough job well. But not all of them were so kind.

I got a couple of stinkers: critics writing that I wasn't up to the role. That I couldn't hack it. I tried to put them behind me. *It's tomorrow's chip paper*, I'd tell myself. Peter Prichard, my manager, told me to ignore them, and I convinced myself that I didn't care what they wrote. But that wasn't always true.

That kind of public criticism can knock your confidence. After one bad write-up, I went to see Lew Grade. 'I just want to check that you're happy with me?' I asked.

'Delighted, Jimmy,' replied Lew. 'You're doing a brilliant job. Just stop doing all those in-jokes with the orchestra ...'

One day, towards the end of the first Palladium series, I needed to go to Elstree Studios for some reason. In the canteen, I bumped into a pal, the writer Johnny Speight (with whom I was about to do some work – I'll come to that shortly). He introduced me to a guy sitting at the table with him.

I didn't catch what Johnny had said. 'Sorry, what's your name?' I asked the feller.

The feller said his name, and as soon as I heard it, the red mist descended. 'Not the TV critic from the *Daily Mirror*?'

'Er, yes.'

'Oh, I've been wanting to meet *you*,' I said. Because the bastard had torn me to bits in his paper a few weeks earlier. 'You're the one that said I'm not funny. Are *you* bloody funny then, eh?'

'Er ... er ... no!' he stammered. 'I'm sorry! I never meant to ...'

'J-Jimmy! Leave it!' Johnny Speight stuttered (he always had a stutter). But my hackles were up. I was rolling my sleeves up. The Liverpool came out of me. 'If I were you, I'd get out before I give you a smack in the mouth,' I told the twitching hack. He took me at my word, jumped up, and scarpered.

So, you know what? Maybe I *did* care a bit more than I thought.

Because, no matter how easy I may have made it look, hosting the Palladium show was a difficult gig. Making people laugh, and keeping a variety show moving along on live telly, is no easy task, whatever anyone might think.

Once, a club comic wrote in to Lew Grade, criticising my performance and saying that he could do better. Lew laughed when he showed me the letter. And a lightbulb came on over my head. 'Invite him down,' I said. 'Let him do the warm-up before next week's show.'

Well, Lew did exactly that. The feller came in all excited but I could see that he was shitting himself as he tried to get the crowd going before the broadcast. He never raised so much as a titter. I admit that I enjoyed watching him die on his arse. 'Not so easy, is it, mate?' I asked as he came off.

But such negativity was rare. Nearly all of my memories of the Sunday Palladium show are incredibly happy. I was having the time of my life and meeting the cream of the showbiz world. Think of any big name from that golden era, and I got to work with them. *What was not to like?*

I'll never forget the first ever colour broadcast of the show in March 1966. Because of the technical challenges, the TV broadcast didn't go out live, for once: it was on a one-hour delay. It was a big news event, very exciting, and Lew Grade himself came down to watch the show.

It was an important event so we had an important head-liner: Roy Orbison. Now, Roy was not just a huge talent, and an icon of rock and roll, but a delightful man. He went down a storm: the audience loved him singing 'Pretty Woman' and 'In Dreams'. But Lew Grade had identified a flaw in our American star's appearance.

'This is our first colour broadcast,' he told a colleague in the audience. 'And this man is wearing a black suit and tie, black glasses, has dyed black hair, and is playing a black guitar. Who on earth booked him for this show?'

'Er, you did, Mr Grade,' his colleague reminded him.

'Ah, yes. A splendid idea!' said Lew.

Meeting Roy Orbison. Wow! It was one of the many evenings I encountered greatness on the stage of the London Palladium. One of the many times, as a starstruck young lad, that I met some of the biggest international stars in the world of showbiz. And, you know what? I was about to meet a whole load more.

CHAPTER 8

Hair like a lavatory brush

In the spring of 1966, Lew Grade gave me another short series of televised variety shows to host. It was at the Prince of Wales Theatre, close to Piccadilly Circus. I was amazed – and honoured – when Lew actually put my name in the title of the show: *Tarbuck at the Prince of Wales*. It made me feel like I'd properly arrived.

It was a very similar show to the Palladium and it had exactly the same very high calibre of guests. An up-and-coming New York comedian and film director named Woody Allen flew in to do the show. I spent the day with him. Woody was wearing a scruffy green corduroy suit and he was hilarious as we did the rehearsal.

After we'd done the run-through, he asked me, 'What goes on now, Jim?'

'You've got two hours to kill,' I told him. 'Have a sit down backstage. Relax, then put your tuxedo on just before it's time to go on.

Woody looked at me like I was mad. 'Tuxedo? *What* tuxedo?' he asked. All he had with him were the clothes he was standing up in. He went on in the same green corduroy suit, and he was fantastic. I was pissing myself laughing. A few weeks later, I went to watch him perform at the Playboy Club, which had just opened. He was just as funny there.

Dudley Moore came on the show. This time, it wasn't with Peter Cook: it was with his band, The Dudley Moore Trio. He told a few gags but mostly he just played music. It was superb: Dudley was a brilliant jazz pianist. Another terrific talent who came on was Lulu, who brought the house down. She and I were to become good mates.

On the nights that I wasn't on at the Prince of Wales, Barbra Streisand was there starring in *Funny Girl*. I was hanging out with Tommy Steele a lot at that time so we went to see it. It's funny, the things that stick in your mind: I remember the tickets were two pounds ten shillings (£2.50). The next time Streisand was in town, they cost a damn sight more than that!

The show was great. Afterwards, Tommy and I went backstage and met Barbra and her husband, Elliott Gould. We all had a few drinks and ended up at Tommy's mum's house, out in the sticks. Funny to think about that now! Barbra and Elliott took it all in their stride and were lovely.

Back at the Palladium, Liza Minnelli came over to do the show. She'd only just turned twenty, but had already done a lot of work in America, making albums and appearing on Broadway. And, I'll tell you this, it was obvious to everyone what a huge superstar she was to grow into. She was an incredible performer.

It wasn't Liza's first time at the Palladium. The year before, she'd done a joint show with her mother, Judy Garland. I'd gone to see it. They were both great but Liza had virtually stolen the show. She went down so well that her mum had jokingly ushered her off the stage: 'OK, you can go now, Liza. This is *my* night.'

Liza was just as captivating when she was on with me at the Palladium. She was so vivacious and had star quality to burn. While she was over, Tommy Steele and I went to see her play a little theatre in Leicester Square. Guess what? Liza ended up drinking with us two back at Tommy's mum's, as well.

I was meeting incredible people like that on a weekly basis. The Canadian actor Lorne Greene, star of the US cowboy series *Bonanza*, came to the Palladium. He got an ovation just for walking on. He and I did a skit together. We stood in front of the closed stage curtains and Lorne told me, 'Jimmy, I'm looking for a man to fight.'

The curtains parted, and out walked Henry Cooper. 'So am I,' he said.

Henry was about to fight Muhammad Ali in London for the second time. We all went to the weigh-in. Ali was hilarious. He asked Lorne Greene to punch him on the chin and, for some reason, Lorne gave him a right old wallop. Ali joked that it was one of the hardest punches he'd ever been hit with.

I was a bit overawed to meet Ali – *it's Muhammad Ali!* – but he put me at my ease. He asked me to thump him on the chin, as well. 'No, I can't knock you out!' I answered. 'I respect you too much.' But someone took a great snap of me pretending to lamp him. Where's that photo now? Framed in my downstairs loo at home.

When that series of Palladium/Prince of Wales TV shows finished in the summer of 1966, I went straight into a variety revue show, again at the Palladium, called *London Laughs*. And I look back on that experience now, sixty years later, as six months of absolute paradise. One of the best times of my life.

Why so? Mostly because of my co-star, Harry Secombe. Harry was a joy to work with. A truly likable, decent man. He was so funny that he would have me weeping with laughter whenever I was onstage with him. And the main reason for that was that he had one particularly deadly talent.

Harry could pass wind at will. During the show, he entered, via the revolving stage, in a stagecoach as Mr Pickwick. As the coach came to a halt, you'd hear a resounding fart from inside it. 'Uh-oh!' Harry would yell, in that stentorian roar. 'Here comes another one!' And he'd let rip again. The crowd would be in stitches.

Later in the show, he'd do his big hit, 'If I Ruled the World'. It would go down a storm and at the end, as the audience were applauding him, Harry would whisper to me: 'Look out, I've got one on the way!' I couldn't keep a straight face because I knew what was coming next. And where it was coming from. It was quite the party piece.

For such a household name, Harry was a remarkably humble man. I remember him giving me a tip: 'Jim, you're going to be a big star, but remember: it's nice to be big, but you don't have to be big to be nice.' And I reckon that's not bad advice. I've always tried to follow it.

London Laughs was a joy to be in. I got togged up in my best Carnaby Street gear to sing The Kinks song 'Dedicated Follower of Fashion', as well as duetting with Harry and Nicky Henson. Russ Conway, the pianist, was in the show, as was the smashing Thora Hird. There wasn't a bad 'un among 'em.

We had a Cockney sing-along in the revue, with Harry and Thora dressed as a Pearly King and Queen in a donkey-drawn cart. This meant having a real donkey onstage. One night, as we stood on the revolving stage, I complimented the man who looked after the mule on how well behaved it was every night.

'Oh, yes,' he said. 'He's well trained. The only thing you have to be careful of is not to give them sweets before they go on.'

'Oh, really? Why's that?' I asked.

'Because they go right through them. They get onstage, get excited, and drop their guts!'

A-ha! This felt like useful information. The next day, I went next door to Liberty's and bought a box of liquorice allsorts to take to the theatre. I waited until Eeyore was on his own then fed him some. Sure enough, as soon as he got onstage, his tail went up and, not to put too fine a point on it, he crapped all over the place.

The audience roared, but poor Thora Hird was sitting right next to the donkey's rear end. 'Yuk!' she said, pulling a face. Later, she asked me, backstage: 'Wasn't it awful, Jimmy, that donkey doing its business like that?' I kept a straight face as I agreed that, yes, it was.

For the next few evenings, I gave sneaky Bassett's treats to the mule every night. It was certainly enjoying them, its onstage deposits multiplied, and Thora got more and more dismayed. I went on until suspicions arose that a cast member was giving the donkey sweets … and it might be J. Tarbuck. At which point, I thought I'd better stop.

When *London Laughs* came to an end, Harry Secombe asked what I was going to do next. I wasn't sure. 'I dunno,' I replied. 'Maybe a holiday?'

'Well, I'm taking my family to Barbados,' Harry told me. 'Why not fly out and join us?' I liked him so much that I booked it up straight away.

The trip didn't get off to a great start. Pauline, the girls and I landed in Barbados after dark. Well, I say *dark*: it was pitch black. You couldn't see your hand in front of your face. Yet it was still so hot that you were sweating as soon as you got off the plane. 'I don't like this,' I grumbled to Pauline, on the bus to the hotel. 'We're not staying here long.'

That all changed the next morning when I got up and opened our hotel curtains.

'Bloody hell!' I yelped. 'Pauline, come and look at this!'

The view was magnificent. All you could see was a perfect cloudless blue sky, turquoise sea, golden sands and palm trees. As Pauline and I gawped out of the window, it felt impossible to imagine a more beautiful scene on the planet. We were in paradise. And we had the best time in Barbados.

We swam in the warm sea every day. I went scuba diving for the first time over the wreck of a sunken ship. We got on great with Harry's family – his wife, Myra, and their kids – and Harry was a riot wherever we went, exactly the same as he was in England. He kept breaking into song. Thankfully, he kept his farting to a minimum.

* * *

When I first got on the telly and started making money, I bought houses for my family. I got Mum and Dad a place in Liverpool, and one for our Norma. I got Pauline's mum and dad a place up there as well. In fact, just about the only people in my family that I hadn't bought a house for were Pauline and me.

We were still living in the flat in the White House in central London. It was a lovely gaff, but we fancied a change. It felt daft that we were still renting and I was tired of waking up in a noisy city. I'd always rather live in the country, given the choice. So, Pauline and I began scouring the property ads.

We spotted an advert for a house called Glen Cottage in a village called Trout Rise near Loudwater in Hertfordshire. It sounded nice so I decided to go and have a butcher's. *Wow!* It was a pretty thatched cottage by a stream in a picturesque valley. It looked like it belonged on a chocolate box. I fell in love as soon as I saw it.

Pauline loved the place just as much when she came out to view it. There were great schools for the girls nearby and, really, it was a total no-brainer for us to buy it. We moved in and I have to say that we were blissfully happy there from day one.

There was one drawback to Glen Cottage. We wanted to extend it but, because of the thatched roof, we weren't allowed to. Apart from that, everything was grand. We even knew some of the neighbours already. Val Doonican was just up the hill from us, and Bruce Forsyth wasn't far away.

Frankie Vaughan was a short car journey away in posh Totteridge. I saw a lot of him. One night, I was at the Palladium and Frankie was playing the Talk of the Town. He asked if I could give him a lift home at the end of the night. I finished first, so I changed into jeans and a tatty old T-shirt, went to the Talk stage door, and stood in the wings to wait for him.

Frankie was singing on my side of the stage. When he finished, I said – just loud enough for him to hear – 'Come on, Mr Vaughan, you're not trying!' Frankie saw me and smiled.

'Oh, it's *you*, Sweet Lips!' he said, before turning to the audience. 'I've got a pal in the wings,' he told them. 'Would you like to see him?' They all cheered.

I shook my head. 'No! I can't come on dressed like this.' But Frankie couldn't have cared less.

'It's Mr Jimmy Tarbuck!' he grinned. 'Come on, Jimmy!' I had to walk on, looking as if I'd come to fix the theatre's drains. I hated doing that. Frankie was pissing himself. And I wanted revenge.

I knew Frankie's act inside-out so I knew his big closing number was 'Hello, Dolly'. I went over to the orchestra. 'OK, play "Dolly"!' I told them.

Frankie looked horrified: 'No, no, not yet!' he protested. But the pit band grinned and struck it up. He had no choice but to duet with me. I got the band to play it four times. *That* showed the bugger.

Frankie lived at the side of a golf course in Totteridge but he wasn't allowed to join it because he was Jewish. That was the first time that I saw bigotry like that. But I quickly joined my new local course, Moor Park in Rickmansworth, and I invited Frankie to play with me there.

I enjoyed those games because, among all the madness that was going on in my life, I'd got a lot better at golf. I'd taken lessons, both in London and when I was visiting my folks in Liverpool. A feller up there called Bill Large had coached me. And, in 1966, I got asked to enter my first pro-am tournament.

It was at Sunningdale, the beautiful course in Berkshire. I was nervous because I'd never played in front of a crowd. I had a couple of playing partners: a fine professional golfer named Harry Weetman and a well-spoken fellow amateur who introduced himself as Anthony Tate.

'I understand you come from Liverpool?' asked Mr Tate, as we made our way around the course. 'Which area?'

'Well, I grew up in Wavertree,' I replied. 'But I spent a lot of time hanging out with a good friend, Bobby Campbell, in Scotland Road.'

'Oh, we own a family business in Scotland Road,' he nodded. 'It's just by the roundabout on the dock road.'

I was puzzled. 'But that's Tate & Lyle?' I said.

'Yes,' he confirmed. 'That's our family business.'

'Bloody hell!' I exclaimed. 'I'm playing golf with royalty!' But Anthony Tate was a nice guy. He brought his family to see my show and we got friendly.

Just after Pauline and I moved to Glen Cottage, we had a small house built in Marbella. It was great. Sean Connery had a place there and a few years later, after Cilla and her hubby Bobby came to stay with Pauline and me, she bought one as well. We all loved it out there, and it was a fantastic place to escape to for a week or two to get away from the British winter.

* * *

You've got to give me this: I've always been a trier. Early in 1967, I put out another couple of pop singles. One was my take on an old folk song called 'Stewball' about a racehorse who 'didn't drink water, he only drank wine'. The other was a cover of Anthony Newley's 'Doctor Dolittle'. How did they do? Exactly the same as my previous effort.

Around the same time, I got wind of a short film being made that sounded a right lark. It was called *The Plank* and was being written and directed by Eric Sykes. It starred him and Tommy Cooper as two clumsy workmen trying to find a plank to fix a hole in a floor. And it sounded like a Who's Who of British comedy.

As well as Eric and Tommy, Jimmy Edwards was in it, as were Roy Castle, Jim Dale, Bill Oddie, John Junkin, Hattie Jacques, and my old mucker Kenny Lynch. So I phoned Eric and asked if I could be involved. 'OK, I can write you a part,' Eric offered. 'But I can't pay you.

'That's fine,' I answered. 'I just want to be in it.'

The Plank was dead short (it only just filled the hole – ho ho!) but a bit of a classic. It was pure slapstick, really, all about

Eric and Tommy's misadventures trying to get the piece of wood from A to B. Kenny Lynch played a binman who tipped a load of rubbish on Roy Castle after he fell into the dustcart.

I was a barman: my part was so small that if you blinked, you'd miss it. They repeated *The Plank* on telly some years back. I pointed myself out to my grandkids: 'Look, that's your grandad there!' They could hardly believe it because I'd got a mad moptop of Beatles hair. Oh yeah, and because I was skinny.

I did my bit in *The Plank* in just one day, which I liked. No messing about. At the end, Eric Sykes thanked me and said, 'Jim, I've got something for you in my car.' He'd bought me a case of whisky. So he *did* pay me, after all. That was nice of him. Even though I didn't like whisky.

And then, pretty much straight away, I got a very different acting job.

My mate Johnny Speight (who was also in *The Plank*) asked me if I'd consider taking the lead role in a sitcom pilot he was writing for the BBC. It was for a drama series called *Comedy Playhouse* and it was to be titled *To Lucifer: A Son*. I would play Satan's son, whose name was, apparently, Nick.

It was a weird offer, and a long way from my normal shtick, but I just figured, *why not?* I liked Johnny, and I've always enjoyed working with people I admire and respect, so I decided I'd give it a go. I didn't know if the script was good or bad: I found it impossible to judge. But I said I was in.

The filming was a hoot. I wore red plastic devil horns. John Le Mesurier was Lucifer. He was a toff, a gentle soul who called me 'Dear boy'. Dermot Kelly was Saint Patrick, and Pat Coombs and Arthur English were in it. We never actually saw God on screen but we all talked about him as 'The Big G'.

The BBC didn't like our finished programme. They said they weren't going to put it out, but we insisted: 'Oi! We've got contracts!' When they *did* broadcast it, the reviews weren't good. It didn't really bother me: I hadn't written it. And it didn't diminish Johnny Speight's other great achievements.

Johnny's most famous creation, of course, was *Till Death Us Do Part* (which had also started as a *Comedy Playhouse*). Right after we'd filmed *To Lucifer: A Son*, Johnny asked me if I'd appear, as myself, in a special episode called 'Till Closing Time Us Do Part'. And my answer was exactly the same: *Sure! Why not?*

The storyline was that me, Kenny Lynch and the Australian actor Ray Barrett, who was well known for playing a doctor in the medical soap opera *Emergency Ward 10*, were in a pub having a drink. We got recognised and buttonholed by Alf Garnett, the bigoted paterfamilias of *Till Death Us Do Part*, played by Warren Mitchell.*

Alf insulted the lot of us. He called Ray, who had a few pockmarks, 'the bloke with the holes in his face' and told me I had hair like a lavatory brush (and, you know what, he may have had a point). And he called Kenny a 'darkie'.

---

* The irony was that Warren's politics were the exact opposite of Alf's. He was very much a socialist: there for his fellow man.

Now, you'd never hear that on telly nowadays, of course, and nor should you. It sounds terrible to modern ears. But Kipper just didn't care. I never once heard him complain about racism, although he must have grown up among it, as a Black kid in east London in the fifties and sixties. I hated any racism. If I came across it, I told people where to go.

After my brush with Alf Garnett, my next TV appearance was on a chat show. In the June of 1967, I was invited onto the *Eamonn Andrews Show*. Eamonn was a good guy, but I was mostly excited because I was to be on with Hollywood royalty: Bob Hope and Bing Crosby.

Bob Hope and Bing Crosby! I couldn't believe I was going to be breathing the same air. I was particularly thrilled to meet Bob, because I'd admired his comedy, and his style, ever since I'd seen him at Liverpool Empire when I was fourteen. And I'm happy to say that neither of them disappointed.

Bob and Bing were both charming to me. Bob even took me to one side to have a word. 'You're doing very well, young man,' he told me. 'Let me give you some advice. When you walk onstage, give them two minutes to look at the suit.' Ha! They were the same words I'd read him saying in that inter-view, years ago. And they still rang true.

Bob went further. 'I hear you like golf?' he said. 'You must come to the States, play in my classic event, and be on my TV show!' Wow! *There* were two mind-blowing offers, right there! We didn't fix a date there and then, but I couldn't get the words out fast enough as I said, 'Yes, I'll take you up on that.'

That summer, I was back in Blackpool for a summer season at the ABC with Frank Ifield, the yodelling Australian country singer. He was a nice guy. Supporting us were The Barron Knights, a novelty musical group. They were a good act but I kept away from them because they were a bunch of lunatics. Let's just say they liked a bevvy.

Also on the bill was a German feller called Jenda Smaha. Not that you saw his name on the posters. Mr Smaha was an elephant trainer from a legendary European circus family, and he was in Blackpool with his latest performing animal, who was billed as Tanya, the adorable baby elephant.

Was Tanya adorable? Sort of. On command, she'd stand up on her hind legs and fill her trunk with water. She sprayed her trainer with it at the end. The kids all loved her. But they didn't see the whole story. Jenda would tap her with a stick – but in rehearsals, he'd use an *electric* stick. Very cruel. It would be banned today.

I remember that Alec Fyne from ATV came up from London to see the show. Afterwards, I joked that I had to share my dressing room with Tanya.

'I'm sorry to hear that,' replied Alec.

'It's OK, I don't mind,' I said.

'No – I feel sorry for the poor elephant.'

While I was in Blackpool, Bruce Forsyth was also in town doing a summer season at the Opera House. Bruce and I shared a house for a few weeks, before our families came up to join us. And we had a cracking time.

Bruce was as much fun as a housemate as you'd expect. I've always said the amazing thing about Bruce Forsyth was that he wasn't the most handsome man in the world, but he always pulled beautiful women. The difference between Bruce and most other men was that he always married them!

He and I played golf every morning at Royal Lytham & St Annes. They were competitive games. I loved that, because I normally won. I was putting my heart and soul into my golf by now and I'd become too good for Bruce. Some days, he'd go into a right sulk as I beat him.

That year, I won my first pro-am on that course. There again, that was largely down to my partner, the brilliant Irish pro Christy O'Connor. Christy gave me tips as we went round the course: 'Eyes up, Jimmy. Knees bent. Elbow in.' I was dead grateful. I soaked up his wisdom like a sponge.

When the school holidays started, I moved out of Bruce's gaff and Pauline brought Cheryl and baby Liza to Blackpool. Louis the labrador came along again. Louis didn't terrorise any more horse-drawn carriages, but the silly mutt developed a bad habit of wandering off and getting lost on the seafront.

I grew wearily used to phone calls from the cop shop: 'He's here again, Jimmy.'

'Bloody hell,' I'd say. 'OK, I'll come and get 'im.'

* * *

Most people go to Blackpool for holidays. Entertainers go there to work. We had a good summer season but by the end I felt like a break myself. We got one: Tommy Steele very kindly invited us to his holiday home in Jamaica with his family (which must have cost more than half a sixpence, boom boom!). We had a cracking time there.

Back in England, late in 1967, Lew Grade cancelled the Sunday night Palladium show. Why? I think he'd read too many know-it-all newspaper critics, like the feller I'd chased out of Elstree, saying the show was old-fashioned and old hat. They were wrong. Lew was later to admit that dropping it was one of his biggest mistakes.

He'd been using guest hosts for a few weeks. Bob Monkhouse hosted the final show, and Bob, Bruce, Norman Vaughan and I – the show had made stars of all four of us – got together and did a song. It felt like the end of an era. That was because it was.

We had good family news: Pauline was expecting again. And I rounded off the year with another trip to Coventry. It was panto again, this time as Buttons in *Cinderella* with Anita Harris. Anita was fun to work with, and I was to do so a lot in the coming years. Richard Hearne was in the panto as well, doing his Mr Pastry turn, as was that great female comic Audrey Jeans.

Our *Cinderella* was a success – *oh, yes it was!* – but not without its critics. A Coventry priest wrote to the local paper to complain. He said he'd been to see it, and it was 'an orgy of verbal indecency'. I mean, blimey! That silly sod must have led a sheltered life, even for a vicar!

It brought to an end what had been a crazily frantic year for me. I ended it thinking that there was no way 1968 would be remotely as hectic or as eventful.

How wrong can you be?

CHAPTER 9

The man who runs the Palladium

I must have been doing something right because Lew Grade gave me a new ATV show. The title was to be what every entertainer dreams of: simply my name. *The Jimmy Tarbuck Show*. It was dead exciting news. But firstly, I had some other business to be getting on with.

Despite the Great British public's apparent lack of interest in my musical career, I recorded not only a new single – Hank Williams's 'Your Cheatin' Heart' – but an album, *Jimmy Tarbuck*. I covered 'King of the Road', 'Little Green Apples' and my pal Tom's 'Green, Green Grass of Home'. The Great British public remained indifferent.

It was summer season time and in 1968 I was back in Great Yarmouth, this time at the ABC with Anita Harris and Kenneth McKellar, the Scottish singer. Kenneth was a lovely feller. That's always been my yardstick: I like working with nice people. I can't be doing with miserable buggers.

On 12 June, I did the normal two shows in Yarmouth and went to bed. I was fast asleep when the phone rang. I looked at the clock by the bed – 5am. *Huh? What the bloody hell?*

I picked up. 'Hello?'

'Hello.' It was Pauline, who was due to have our third nipper any day.

'Have you gone in yet?' I asked.

'I have. I'm in hospital in Watford. Oh, and there's one more thing …'

'What's that?'

'I've got a little boy in the bed next to me.'

What? Pauline and I hadn't known if she was having a boy or a girl, we never did, but after Cheryl and Liza, I'd assumed she'd have another lass. This news blew my socks off. Well, it would have done, if I wore them with pyjamas.

'I'm on my way!' I said. I bounced out of bed like Zebedee, washed, dressed and was in the car in ten minutes. There was no traffic around and I set a new world-record time for a drive from Great Yarmouth to Watford. And there he was. My gorgeous lad.

Pauline and I decided to call him James. I'd always wanted a son named after me. I had a lovely few hours holding my boy before I had to get back to Yarmouth for that evening's shows. Pauline took James home and Cheryl and Liza doted on their little brother. As did his parents. He had completed our family.

At the end of the summer season, just as colour telly was launching properly, I got back to London and started work on *The Jimmy Tarbuck Show*. It was another sketch and stand-up show like *It's Tarbuck*. But I felt different. When I'd made *It's Tarbuck*, I'd still been wet behind the ears. Now, four years on, I felt that I knew what I was doing.

We did six weeks of shows and no sooner was I finished than … guess what? Panto time again. At least I didn't have to go away this year: I had the lead part of Jack in *Jack and the Beanstalk* at my home-from-home, the London Palladium. The part of my mum, Martha, was to be taken by the best pantomime dame in history: the British showbiz legend that was Arthur Askey.

Jack and the Beanstalk was fun. *At first*. Tommy Steele and I used to wind each other up with practical jokes. He was in his own show in town, and he and I began ordering things to be delivered to each other's dressing rooms. Sofas. Televisions. Fridges. You name it, the unwanted gear kept showing up.

One day, Tommy and I met up in a coffee bar after our matinees. Tommy had interesting news. He told me that a men's store on Oxford Street was selling cashmere sweaters at half-price. Well, I've always had an eye both for a bargain and a nice bit of smart casual knitwear, so I headed straight down there.

I bought a couple of jerseys and meandered back to the Palladium. You were supposed to always be in the theatre by half an hour before showtime, but Jack wasn't onstage until twenty minutes into the panto, so I left it a bit later. But as I walked backstage, I was greeted by pandemonium.

The director was tearing his hair out. The producers were running everywhere. And there was my understudy, in full costume, reading over his lines, all set to go on. When they saw me, everybody stopped. 'Where the hell have *you* been?' the director asked.

'Just out,' I replied. 'What's going on? What's the panic?'

'Oh, just that we had a phone call from the Metropolitan Police, saying that you'd been knocked down by a bus on Oxford Street and broken both legs!' snapped the director. And I knew immediately which 'copper' had made that call. Tommy bloody Steele.

I apologised profusely, promised it wouldn't happen again, got into my costume and did the show. And, actually, Tommy and I fell out over that jape. I thought he'd gone too far, landed me in too much trouble, and caused my show too much grief. We didn't speak for years. Happily, we're over it and we can laugh about it now. Finally!

Jack and the Beanstalk had a good cast and was a good production, but my God, that Christmas panto dragged on. The tickets kept selling so the theatre kept adding dates. I'm sure the bugger was still going as Easter neared. It all got a bit too much, for all of us.

'I can't keep doing this,' I sighed to my stage mother as we sat in make-up, prior to yet another matinee performance. And poor old Arthur Askey stared at me, glumly, as a lass painted his familiar rouge circles on his cheeks.

'Nor can I, son,' he agreed. 'This one's gone on too long.'

* * *

I suppose the one good thing about spending week after week in the Palladium was that it was easy for Lew Grade to get hold of me. He always knew where I was. One afternoon he turned up out of the blue and told me that he wanted a word with me. I followed him to his office.

'I want to put on a special *Sunday Night at the London Palladium* next week,' he began. 'Would you be available to present it?'

Lew hardly needed to ask. He knew that hosting Palladium shows was my favourite job of all. I'd always drop everything to do them.

'Of course,' I replied. 'Who's the headline?'

'Well, it was going to be Lena Horne,' he said. 'But she's ill and she's had to drop out. So it's going to be Judy Garland.'

Crikey! This was a big one. Judy was in town doing five weeks at the Talk of the Town. Her fortunes had been mixed. She was still only in her mid-forties but she wasn't in great health. There were rumours that she was drinking heavily, and worse, and some of the reviews of her shows had been dodgy.

I'd seen how things were myself, close-up. One night at the Talk, Miss Garland had said she was unable to go on. The promoter had put in an emergency call to me to fill in. I can still remember standing in the wings and listening to the audience reaction to the pre-show announcement:

'Ladies and gentlemen, we regret to inform you that, due to illness, Miss Judy Garland cannot appear tonight.'

The crowd signed, and groaned.

'But we have a replacement. From the London Palladium – Mr Jimmy Tarbuck!'

More sighs and groans (well, and some half-hearted applause, at least).

I began my act. Half an hour in, out of the blue, the crowd suddenly started cheering and clapping. *Huh?* I turned around to see that Judy Garland had materialised onstage behind me. As I greeted her, she whispered to me: 'Don't leave me alone up here.'

I stayed with her and held her hand as she sang. She was a little unsteady but she got through the set – and she was still a superstar, and a Hollywood legend. So, once it was announced, the levels of interest in her Palladium appearance were sky-high.

On the day, she arrived at the theatre in mid-afternoon. She was very frail and looked a tad shaky in rehearsals, then retired to her dressing room. Then, not long before she was due to begin her set, I became aware of a commotion back-stage. Something clearly wasn't right.

Bill Ward, the show's executive producer, came up to me.

'The bitch says she isn't going on,' he moaned.

I was a bit shocked by this. 'Nor would *I*, Bill, if you talked about me like that,' I said. 'I'll try to have a word with her.' And I had an idea.

Judy Garland was a star who was used to being treated like a star. So, I asked all of the show's producers, stagehands and technicians to stand in line alongside the walk from her dressing room to the stage. Miss Garland had insisted that her three-minute intro be played in full. As Jack Parnell and his Orchestra struck up, I tapped on her door.

'Come in!'

I popped my head around the door.

'Ah, it's you again! Hello, young man!'

'Miss Garland, I've introduced you,' I said. 'They're playing your overture. Walk to the stage with me. If you don't want to go on when we get there, that's fine, I'll go on instead.'

She got up and took my arm. She was leaning on me, I think for physical *and* emotional support, as we walked through the tunnel of lined-up theatre staff. As we made our way, they all clapped and encouraged her:

'Welcome back, Miss Garland!'

'Good luck, Judy!'

'You'll be great!'

'Thank you, thank you, darlings!' By now she was smiling. By the time we got to the stage she was ready to go on.

She asked me to accompany her again, and I did. And, as I held her hand, Judy Garland was magnificent. She knocked them dead. She made it through: as the old showbiz saying goes, the show had gone on. And gone on extremely well.

At the end, as all the performers stood on the revolving stage, she took my arm again and kissed me on the cheek.

'You, young man,' she said, 'have got a lot of class.'

Of course, the press being what they are, the papers were itching to run stories that Judy Garland had been unfit to go onstage at the Palladium. Journalists called me up asking if I had stood with her because she was drunk, or off her head. I gave them nothing.

'That's bullshit!' I said. 'That was how she wanted to perform, and how we rehearsed it. She was great. And if you print any of that crap, you'll be hearing from our lawyers.' They never did.

Judy Garland didn't make it home to America. She was to be found dead, in London, mere months later. I still have my photograph of her kissing me at the Palladium. Every time I look at it, it brings back so many memories for me. Because Miss Garland had a lot of class, too. And even in her sadly diminished state, I'd known one thing for sure:

That I was in the presence of greatness.

* * *

After *Jack and the Beanstalk* had finally ended I had some rare free time, and I knew exactly what I needed: a holiday. And I knew exactly where I wanted to go for it. Pauline and I flew back to Barbados. It was just what the doctor ordered: beautiful, tranquil and very relaxing. Paradise hadn't changed.

We were flying home from Miami so we sailed there from Barbados. I remember that on the boat we met Lester Piggott, the jockey. I didn't know him but he probably knew from my interviews that my dad was a bookie and I liked the gee-gees. Lester said he could sort us tickets to see some racing in Miami.

We had a couple of days before we flew back so this sounded a cracking idea. The next morning, Pauline and I eagerly headed off to the racecourse … only to get turned away. It appeared American racetracks had stringent dress codes. Pauline was in a trouser suit so they wouldn't let us in. Snotty buggers.

Our disappointment wasn't to last long. Because we were about to have an unbelievable encounter. And I *mean* unbelievable.

We were staying at the gorgeous Fontainebleau Hotel on Miami Beach, which had been recommended to us before we left. As we were walking through the foyer, who should we bump into but George Raft. That was where he hung out when he was in Miami. We had a nice chit-chat, then Pauline and I headed out to the pool.

We were basking in the sun on our recliners when a guy came up to us, immaculately dressed in suit and tie. As he crouched down to speak to me, I couldn't help but notice the tell-tale bulge in his inner jacket pocket that showed that he was packing a pistol.

'Are you Jimmy Tarbuck?' he asked me.

'Yes.'

'From the London Palladium?'

'Yes. Why?'

'The Man wants a word with you.'

'Eh? What man?'

He gave me a small smile. 'There's only one Man in Miami.'

'You don't mean ... Frank Sinatra?'

'That's him. Go meet him in the lounge bar.'

Well, Pauline and I were up off those loungers like a pair of rockets! We scurried up to our room and quickly got changed out of our swimming gear into our best togs. In the lift down to reception, I couldn't believe what was happening. *Huh? Is this a dream?* And it felt even more like one when we walked into the lavish bar.

Frank Sinatra was sitting with a couple of guys. He looked like a million dollars, as the Yanks say. It was like a scene from his

Pal Joey movie. As soon as he saw us come in, he jumped up from his seat and walked up to us, his hand outstretched for shaking.

'Hey, Jimmy, how ya doing?' he asked.

'F-fine, Mr Sinatra,' I stuttered. 'Lovely to meet you. This is my wife, Pauline.'

'Delighted, ma'am.' He smiled at her, then turned his attention back to me. 'Don't call me Mr Sinatra – call me Frank. So, you're the guy who runs the London Palladium, huh?'

'Er, yes, sort of,' I said. (I wasn't sure what Lew Grade and Val Parnell would make of that description, but I decided to run with it.)

'My friend, George Raft, has told me all about how well you look after him in London,' Sinatra continued. 'Can I get you guys a drink?'

'That would be great, thanks.'

A waiter glided over to us. 'I'll take a JD,' Sinatra told him. Now, I hardly drank in those days, but I decided my best move would be to do exactly the same as Frank.

'Yeah, I'll have a JD too.'

'Oh, you're a bourbon man too, huh, Jim?' he asked.

'Yes. That's right.'

Pauline raised an eyebrow at me as if to say, *Oh, really?* She asked for a glass of wine. The waiter brought our drinks. The glasses were long, and very full. Sinatra swirled the ice around his glass, tipped his head back and drained it in one. So, I did the same.

Yikes! I had no idea what Jack Daniels was like. That bourbon went down my throat, past my backside and my knees, hit my ankles and came shooting back up. It nearly choked me. I started coughing and spluttering. Sinatra couldn't help laughing. He could tell that was the first – and probably last – JD of my life.

'You guys must join me for dinner tonight,' he said. 'I'll see you at seven.'

And that was what we did. Pauline and I spent the most fantastic evening with Frank Sinatra and one of his associates. He was the most charming, entertaining company. As you'd expect, he had stories about every A-lister in American show-biz. And he had the most amazing offer for us.

'I'm playing a show here in three weeks to warm up for my American tour,' he said. 'You guys must come back and see it. There'll be a table in your name, Jimmy.' Well, I floated back up to our hotel room. The next day, I hardly needed a plane to get back across the Atlantic.

There was no way I was going to pass up an invitation from Frank Sinatra. I was definitely going back, but Pauline wasn't. She didn't want to return to America so soon, and said she'd rather stay home with the kids. 'But *you* must go, Jimmy,' she urged. 'You'll be in heaven.' And I wasn't about to argue with her.

Back in London, I went for a coffee with a pal, Billy Smart Jr, from the legendary circus family. I'd met Billy at a charity event organised by my old boss, Billy Butlin, and we'd got on well and become pals. I told him about my encounter with Frank Sinatra in Miami, and that I was about to go back to see him perform. Billy's eyes widened.

'Wow! Can I come with you?' he asked.

'Sure, if you want to.'

I got a suit made in Savile Row especially for the occasion. It was a cracker: a black silk job with a waistcoat with a little watch. And Billy and I flew to Florida. Everything at the Fontainebleau was just as Sinatra had promised. There was a table in my name. We were his personal guests, so the staff arse-kissed us to it. We took our seats.

The lights went down. An announcement began. 'Ladies and gentlemen, the music is Mr Nelson Riddle.' Violins struck up. 'The voice is Mr Frank Sinatra.' The orchestra started playing 'Strangers in the Night'. And Sinatra's unmistakable drawl came over the Tannoy: 'Jesus Christ, I hate that song!'

Everybody in the venue fell about. The curtain went up, and *there he was*, onstage: The Man. Frank Sinatra. And you couldn't take your eyes off him. What a performer he was. Hypnotic, mesmeric, and above all … *that voice*. It was like liquid gold. Sinatra sang three or four songs before he spoke to the audience.

'I'm honoured to have some special guests here tonight,' he announced. 'Ladies and gentlemen, please welcome Mr Ed Sullivan!'

The host of America's most important light-entertainment show got up from his table and took the crowd's applause.

'Mr Steve Lawrence and Mrs Eydie Gormé!' Sinatra continued. The married superstar American singers took a bow.

'And,' said Sinatra, 'all the way from London, England, the man who runs the greatest theatre in the world, the London Palladium … Mr Jimmy Tarbuck!'

Huh? Did I hear that right? A spotlight picked out our table. I was frozen to my chair. Billy Smart kicked me under the table. 'Stand up!' he hissed. And I rose, waved, and took the Fontainebleau's applause for, er, running the Palladium. It didn't feel the right time to try to explain that wasn't entirely correct.

I was in a daze for the rest of the show. At the end, we were invited for after-show drinks. Sinatra was charm itself, a total gent, and seemed delighted to see me again: 'Hey, Jimmy! Enjoy the show?' But I also saw another side of him. A side that said it would not be a good idea to cross him.

We were having a drink (*not* JD, in my case) and chatting when a guy approached us. He must have had a recent fall-out with Sinatra because he looked a bit nervous as he said, 'Hey, Frank? No hard feelings?'

'None at all,' said Sinatra, turning to a passing waiter. 'Get this man a drink.' When the waiter came back, Frank took the drink off him ... and chucked it in the guest's face. Then, just for good measure, he threw the glass against the wall. It smashed.

'Blow!' Sinatra snapped at the guy.

The shell-shocked feller was trying to say something. He didn't get the chance. One of Sinatra's heavies stepped in. 'You'd best leave,' he told him. And the guy did.

So, there was that element to Frank Sinatra. But he was never anything but sweetness and light with me. A few years later, he came over to play the Palladium. I got tickets to see him. I didn't try to contact him; I didn't even know if he'd remember me ... until a feller came to my seat and asked me to go backstage.

Frank was sitting in his dressing room. 'Jimmy!' he said. 'How ya doin'? They told me you were in tonight. You didn't wanna say hello?'

'I didn't want to intrude,' I confessed.

'Ah, don't give me that shit!' laughed Frank Sinatra. 'Come back here and we'll talk after the show.' So, we did. And, inside of me, there was that feeling again, the same that I'd had with Judy Garland: the knowledge that I was in the presence of greatness. Those two encounters will live with me forever.

CHAPTER 10

Look at Buttons. He's pissed!

When I was on the way up and getting famous, I'd always appreciated established stars who took the time to take an interest and help me. I'll never forget Eric Morecambe and Tommy Cooper encouraging me as I stood nervously in the wings before my first Royal Command Performance. That kind of thing meant a lot.

Not everybody was so kind or as generous with their time. Some performers seemed to regard newcomers and rising stars as a threat to their own status. They'd been wary of me. I have to say that one particular legendary Liverpool comedian, Ken Dodd, was a bit like that with me.

When I was first playing the clubs, I'd seen Ken's act and thought he was fantastic. He might still be the best stage comic I've ever seen live (although, let's face it, he did go on a bit). But when I actually met Doddy, he wasn't very warm with me. I think he wanted to be the biggest thing to come out of Liverpool* and didn't like any competition.

There again, Ken Dodd was never actually hostile or nasty to me. And that wasn't true of everyone.

I've always thought entertainers who are lucky enough to make it like I have should use their fame to give something back. So I was pleased, and flattered, at the end of the sixties when Frankie Vaughan suggested that I should become a member of the Grand Order of Water Rats.

The Water Rats is a showbiz social group and charitable organisation that raises money for all kinds of worthy and good causes. Frankie proposed me for membership and then I had to get seconded, discussed and accepted by what they call the Grand Council of senior members. So, it was a thrill to be told that I'd been accepted.

I went along to my first lodge meeting in London. I was still only in my late twenties and found myself mixing with established household names and performers who'd been members of the Rats for decades. Most of them were dead nice and welcoming. But one feller made a point of coming up and buttonholing me.

His name was Charlie Chester and he'd been famous as a singer, comic and radio star since he'd started out during the war. He was now a popular radio DJ whose show had carried over from the old BBC Light Programme to the new Radio 2.

---

* And let's face it, that was never going to happen when The Beatles were around.

Charlie was nearly sixty by now, and he wanted to share his opinion of me.

'I've seen you on the telly,' he told me. 'Can I tell you something?'

'Yes.'

'You fluff too many jokes. Far too many.'

Well, this got my hackles rising. Once again, it brought the Liverpool out in me.

'Oh, I saw another comic who used to do that all the time,' I said.

'Who was that?'

'You.'

Well, Charlie didn't like that! He went red in the face and started giving it me with both barrels. 'Who are *you* to talk to *me*?' he snarled. 'You've had it all on a plate. I never got given a chance on TV.' But I wasn't about to back down.

'Well, you've had more than enough chances on the radio, haven't you?' I asked. 'Envy is a terrible thing.'

It could have got proper nasty but some of the other Water Rats saw what was going on, came over, turned it into a joke and smoothed things over. One or two of them had a quiet word with me afterwards. 'Take no notice of Charlie,' they said. 'He's a bitter man.'

It may not have pleased Charlie Chester, but I was doing well. I was still doing stand-up gigs, and returned to the City Varieties Theatre in Leeds to appear on *The Good Old Days* TV show. Barbara Windsor was on as well. Barbara was great, a smashing girl. Sid James certainly always thought so.

I also headlined a run of variety shows at the lovely old Opera House in Manchester. Eartha Kitt was on the bill with me. Eartha had a daughter who was about eight years old and was a sweet little girl. Once or twice she came to my dressing room, drank a Coca-Cola and sat and chatted to me.

I can't say her mum was my cup of tea, though. Eartha Kitt was (or had been) a big star but she had an attitude. In fact, she was bloody hard work. One evening, she just walked in on me, looked around, and growled, '*I* should be in this dressing room, not you.'

'Sorry, luv, just check the billing,' I replied. I wasn't about to back down.

That Christmas of 1969, I did my first big show for the BBC. I was back in *Jack in the Beanstalk*, this time as Buttons, for the Beeb's Christmas panto, broadcast at 5pm on Christmas Day. My old pal Anita Harris was Cinders, and the cast included someone who said, 'Boom boom!' even more than me: Basil Brush. A nice fox, he was.

Beryl Reid was playing one of the Ugly Sisters. Beryl was a hoot: I absolutely loved her. She didn't give a bugger about anything. We were recording the panto at a theatre in Golders Green up in north London, and one day Beryl asked me if I fancied getting a bit of lunch.

'Yeah, why not?' I said.

'I know a place,' Beryl told me. She took me to an Italian restaurant round the corner from the rehearsals. Very nice: red-checked tablecloths, the works. 'Do you like Valpolicella, dear?' she asked as we sat down. Well, I had no idea what the hell it was, but I was willing to give it a go.

Valpolicella, of course, is an Italian red wine. A delicious and, it turns out, very *strong* Italian red wine. Beryl and I were having a right laugh as we knocked it back. A second bottle followed the first down the hatch. There may have been a third. Golders Green was very fuzzy around the edges as we lurched back to the theatre an hour late.

Freddie Carpenter, the producer, was waiting when we arrived. 'Miss Reid! Where have you been?' he asked. 'This is disgraceful!'

'It's not me you have to worry about, darling,' laughed Beryl. 'Look at Buttons. He's pissed!' *And ssho I wassh.* They sent me home in a car, and I had to tell Pauline that I'd been outdrunk by a demure middle-aged lady of five foot two. Still, at least I only had to record that TV panto once, rather than doing it night after night for weeks on end …

* * *

The Beeb must have forgiven Buttons for getting bladdered because, as the seventies dawned, they gave me a one-off telly show. It was called *Tarbuck's Luck*, and as well as me doing my usual gags and hosting, it featured Lionel Blair choreograph-ing his dancers in routines that I was supposed to join in with.

Now, as I've said, I could cut a bit of a rug in those days but I was no Fred Astaire, so I decided to put a lid on that side of things. I took good old Lionel aside for a quiet word. 'Look, mate, don't give me any dance moves,' I told him. 'Let the girls dance around me.' So, they did that, and I just shim-mied my hips occasionally. Result!

I'm not saying that I was starting to take golf very seriously at this point in my life, but in 1970 I was doing a summer season in Bournemouth, with Kenneth McKellar, and I made Peter Prichard negotiate a clause in my contract that I got one particular Saturday off. Why? Because there was a golf pro-am that I wasn't going to miss.

Sean Connery was organising a two-day tournament in Troon and he told me that if I could make it, I'd be partnering one of the greatest golfers of all time: the South African legend Gary Player. *What? I'm there!* I hired a plane specially, flew up to Scotland, and played a round with Gary and the Scottish football great, Ronnie Simpson.

Let me tell you, it's hard to play golf when your knees are knocking! But that was only for the first few holes. Gary was a gent, put me at my ease, and it was a thrill to watch such a golfing genius at close quarters. After I finished my round, I flew straight back to the south coast. My Bournemouth understudy only had to cover for me for one show.

Golf was taking a bigger role in my life. One of my many playing partners was Val Parnell, the Palladium boss, who had taken me down to his beautiful golf club at Coombe Hill, near Kingston in Surrey. The first time I went there to play with Val, I walked into the reception and put my clubs down. A feller glided over and picked them up. I asked him: 'Eh, where d'you think you're going with those?'

'I'm taking them for you, sir,' he murmured.

'You're taking them, but will I get them back?' I asked. 'Because I might not in Liverpool!' I wouldn't say the guy roared, but at least he smiled.

I loved playing at Coombe Hill with Val Parnell so much that he offered to put me up for membership. Initially I was a five-day member, meaning I couldn't play at weekends, but they quickly made me a full member. And, once that had happened, I played there as often as was humanly possible.

I brought some mates down to play who also ended up joining the club. Stanley Baker was a member, as was Sean Connery. I played with Harry Secombe a few times. Harry couldn't play golf for toffee but he was a big bloke. When he hit the ball, it stayed hit. It would go for bloody miles in random directions.

And, in 1971, I got a new home because of the club. I noticed there was a big house for sale right next to it. Just out of interest, I had a nosey around the place. It was gorgeous. I told everybody I met at the cub how nice it was and, when I went into the bar after I'd finished my round, a feller that I didn't know collared me.

'I hear you like my house?' he said.

'Oh, is that yours?' I replied. 'It's fantastic. Why are you selling it?'

'My wife hates it,' he sighed. And, right there and then, without even thinking what I was saying, some words came out of my mouth. 'I'll buy it,' I said. 'I'll give you £1,000 for the contract and then we'll agree a price.'

The guy held out his hand. 'You've got a deal,' he said.

Brilliant! Of course, there was the little matter of telling Pauline what I'd done. I sank a celebration drink and then made a slightly nervous phone call home to my wife.

'Hello, love,' I said. 'You'll never guess what? I've just bought a house.'

The news got a strong reaction: 'You've done bloody what? Are you mad?'

'No, you have to see it. Come down right now!'

And Pauline got in her car and drove straight there from Loudwater. And, like me, she loved the place the second that she saw it: 'Ooh, look, it's got a drive in and a drive out!' If I remember correctly, we paid £21,000 for it. Fifty-four years later, we're still living there today.

I suppose it was a posh house for a feller from Liverpool to buy, but it didn't change me at all. Why would it? Just after we moved into the gaff, my brother, Kenneth, came down from Liverpool to see it. He was still working for Tate & Lyle at the time, so he drove down in his lorry. But when he rang the bell, and I opened the door, it was nowhere to be seen.

'Eh? Where's your wagon, Ken?' I asked him.

'I didn't want to embarrass you,' he replied, 'so I left it down the road.'

'Don't be daft!' I said. 'Go and get the bugger and stick it here!' And Ken went and got his eight-wheeler and parked it on my gravel drive.

The luck was with me in those days. I still had the love of the horses that I'd got from my dad, so I used to go racing a couple of times a week. In 1971, I went to the Epsom Derby and bumped into a jockey that I knew, Geoff Lewis. He was about to ride a horse called Mill Reef in the big race.

Geoff told me that Lester Piggott had called Mill Reef's owners a few days earlier to say that he wanted the ride if

Geoff couldn't do it. 'I think we've got a real chance, Jimmy,' he said. Well, that was good enough for me. I bet a load more on the horse than I normally would, and picked up my binoculars.

Geoff was in the middle of the pack as it neared Tattenham Corner. He hadn't touched his whip. Then he gave Mill Reef a couple of light licks, and … *bang!* He took off like a rocket. He shot past the other horses as if they were going in slow motion. As Geoff passed another jockey, Joe Mercer, I could have sworn I saw him speak to him.

Mill Reef* won easily, by two lengths. After I'd picked up my winnings, I met Geoff in the paddock. 'What did you say to Joe Mercer?' I asked him.

'I just said, "Bye!"' He grinned. 'It really pissed him off.'

Talking about luck … the BBC had liked the one-off *Tarbuck's Luck* show I'd done for them, and early in 1972 they brought it back as a series. I got some cracking guests to come on it: June Whitfield, Joan Sims and Lulu. You know what they all had in common? They were nice people. Because I can't be doing with smartarses.

The Beeb commissioned a song for the show's theme tune. It was called 'Lucky Jim' and was written by a pair of famous songwriters, Roger Cook and Roger Greenaway, who'd previously written hits for stars including Cliff, Cilla

---

* Mill Reef was one of the greatest racehorses of all time. In 1971, he went on to win the Eclipse Stakes, the King George VI and Queen Elizabeth Stakes, and the Prix de l'Arc de Triomphe. Then he broke his leg and got put out to stud. Which sounds an OK life to me.

and Engelbert Humperdinck. I sang the theme song, and I felt like it summed up my life in those days:

> *I'm a lucky, lucky Jim, the people all say,*
> *'Just look at him,*
> *What has he got that keeps him smiling every day*
> *of the week?'*

* * *

While this was all going on, I hadn't forgotten that Bob Hope had invited me out to America to play golf with him and go on his TV show. How could I? It was an offer in a million. I'd kept in loose touch with Bob after I'd met him on Eamonn Andrews's TV show, and early in 1972 I finally got the opportunity to take him up on his kind offer.

I flew out to sun-drenched California and Bob told me to meet him at his golf club. I was so keen that I got there early. As I walked in, I got stopped by a rather officious member of the club staff.

'Excuse me, sir,' he asked. 'Are you a member here?'

'No, I'm not.'

'And are you playing with a member today?'

'Yes, I am.'

The guy clearly didn't believe me. 'And would you care to tell me which member it is?' he sniffed, with one eyebrow raised.

'He's with me,' said a voice behind me. And there was Bob Hope.

Well, the snotty feller almost bowed when he saw him: 'Oh, I'm *so* sorry, Mr Hope. I had no idea.' Because Bob Hope was royalty in those parts. All over America, in fact.

We played a round. Bob was a great golfer; he'd already begun running his US Bob Hope Classic pro-am tournament. But I'd got good enough by then to give him a decent game. Bob must have been impressed, because he said, 'Jimmy, you must come and play my Classic one year.' And I said the same thing that I'd told him five years earlier:

'Yes, I'll take you up on that.'

While I was in California, I did a set at Bob's golf club, which he put on his TV show. I also had a walk-on part on his friend Don Rickles's telly show. Rickles was known as 'the insult comic' because he insulted all of his guests. I was unknown in America, but that didn't stop Don taking the piss out of me.

'This is Jimmy Tarbuck,' he told his viewers. 'And if you don't know who he is, he'll soon tell you. Because all he ever says is, 'I'm Jimmy Tarbuck. Jimmy Tarbuck. Jimmy Tarbuck from the London Palladium. Jimmy Tarbuck. London Palladium …'

It was a brilliant trip to America – so exciting that I went back just a few weeks later. And, let me tell you, this trip was even more memorable.

By the early seventies, I was proper big mates with Tom Jones. Jonesy had made it massive in America, and by now he was doing months-long residencies in Las Vegas. And he invited me over to see him play at Caesars Palace. *Yes, please!*

The girls were in school, so Pauline and I left the kids with her parents and flew into Vegas. Jonesy looked after us well: we got picked up at the airport in a Lincoln limo and driven to our hotel on the Strip. Now, I've heard that Vegas is very tacky nowadays, but it wasn't so gaudy back then. I was surprised by how small it was.

Pauline and I had our gobs hanging open at some of the big American stars who were performing on the Strip: Frankie Laine, who was a brilliant singer; Phyllis Diller, a fantastic comedian; Jimmy Durante, the legendary comic. Pauline and I went to see all of them. Durante was nearly eighty by then, and he was sensational.

But one name towered over all the others. Elvis Presley was making his big comeback in Vegas at the time. He was doing two performances a night at the International Hotel. The shows were all long sold out, of course, but I *had* to see him. *This. Is. Elvis. Presley!* No way was I going to go to Vegas and miss him.

Now, say what you like about old Tarby, but I've always been resourceful. I'm also pretty good at doing accents. So, I got on the phone to the International and, in my best Welsh impersonation, asked for the promoter of the Elvis show. I got put through.

'Hello, can I help you?'

'Hello, boyo, this is Tom Jones,' I growled, in what I hoped was a Valleys baritone.

'Mr Jones, sir! What an honour to speak to you. How can I help you?'

'I have a friend over called Jimmy Tarbuck. He's a very, very big star in England. He's here with his wife and they would love to see Elvis Presley tonight. Can you help them?'

'Of course, Mr Jones! We'll give them VIP tickets. Leave it to us.'

So, Pauline and I showed up at the International for Elvis's early evening show. The venue treated us like super-stars. They showed us to a fantastic table and gave us free Champagne. And, as we drank it, our eyes were glued to the stage. Because Elvis Presley was magnificent.

I didn't much care for his dress sense – a zip-up white jumpsuit with black pockets – but even in that, Elvis looked marvellous. He hadn't yet got into the pills and the burgers and he was in fantastic shape. He opened his set with 'Mystery Train' and it never let up. He was mesmeric: pure charisma. I spent the whole show thinking: *Wow! This is Elvis!*

Pauline and I were meeting Tom for dinner. When we got there, he asked, 'What have you two been doing, then?'

Well, I could hardly say, 'Impersonating you, in order to ponce in to see Elvis,' so I answered, 'Oh, just going down the Strip. We saw Jimmy Durante.' And bugger me if Tom didn't have a surprise planned.

'Guess what? I've got us tickets to see Elvis Presley's second show tonight,' he told us, over dinner. 'I've seen it a few times. It's fantastic.' And I thought, *Yes, we know!*

So, later that night, it was back to the International for Pauline and me. We were with Tom, his wife, his parents and his sister. I still hadn't let on to Tom that I'd bullshitted my way into the first show. As we trooped back in, I hid my face behind a hanky in case the staff recognised me and said, 'Ah, hello, Mr Tarbuck! Back for more?'

This time, because we were with Tom, we had the best table in the house. Jonesy was so huge in Vegas that he got treated like Jesus. Elvis was just as tremendous as he'd been at the first show. Absolutely wonderful. And, at the end, Tom had another surprise for us.

'Come on, Jimmy,' he said. 'Let's go and say hello to him.'

'Who?'

'Elvis. Let's go his dressing room. He knows I'm in.'

Bloody hell!

We all got led backstage. The ways parted for Tom. When we got to the dressing room, Elvis was still in his jumpsuit, relaxing with his entourage. As soon as he spotted Tom, he jumped up and came over. You could tell that they were properly close.

'Great show, Elvis!' said Tom. 'Hey, I want you to meet a good pal of mine. This is Jimmy Tarbuck, from the Palladium in London.'

And Elvis Presley shook my hand. It was hard to believe but, close up, he looked even better than he had onstage. He had the most piercing blue eyes, under that famous kiss curl hanging over his forehead. As he said hello to Tom's family, Jonesy nudged me and handed me a lemonade.

'Pass that to Elvis, will you?' he asked.

I couldn't. I seemed to have lost the power of both speech and movement. I stood there like a statue. Tom noticed, and laughed.

'What's the matter with you?' he asked. 'You're acting like a schoolgirl. Just give him the bloody drink!'

'But … *he's Elvis Presley*!' I whispered.

'So what? *I'm Tom Jones*!'

'Yes, but you're not Elvis Presley! "Heartbreak Hotel" is the first record I ever bought as a kid. And now he's standing right here!' Pauline rolled her eyes, took the lemonade off me and handed it to Elvis herself. And The King started talking to me.

'So, how are you doing, Jimmy?' he asked, in that legendary drawl. 'Where are you from?'

'Liverpool, England.' I said. 'When are you coming over to play for us?'

Elvis looked taken aback. '*Me*? Where would *I* play in England?'

'Wembley Stadium,' I said.

'Huh? What's that?'

'It's a football stadium,' I told him. 'Well, what you'd call a soccer stadium.'

'How many people does it hold?'

'One hundred thousand.'

Elvis laughed, as if it was the most ridiculous thing he'd ever heard. 'Oh, come on!' he said. 'I'd never get a hundred thousand people to see me.'

'No,' I replied. 'You'd get *five* hundred thousand. People love you over there.' Yet he still looked as if he didn't believe a word of it. 'It's very nice of you to say so, and very nice to meet you,' he said with a smile, shaking my hand once more as he moved away.

We stayed in Elvis's dressing room for an hour or so. He was charm itself. He was what Americans call a Southern gentleman: at the end of the night, he went right around the room, kissing every lady's hand and saying, 'Goodnight, ma'am.' They were all wetting themselves. And, to be frank, so was I.

The following night, Tom gave Pauline and me tickets for his own show at Caesars Palace. Tom was fantastic as well. Knickers were flying everywhere (well, not mine).* And, after the show, bugger me if Elvis didn't show up in Tom's dressing room. He greeted Pauline and me like old friends. He was one class act.

It's a tragedy Elvis never made it to Britain. I stand by what I said to him: he could have headlined Wembley as many nights as he wanted. He'd have pulled the crowds like The Beatles did, or like Oasis do today. When I was with Elvis Presley, I got that same feeling that I did with Judy and Frank, the feeling I've only had three or four times in my life:

I was in the presence of greatness.

* * *

Back in England, it was summer season time again, and I was back in Bournemouth, this time with Kenny Lynch. Now, as I've said, I loved Lynchy to bits. He was my best mate in showbiz, and probably in the whole world. But that didn't mean he wasn't an infuriating sod to work with.

---

* I was too busy picking them up, boom boom!

Why? He was always late. And I mean, *always*. For everything. Kipper was notorious for it. Time didn't mean a lot to him, especially if he was on the old wacky baccy. Which he often was. He was a wonderful feller, but he was always flying by the seat of his pants.

One night in Bournemouth, he turned up late yet again, almost missing the start of the show. I was pissed off, and tore him off a strip. 'Kipper, take a look at yourself, mate,' I said. 'You're unprofessional. You never learn.' Kenny was blithely unconcerned.

'I'm here now, aren't I?' he reasoned. 'There's nothing wrong with me. *You're* the one with the problem. Just look at you: all tense and worried. I don't worry about anything. You need to learn to relax, Tarby.'

Well, I admit, this got my goat. 'Oh, you never worry about anything, Kipper?' I asked. 'Yeah. That's right.' And I went away thinking, *we'll see about that* …

We had a full orchestra for the shows. The next night, before Lynchy did his slot, I had a word with the band leader. 'Kenny asked me to tell you that he wants to reverse his show tonight,' I said. 'He wants to do his first song last and do the whole set backwards.' The feller looked surprised, but nodded. 'No problem,' he said.

Well, that night Kenny didn't know what had hit him. He was thrown from the opening note. He had no bloody idea what was coming next. I was pissing myself in the wings as I watched him flailing about. He spotted me, and put two and two together. When he came off at the end (or was it the start?), he was bloody furious.

'You bastard!' he yelled at me. 'I'll bloody kill you ...'

'Ah, look at you, all tense and worried!' I laughed. 'I thought that you never worry about anything? You need to learn to relax, Kipper ...'

Sometimes, when things went wrong onstage, it was down to pranks like that. At other times, it was a pure accident. By the end of 1972, I was back in breeches and jerkin for another panto: being Jack yet again in another production of *Jack and the Beanstalk*, this time at the Wimbledon Theatre.

Also in the cast was Hugh Lloyd, a veteran comic actor who'd made his name in series such as *Hancock's Half Hour* (he was in the famous blood-donor sketch). Hugh was a lovely guy but he'd just had to have a week off the show with a bad case of the flu. And I think he'd returned before he was properly well again.

Hugh used to sing an old music-hall number early in the panto: 'Hello, Hello, Who's Your Lady Friend?' On his first night back, he made his big entrance, ran across the stage as he sang the song ... and went arse-over-tit over the front lights and into the pit. The crowd roared with laughter – well, until Hugh failed to resurface.

It was panto-monium. I went onstage to see a groggy Hugh being carried out of the pit by security. We had to close the curtain, wait for Hugh's understudy to quickly climb into his costume, and start the show all over again. And poor old Hugh was off again, for a day or two. Well, you know what they say, don't you? *That's showbiz!*

CHAPTER 11

A difference of opinion, Geoffrey

As we moved into the mid-seventies, I had a nice work routine going. I'd generally have a TV show on the go. There would be a summer season, more often than not. The end of the year normally meant a panto. And pretty much any time that I had a day off, you'd find me on a golf course. *Oh, yes.* It was a life that suited me.

My telly shows tended to have my name in the title. That wasn't my doing. The telly companies and commissioning executives would think them up, run them past me, and I'd say, 'Yep, that sounds fine to me.' It was a system that worked well and I was happy with it.

The start of 1973 brought a one-off BBC special called *The Tarbuck Follies.* It was me as the host of a modern music-hall show, with the singer Clodagh Rodgers and a burlesque troupe called the Tarbuck Girls. Lionel Blair was also on it, working out yet more ways for his girls to dance around me as I stood still and swayed.

I also did a new, third series of *It's Tarbuck* for ITV. The sketch-and-stand-up format was the same as the original 1964 series, but Ronnie Corbett and Amanda Barrie had moved on and been replaced by Frank Williams and Josephine Tewson. They were a pair of very professional comic actors who were a pleasure to work with.

After I recorded shows like that, I'd often end up in Tramp nightclub late in the evening. I liked the guy who ran it, Johnny Gold: his dad was a bookie, just like mine. Tramp was a big place at the time. Everyone went there, from rock stars to royalty. You were equally likely to bump into John Lennon or Princess Margaret.

I wasn't a big drinker but the place was such good fun that I'd still get home in the early hours of the morning. Pauline would sometimes wake up and give me a bollocking:

'What time do you call this? Where the hell have you been?'

'Oh, I just went for a bite to eat …' The following morning, I'd be up at seven, bleary-eyed after four hours' sleep, to help her get the kids ready for school.

My career was going well, but my favourite job was still hosting shows at the London Palladium. I hadn't done it for a few years, and I missed it. Yet in the autumn of 1973, when ATV brought back *Sunday Night at the London Palladium*, they didn't ask me to present it. Instead, it was hosted by Jim Dale and Ted Rogers.

Maybe I would have liked to have been asked, but when I watched it, I was glad that I wasn't. It just didn't work. It wasn't as spectacular, as if the bosses were cutting corners and trying to save money, and it lacked the old warmth. I can't say that I was surprised when it only lasted one series.

Instead, ATV gave me a six-part series (with my name in the title, yet again): *Tell Tarby*. It went out on Monday nights and it was more of a sketch show than telling gags. I did it with the lovely Lynda Bellingham and a bonkers comic called Stanley Unwin, who used to talk backwards. God knows how he did it, but he'd have me crying with laughter.

But I was doing plenty of crying, and no laughing at all, at another event in 1973 – a tragic one. Because my mum died.

Mum hadn't always been well. Like a lot of people of her generation, she'd smoked for her entire life (I'd dabbled in my youth, but never taken it up because of playing football). And now she had stomach cancer. We never told her about the diagnosis because we didn't want to upset her. Mum thought she just had shingles.

She was in hospital in Liverpool and I was going up to see her. One day, I went to the hospital with Kenneth. He and I went for a drink that evening, then I really wanted to go back to see Mum again. She was lying in bed, mostly unconscious, but would occasionally come to. At least I could see that she wasn't suffering.

As I sat quietly by her bed, Mum opened her eyes and looked at me. 'Jimmy, you've been nothing but a heartache my entire life, you bugger!' she said. But that was her sense of humour for you. She had a smile on her face as she said it: a smile of pure love. That was the last time I saw her before she passed.

Mum was a great lady. Her death took a lot of getting over for all of us. But, obviously, it affected Dad the worst. He had loved Mum with all his heart, and most of all he'd loved the companionship they shared. Dad became a broken man. On his wreath at Mum's funeral, he wrote three simple words: 'See you soon'.

* * *

Sometimes, when you've had heartbreak and tragedy in your life, it's good to just throw yourself into something that's fun and silly. At the end of 1973, I was almost glad when panto season came around (*Oh yes, I was!*): Jack in *Jack and the Beanstalk*, yet again, this time at the Alexandra Theatre in Birmingham.

I've always liked Brum and I had a happy time in that show. My main co-stars were a pretty crazy five-piece comedy and music band called The Grumbleweeds. I used to laugh when I worked with those guys, and I took any opportunity I got to prank them and wind them up.

In one scene, The Grumbleweeds had to exit through a door in the stage set. I wasn't on for that bit, so I locked the door from backstage. I heard them say, 'We're off!' then I stood behind the door, pissing myself laughing, as I heard them rattling the handle and mumbling to each other:

'What the hell are you doing? Open it!'

'I can't – it's locked!'

'Gah! I bet that bastard Tarbuck's locked it …'

I'd done *Jack and the Beanstalk* so many times by now that I just messed about most of the time and said whatever

I felt like. The audiences seemed to enjoy it, so it was OK. The theatre was owned by two brothers, and at the last-night party, one of them said to me, 'Thank you, Jimmy. You must try actually doing a *panto* here some time ...'

The following year I was back in summer season again, this time in Margate with good old Arthur Askey. Arthur was well into his seventies by now but he gave the show his all: he was a textbook definition of a good, old-fashioned showbiz trouper. But when the season had finished, and I was back in London, Pauline and I had a terrible time.

Pauline's father, Barney, dropped dead. Barney was a good man. He'd always been like a second dad to me and was a fantastic grandfather to our kids, who all loved him to bits. Barney had been very ill, so it wasn't totally out of the blue, but it was still a shock. And then, the very next day, my dad died.

What were the odds? Our two dads going, one day apart? After I got the news about Fred, I remember being out in our garden with Liza, who would have been nine then. 'Dad, I'm sorry I can't cry about Grandad Fred,' she apologised to me, sweetly. 'But I've used up all my tears on Grandad Barney.'

Dad had written 'See you soon' on Mum's funeral wreath and he was right. He'd been poorly for a while but, if I'm honest, I think he just gave up and turned it in when Mum died. He didn't want to go on without her. They were both only in their early seventies when they passed. That seemed a good innings at the time. It seems nothing nowadays.

The undertakers offered me the chance to see Dad in the morgue but I couldn't do it. I didn't want to. I was used to seeing him laughing and joking, with a pint in his hand, and *that* was how I wanted to remember him: not lying cold on a slab. I said goodbye to him in my own way, internally. I never visit Liverpool without going to his grave.

I loved my parents and I am so grateful to them for everything they did. They made me what, and who, I am.

* * *

As I said, I had a nice, steady work routine going at this point in my life, but now and then I liked to do something different. My success had nearly all come in Britain, and I got to wondering about whether I might be able to work abroad. So, at the start of 1975, I set off on a bit of an adventure.

I went on a trip with Ken Hatton, the pal I'd met when he was the camp barber at Butlin's all those years ago. It was a mix of work and pleasure. We started in California then went on to Hawaii, where we visited the memorial of the USS *Arizona*, the battleship that was sunk at Pearl Harbor and lies on the seabed, the bodies of its crew still on board.

Ken and I flew from there to Sydney. I was going to do a couple of cabaret shows there, one of them covering for Max Bygraves, who couldn't make it. It was a long flight and I was unshaven and wearing a scruffy jean suit for travelling. By the time I got there, I was shagged out.

I wasn't well known in Australia then. Or, at least, I didn't think I was. Aussie telly had shown one or two of my shows, but that was it. So I thought nothing of it when we wheeled our luggage trolleys out of immigration and Ken said, 'Jim, there's loads of reporters here for you.'

'It can't be for me,' I replied. 'It must be for someone else.'

'No, it's definitely you, Jim.' And he was right. As soon as we got through customs, *bam!* There were paparazzi flashing away. Some tall feller in a dodgy safari suit stuck a big microphone in my face as his cameraman filmed us.

'Well, Jimmy Tarbuck is here,' he said. 'So, you're England's leading comedian, are you?'

I was knackered, and I didn't really need this. 'So they say,' I replied.

'Well, make me laugh, then,' he sneered.

Oh, you're a smartarse, are you? I thought. 'Tell you what,' I answered. 'Let's have a good look at your suit, and we can all piss ourselves.' He didn't like that.

Once I'd settled in and got over the jet lag, Ken and I had a great time in Australia. We were there for four weeks and we fell in with a group of guys who liked golf and liked beer. From day one, the Aussies' laid-back way of life fitted me like a glove.

Peter Prichard had fixed me up a few gigs while I was out there. I went on a telly show with Yvonne De Carlo, the veteran Hollywood movie star, and played a charity show for Aboriginal Australians, who weren't treated well in those days. And I did a gig at a cabaret club that was the dictionary definition of the phrase 'tough crowd'.

The promoter said they had a big stag party in. 'Be as blue and go as rough as you want, mate!' he encouraged me.

'That's not my thing,' I replied. 'I did that stuff a bit when I was starting out, but not any more.'

He shrugged: 'Suit yourself, cobber.' And I walked out to a crowd of baying, shouting, pissed-up blokes.

'Good evening, it's great to be here …' I began. And the heckling started.

'Piss off!'

'Gerroff!'

'Make us laugh, you bloody Pom!'

Well, I wasn't taking that. *You want some? OK, let's do this.*

'I've got Aussies living either side of me in London,' I began. 'I'm glad. It keeps all the flies out of my place …'

They roared at that, and I was off. For the next forty-five minutes, I gave it them with both barrels. I was effing and blinding my head off, I was winding them up, I was blue, I was raw. I did the roughest, rudest stand-up I'd done since I was in the northern working men's clubs fifteen years earlier. Bernard Manning might have blushed. It was brutal.

The crowd loved it. I could hear them yelling, 'Go on, you Pommie bastard!'

When I came off, dripping with sweat, the promoter was waiting for me. 'That was great, mate!' He beamed. 'Can you do next weekend as well?'

'No, thank you,' I told him. 'I think once is quite enough.'

From Australia, I stopped off in Hong Kong. The kids were on school holiday by now so Pauline brought them out to join me. We were in a lovely hotel, and part of the deal was that I played a show in their theatre while I was there. At the end of it, an English feller came up and introduced himself.

'I saw you playing a charity football match in Liverpool years ago,' he said. 'You were good. My team has got a cup game tomorrow and a bloke has just dropped out – will you play?'

One thing about me has never changed. I never turn down a game of football. 'Sure,' I said. The guy went away and I had a drink and promptly forgot all about our conversation.

The next day, I was hanging out in our suite with Pauline and the kids, stuffing down ham and eggs for lunch, when there came a knock at the door. It was one of the hotel staff. 'Sir, there is a car for you downstairs, waiting to take you to a football match,' he told me.

Bloody hell! I had no choice but to go down and get in. The family came along. I had bugger-all with me: no boots, nothing. The car drove us to Hong Kong National Stadium. It was packed. *Eh? This looks like a big deal!* Pauline and the kids joined the crowd and I was led to a dressing room, where the feller from the night before was waiting for me.

'Thanks for doing this, Jimmy,' he said, as he sorted me out for boots and kit. 'Where do you play?'

'Just stick me behind the forwards on the right,' I said.

The game started. It was the biggest crowd I'd ever played in front of. After about twenty minutes, the ball came to me. I slipped a good pass through to our right winger and he ran through and scored. 'Great ball, Scouse!' he yelled as he ran over and hugged me. 'Keep it up!'

No way. I couldn't. I was struggling: struggling very badly. I hadn't been expecting to play football so I'd done no training, I'd been on the piss in Australia for the last month, and I was full of ham and eggs. I had an aching stitch and I could hardly move. There was only one thing for it.

'Aaargh!' I yelled, clutching the back of my thigh and falling to the ground dramatically.

A trainer ran on and began massaging my leg. 'I can't feel anything?' he said.

'I've done my hamstring,' I sighed, shaking my head. 'Damn! I'm going to have to come off.'

A sub came on. I pretended to limp down the tunnel, headed to the dressing room, changed and went straight to the car. Pauline and the family were waiting for me. The kids looked worried. 'Are you alright, Dad?' they asked me.

'Yes. Just get in the car,' I whispered. Within twenty minutes, I was back in the hotel suite scoffing a second helping of ham and eggs. Then I did a show that night. *That's* the way to do it.

It was a great trip but it went on a bit too long. If I'm honest, it felt as if it was never going to end. I can remember looking out of the plane window as we neared Heathrow, seeing Big Ben and the Thames, and feeling relieved: *Thank God I'm home!* But what an adventure it had been.

* * *

Once I was back in London, it was telly time again. It was ATV's turn to come up with the title: *Tarbuck and All That!* My main partner in crime on that one was Alison Steadman, who was brilliant. She is a formidable actress. It's the only time I ever worked with Alison but even today, if we bump into one another, we laugh about how much fun it was.

Tarbuck and All That! only ran for one season, but two other series began in 1975 which were to play a rather bigger part in my working life. The first one was a show that BBC2 began running called *International Pro-Celebrity Golf*.

I couldn't believe my luck when that programme started. Why, here was a show that combined my two biggest interests in life, family aside: appearing on television, and playing golf. It could have been custom-made for me. And I made the Beeb very aware that I was available to appear on it absolutely any time they wanted me.

The format was simple: two top golf professionals would play a round each partnered by someone from the world of showbiz. The celebrities read like a list of my best mates and golfing partners. Bruce Forsyth did it, as did Ronnie Corbett, Eric Sykes, Sean Connery and Dickie Henderson, as well as people like Christopher Lee and Bobby Charlton.

The professionals for the first series were the American Tom Weiskopf, who had won the British Open a couple of years earlier, and the Englishman Peter Oosterhuis. They were chalk and cheese. Weiskopf was very confident and outgoing and Oosterhuis was a much quieter lad. I think Tom was the better golfer of the two.

I made my debut in the last episode of the first series, along with an American racing driver called Johnny Rutherford. I had to pinch myself all around the course: *I'm being paid to play golf! International Pro-Celebrity Golf* ran for sixteen series and I'm pretty sure I appeared in virtually all of them.

My other big telly show that launched in 1975 ran for nearly as long and was just as good, and as important, for me. It was a game show called *Winner Takes All*.

Now, some comics can be a bit sniffy about presenting game shows. They think they are somehow a bit beneath them. Well, not me! When I first got offered the opportunity to host *Winner Takes All*, I jumped at it, because I knew, instinctively, that it would suit my personality. And that was exactly how it worked out.

For a working comic, a game show is a wonderful way to be on television. Why? You're not using any material. Think about it. If you do a five-minute stand-up slot on telly, and ten million people watch it, it means they all know those jokes now. You can't ever tell them again. You have to go off and put together a whole new set.

Hosting a game show is different. All you have to do is talk to people and, if I may say so, I'm pretty sure that I'm good at doing that. Whether I'm onstage, on telly, or just in the street, I've always loved having a chat, having a laugh, and jollying things along. My job on *Winner Takes All* was to do that, and to relax the nervous contestants.

How did I do it? Sometimes, I'd crack a gag. Others, I'd turn on the charm: 'Oh, that's a lovely dress, if you don't mind me saying so …' I'd do whatever it took to make sure the show was fun for the people who came on. It wasn't an effort, it came naturally.

The show's format was simple. Two contestants would be given points, get asked a load of questions and be given multiple-choice answers. They'd bet their points on getting the answers right. Each answer had odds, the same as betting on horses: 2–1, 3–1, 5–1 etc. It was simple and it was addictive.

My sidekick on the show was a man called Geoffrey Wheeler. Geoffrey had devised the whole idea and he set the questions every week, but you never actually saw him on the screen. He was a disembodied voice, asking the contestants all of the questions and then giving them the answers. He was a very nice man indeed.

Geoffrey, and *Winner Takes All*, inadvertently gave me a catchphrase. Unlike Bruce, with his 'Nice to see you, to see you, nice!' and 'Good game, good game!', I'd never been big on catchphrases (unless you count 'Oh oh!' or 'Boom boom!'). But I said one phrase so often on the show that I became known for it.

Geoffrey would read out a question. The two contestants would ponder their answers, press their buzzers and choose two different options. One might go for the 2–1 answer and one for the 3–1 shot. And I would look at the scoreboard and say, 'Well, we have a difference of opinion, Geoffrey ...'

I did it without thinking. I didn't even know I was doing it at first. But it quickly caught on, and people started saying it. Folk would shout it at me in the street: 'Oi, Tarby! We have a difference of opinion, Geoffrey!' I didn't mind and, in fact, I started playing up to it and saying it even more on the show. It was a bit of harmless fun.

Winner Takes All was a Yorkshire TV show so we filmed it up in Leeds. I might go up for two or three days at a time, and we'd record three programmes in a day. We had to keep the show looking fresh, so I'd change my tie and blazer between each recording. I'd have a row of them, of all different colours, hanging in my dressing room.

Three shows a day was the norm. Occasionally, we'd manage four. One day, we did five. *Five shows!* That was a lot of hours to spend concentrating under those hot studio lights. As we prepared to begin the last recording of the day, I was exhausted. We had a young runner hanging around the set, and I called him over.

'Would you mind getting me a glass of water, please?' I asked him. Then I beckoned him closer, and whispered, 'Make it a vodka and tonic.'

The kid nodded and vanished backstage, reappearing with a glass a minute later. 'Here's your water, Jimmy,' he said, and set it down between me and a female contestant.

The woman looked at it, and licked her lips. 'I'm gasping as well,' she said. 'Do you mind if I have a sip, Jimmy?'

Before I could say anything, or stop her, the lady raised the glass to her lips and took a proper big swig. Her eyes widened and she spluttered it back out. 'That's a bit fierce! That's not water!' she said, laughing. The studio audience fell about. And I just grinned and thought, *I hope the bosses aren't watching!*

Some of the contestants were a lot better than others. One week, a lovely old lady from Liverpool came on. The question was 'What's the name of the creature that is half-man, half-beast?' The answer we were looking for was centaur. She went for Geoffrey's 10–1 outside shot: Billy the Kid. Everyone fell about.

The show's winners took home £1,000 per week. The losers got nothing at first, and then we started giving them £100. But the winners also had the option of coming back the following week, playing again, and adding to their prize money. The danger with that was that if they lost, they'd forfeit all the money they'd won.

Most people were happy to take the £1,000 but some took the gamble and came back again. And we had one particular elderly gent who loved playing the game, was very good at it, and kept coming back week after week. He was piling up the winnings – but that meant he had a lot to lose if, or when, it went pear-shaped for him.

With all respect, he wasn't the smartest-dressed of fellers. What he turned up wearing wouldn't have looked so good on screen, so the producers gave him a suit and tie to wear. He loved them. He kept coming back, putting them on, and winning again. After five weeks, he was up to £5,000.

Now, that might not sound a lot today, in the age of *Who Wants to Be a Millionaire?*, but in those days, £5,000 was a lot of cash. It would be worth nearly forty grand today. Back then, you could easily have bought a small house with it. And every week the feller kept coming back and risking losing the lot.

As the host, I wasn't allowed to influence the contestants in any of their decisions. But we had meetings about him. The Yorkshire TV bosses were desperate for him to take it. It would be heartbreaking to see this old guy losing all that cash. But it was his decision, and his decision alone.

People were talking about this feller. The word spread. By his sixth show, we were up to number one in the TV ratings. And the chap put his studio suit on, sat down, and won yet again. It was decision time.

'Well, what are you going to do?' I asked him. And I'm sure my eyes were burning into him, saying, *Quit while you're ahead, you silly sod!*

He looked at me. 'You know what? I think I'm going to take the money, Jimmy,' he said. And the place exploded. The studio audience were on their feet, giving him a standing ovation. When it had died down, he smiled at me, and said, 'Something in your face told me you thought I ought to do that.'

'Spot on!' I said. I shook his hand and congratulated him. But, before he left, the old guy had a favour to ask. He gestured at his borrowed clothing.

'Could I buy this suit, please?' he asked.

I couldn't believe my ears. 'No, absolutely not,' I replied.

'I thought you'd say that.' He sighed.

'I'm going to *give* you that suit,' I told him. And I think he looked even more delighted about that than winning the six grand. But the feller had turned *Winner Takes All* into must-see telly. A second-hand suit didn't seem too much for him to ask.

I was on *Winner Takes All* right up until 1986. Then Yorkshire TV decided to stop making it. It was a pity. After I'd left, Geoffrey Wheeler persuaded the studio bosses to give it a bit longer, and he presented the show himself for a little while. But it seemed to have had its day, and they axed it for good.

I'll tell you what, the whole snobbery around hosting game shows is bollocks. It may look an easy job, but it isn't. There is an art to doing it, and a lot of that art is *making* it look easy. I can count the number of people who were, or are, brilliant at it on the fingers of one hand.

Bruce Forsyth was fantastic on *The Generation Game*. Terry Wogan was brilliant on *Blankety Blank*, as was Les Dawson. Nowadays, Bradley Walsh is good on *The Chase*, as is the feller who hosts *The 1% Club*, Lee Mack. I like him because he's very quick, and he gets right in there – *Bang! Bang!*

But if I were forced to name the best game-show host of all time, I think it's easy: Bob Monkhouse. Bob was a genius at it. He was so meticulous, so professional and so funny, whether he was presenting *The Golden Shot*, *Celebrity Squares* or *Bob's Full House*. He was bang on top of his game, week in week out.

The proof of what a tough gig hosting a game show can be is the top entertainers who had trouble with it. Charlie Williams was a good comic but he struggled when he took over *The Golden Shot*. My mate Max Bygraves was a terrific performer but he never looked at home on *Family Fortunes*. It didn't suit him.

I did eleven years on *Winner Takes All* and I loved every minute of it. I thank it every night when I say my prayers because it was wonderful for me. You know what? God bless the show. And I have no difference of opinion about that at all.

CHAPTER 12

I've run out of soap

OK, it's confession time. Looking back, as I am doing for this book, it's very hard for me to deny that I got distracted from my career in the late seventies. And there was one big thing distracting me: *golf*. No question, I became fixated on the sport. For a few years, golf went from being a hobby to an obsession.

It's exaggerating a bit to say I handed my career over to golf. But only a bit. It was all that I thought about. I woke up every day next door to a golf course, at Coombe Hill, and if I could spend that day on the course, I did. Dick Burton, the club pro when I first moved there, used to give me invaluable tips. After Dick sadly passed away, I just carried on practising and practising. Which meant I got rather good.

I wasn't the only Tarbuck getting a bit tasty on the course at Coombe Hill. Pauline was intrigued about why I loved golf so much and sometimes she would come over and play a round herself. She proved to be a natural, a very good golfer, and soon I had myself another talented playing partner.

At this time, I had plenty of chances to play. I had a regular, well-paid gig in *Winner Takes All*, which made me less bothered about chasing summer seasons and pantos. I was spending less time chatting to Peter Prichard about getting me new telly shows. I mean, why bother? I had a golf course at the end of my garden!

There's a great, unique thing about golf as a sport. The handicapping system means you can play the very best and have a chance of beating them. I mean, you'd never be able to outrun Usain Bolt. You couldn't take a set off Novak Djokovic at Wimbledon. At golf, you can play the greatest pros on a level playing field. And I was.

I was still appearing on *International Pro-Celebrity Golf* as often as I could, and avidly watching it the weeks that I couldn't. I think, if I'm honest, that show allowed me to pretend that spending all day playing golf was actually *good* for my career, rather than the opposite. It was a fantasy that I let myself wallow in.

For the third series of the show, in 1977, Bing Crosby became the co-host with the great Henry Longhurst. It was a thrill to hang out with both of them. Even better, Tony Jacklin became the UK team captain. Tony was the best British golfer of his generation: he'd previously won both the British and US Opens.

I loved talking to Tony, watching him play, asking him for tips and simply soaking up his golf knowledge. It was a privilege: *lucky Jim*, again. It was even more special when we became pals and took up socialising and playing golf outside of the show. I reckon I partnered Tony at pro-am more than any other pro.

All of my showbiz golfing pals – Bruce Forsyth, Ronnie Corbett, Henry Cooper, Kenny Lynch, Des O'Connor – came down to Coombe Hill to play me. But our matches had changed. I was playing so much more than any of them that I'd got a lot better than they were. My handicap was down to eight. I'd usually win pretty easily.

If I wasn't thinking about golf, I was thinking about football. I was in my mid-thirties by now but I still loved to have a game. Whenever I was asked to play in a charity match, or a testimonial, I was bang up for it. And I got to meet some players who, for me, were footballing gods.

I played with the great John Charles, in a match at Leyton Orient. I also got a game in a testimonial at Chelsea's ground. I was in the dressing room before the match when a little old feller came in and sat next to me. I put out my hand and introduced myself.

'Jimmy Tarbuck, Liverpool,' I said.

'Ferenc Puskás, Hungary,' he replied.

Wow! Ferenc Puskás! The captain of the Mighty Magyars team who had beaten England 6–3 at Wembley when I was a lad, and one of the greatest players of all time! But by now I knew a few football legends. I had met all of the England 1966 World Cup-winning team. Out of all of them, I was closest to the captain, Bobby Moore.

Bobby was a delightful feller. He was always charming and well dressed, and still a fantastic footballer. I'd never hung out with anybody who excited admiration and turned heads as much as Mooro, yet he was still a humble, down-to-earth character. What a great bloke he was.

I played a lot of testimonials with Bobby. He'd give me advice. I remember once, before a game at Fulham, he told me: 'Jimbo, don't hold on to the ball. As soon as you get it, pass it to a better player.'

'Bloody hell, Bobby,' I said. '*Every* other player is better than me!' And the cheeky sod nodded in agreement.

When the game started, I didn't take his advice. I got the ball and, rather than play it short, I tried a long pass out to our winger. It fell about twenty feet short. Bobby gave me a pitying look. 'It's a long way, isn't it?' he said. I had such laughs with him. *The England World Cup-winning captain*: it still annoys me that he never got a knighthood.

In 1977, Liverpool got to the European Cup final against Borussia Mönchengladbach. I went to the final in Rome. We won 3–1, and our legendary hardman defender, Tommy Smith, scored the second goal with a bullet header in his 600th appearance for the club. And, two days later, I played in Tommy's testimonial in front of 35,000 people at Anfield.

What a hoot that night was. Liverpool drew 9–9 (yes, 9–9) against a Bobby Charlton XI. Tommy stuck our skipper, Emlyn Hughes, in goal, and our keeper, Ray Clemence, up front.* I played in a seven-a-side game during half-time.

---

* Clem scored two goals, as did Tommy Smith, one of them from the most ridiculous penalty I've ever seen given. I still laugh to think about it now.

I scored a cracking goal from an Ian St John pass, and Kenny Lynch got carried off with 'exhaustion'. Happy days.

* * *

Just to make it clear, I hadn't given up on work completely. In 1978 I did a summer season at the Floral Hall in Scarborough with Les Dennis. Les is a great lad: I've worked with him a lot over the years. It was a fun summer because another good mate, Danny La Rue, was appearing down the road at the Futurist Theatre. We all hung out quite a bit. And my family decamped to the seaside for the school holidays as usual, which was nice.

But more than anything, I was all about golf. I wasn't just playing at Coombe Hill by now: I was playing *everywhere*. I entered the Lancôme pro-am in Paris with Tony Jacklin. I had golfing holidays in Spain and Portugal with the likes of Sean Connery, Kenny Lynch and Ronnie Corbett. On one of those, I had a very entertaining incident with little Ronnie.

We were on the gorgeous Penina course in the Algarve, designed and founded by the great Henry Cotton. Henry was giving lessons so he couldn't play the round with us but, to our amazement, he loaned us a donkey who worked at the course, Pacifico, to carry our clubs around.

Well, that was the plan. Pacifico didn't appear to agree. As soon as Henry had left us, the mule pissed gallons all over the first tee, then cantered off, our clubs all strapped to his back. I have an abiding memory of Ronnie Corbett, in plus-fours and golfing cap, chasing that donkey, Benny Hill-style, down a fairway trying to get them back.

I played a fair bit with Terry Wogan. Terry was a smashing guy but not much of a golfer. He did once fluke an incredible hundred-foot putt at Gleneagles, though. He hit the ball and didn't even watch it go: he was talking to a friend. It kept rolling and rolling … closer and closer … rolling … closer … closer … and *plop!* It was in!

Everyone around the green started cheering. Wogan looked up, puzzled. 'What's all the fuss, Jimmy?' he asked. He glanced around: 'And where's my ball?' Tel's face was a picture as the unlikely truth dawned on him. He uttered some immortal words: 'Fuck me! It's in the hole!'

I was playing non-stop and it improved my game still further. I got my handicap down to three. I managed to go round the world-famous 'home of golf', St Andrews in Scotland, in 66 – *66!* – and I even got picked to play a few county matches for Surrey. I was very proud of both of those achievements.

Back on *International Pro-Celebrity Golf*, Lee Trevino and Seve Ballesteros took over as club captains in 1979. Lee was a quick-witted former US and British Open champion from a Mexican family, and he was hilarious. He was a great storyteller and he had a gag for every situation. He could easily have been a comic.

It was just as well that Lee was funny as he never bloody shut up! Tony Jacklin told me a great story about once being partnered with him at a tournament. 'I don't want to talk today, Lee,' he said, hopefully, as they began their round.

And Trevino retorted: 'That's OK, I don't want you to talk. I want you to listen.'

Seve was something else again. He'd come from a very poor family in Spain – his dad was a farm labourer – yet had become the number-one golfer in the world. He was a very likable feller and extremely good-looking. Women were throwing themselves at him and Seve sure took advantage of that.

Yet he was nothing compared to Sean Connery.

I played a lot of golf with Sean over the years. He was an extremely good golfer, the best James Bond there's ever been – and the biggest womaniser I've ever met. Sean was relentless in pursuing women, even ones who happened to be married to his mates. In fact, I soon awarded him a nickname: Soapy.

Let me tell you why. When we played tournaments, or went on golfing holidays, Sean had a bad habit of knocking on his pals' hotel doors when he knew that they were out on the course. When their wives or girlfriends opened the door, he'd smile and say: 'I'm sorry to bother you, but I've run out of soap. Could I get some from your bathroom?'

It was his way of trying to get in the room to chance his arm. Of course, the girls would all tell their partners later what had happened, so word about Sean spread. At one pro-am, he knew that Peter Cook was due on the course at 9am. At 9.05, he tapped on his door. Peter's wife answered it.

'Hello, my dear,' purred Sean, in his smoothest Scottish burr. 'I've run out of soap. Could I ...'

'Oi, you'll have to do better than that, Connery!' came an amused shout from inside the room. Peter's round had been postponed because of fog, so he was still in bed.

Sean varied his script on one golfing holiday in Spain. We'd all rented houses next to the course, yet one morning there was no sign of Sean at our 9am tee-off time. That was because he'd nipped round to Kenny Lynch's house, knowing he'd be out. When Kipper's girlfriend opened the door, Sean asked her, 'Do you dance?'

She politely sent him packing and told Kenny all about it when he got back. That night we were all heading out for dinner. When Connery turned up, Kipper said, 'Aye-aye, here he is, Fred Astaire!' Everyone burst out laughing.

Sean raised one immaculate eyebrow: 'That'sh quite enough of that, thank you!'

Of course, besides his good looks, Sean had one huge advantage when it came to attracting women: *he was James Bond*. Which female was going to resist the chance of a tryst with 007? Sean was well aware of this super-power and he made use of it. If a girl showed the slightest interest in him, he was in like Flynn.

I was once playing a four-ball with him at Sunningdale. A woman was walking her dog next to the course and did a cartoon double-take when she saw Sean: 'Oh, my God, it's James Bond!' He was over to her in a flash: 'Good morning, my love. It's lovely to meet you. Would you care to take a stroll through that wood over there?'

Sean didn't play the next hole because, not to put too fine a point on it, he was shagging the woman against a tree. When he returned, all he said by way of explanation was, 'Sorry, I lost my ball.' The following week, the rest of us went in the wood to see if he'd carved his name on the tree.

Sean didn't restrict his carnal adventures to when he played golf. One night some years earlier, a group of us were going to a Henry Cooper fight at Wembley. We were all meeting up beforehand in one of my mate Cyril Levan's clubs in Soho. As we were having a drink, a beautiful Australian girl behind the bar spotted Sean. Her eyes were on stalks.

Sean purred into action. 'Good evening, my dear. Which part of Australia are you from?' he inquired. 'I know the country a little.'*

Sean was still chatting to her when the call came: 'Everybody to the cars, please, for the Henry Cooper fight.' We all piled into a flight of limousines. Sean wasn't in mine but I assumed he'd got into one of the other cars. But when we got to Wembley, there was still no sign of him.

Three days later, I was playing golf with Sean at Coombe Hill. 'What happened to you at the Cooper fight the other night?' I asked him.

'Oh, I spent some time with the young lady from Australia.'

'What did you do, book into a hotel?'

'No, we went to Hyde Park,' said Sean.

'*Not* against a tree again?'

'Yes.'

When Sean actually made it on to the golf course, he was a very competitive player and a very bad loser. He had a vast

---

* He bloody should have – he was married to an Australian woman! Not that it lasted too long, obviously.

array of clubs: drivers, wedges, putters, the works. That was just as well, as he often snapped them over his knee in a rage if he played a poor shot. His putters got the worst treatment.

I once played a round with him at Guadalmina in Spain. As we passed some rocks by a green, a snake reared its head and hissed at us. Connery's 007 reflexes kicked in. He wheeled around and smashed the snake on the head with his putter, then pounded it until there was no life left in it.

It was only when we got to the green that Sean realised that he'd damaged his club so badly that it now resembled a coiled, twisty metal snake itself. 'Hey, can shomebody lend me a putter?' he requested. He was livid when we all refused and made him putt out with his mangled mess of a club.

In 1980, Bob Hope brought his Desert Classic golf tournament to Britain and invited me to enter. It was smashing to see Bob again and I did so well in the competition that he was impressed and invited me to take part in the American version of the tournament at the start of the following year. There was no way I was missing that.

I flew over to California and went to the course in Palm Springs. When I walked in, I felt like I'd gone to heaven. I was among the best golfers in the world. I knew Lee Trevino and Tom Weiskopf but I was awestruck to see the greatest of them all: Jack Nicklaus. Bob Hope greeted me and said, 'Let me introduce you to your partners.'

The format was that one pro played with three non-pros. My fellow amateurs were a pair of elderly guys who owned pharmaceutical companies. They were both from Canada and they knew each other but they had flown in on separate private jets. 'And who is our pro?' I asked Bob.

'Ah, it's a kid who works in the club shop. He's a junior.'

Huh! I thought. *I've flown all the way to California to play with an assistant pro!* But I hid my disappointment from Bob. 'Come and say hello to him,' he said. He took me across the room to a guy who had his back to us. He turned around ...

... and it was Arnold Palmer.

Good God! Arnold Palmer! The US legend who had been at the apex of the golf world for something like twenty-five years! A man with talent to burn, and even greater charisma! I couldn't believe that he was standing in front of me. I was awestruck. Arnold nodded and shook my hand. 'Hi there, Jimmy,' he said. 'I hear you can play?'

'YesnoyesabitthankyouMrPalmer!' I stuttered.

He smiled. 'Let's have a coffee,' he said. We had a lovely chat then played a great round together. It was a lot of fun and not without incident. At one hole, I went into the rough. The course was out in the desert so there were a load of rocks. I climbed up into them only a find a dozen or more brand-new golf balls that hadn't been retrieved.

Great! I thought. *I'll have a few of these.* (You see, you can take the boy out of Liverpool, but you can't take Liverpool out of the boy.) I was about to pocket them when Arnold yelled to me: 'Jimmy, what the hell are you doing up there? Come down!'

'But there are a load of balls that people have left up here,' I shouted back.

'There's a reason for that,' he said. 'Those rocks are full of sidewinders.'

'Pardon? What are sidewinders?'

'Snakes, you dumb Englishman!'

Aargh! I was out of those rocks like a bat out of hell. Arnold laughed his head off at me. I was nowhere near his league as a golfer, of course, but I held my own during the round. At the end, he complimented me: 'You played very nicely, Jimmy. I enjoyed that. Shall we get a drink?'

A drink with Arnold Palmer? *You bet!* As he strolled towards the clubhouse bar, the awed onlookers before him parted like the Red Sea did for Moses. And I was floating two feet in the air behind him, once again unable to believe my luck.*

I was paired with different pros for the other three days. During one round, I was walking down a fairway when another big-name US golfer, Ben Crenshaw, called over to me. 'Hey, Jimmy!' he said. 'There's a woman says she wants to talk to you. She's sitting over by the side of the course.'

I looked over to where Ben was pointing. There did, indeed, appear to be a young lady sitting in a deckchair. She had a cigarette and a drink on the go and she looked stunning. And there was another rather interesting feature about her. She was topless. Her long hair was draped over her chest and just – *just* – preserving her modesty.

---

* I met Arnold a few more times over the years, including in a hotel during a Scottish golf tournament, where my Jack Russell, Rommel, embarrassed me by pissing on the stairs right in front of him. Arnold thought that was hilarious.

Well, what could a gentleman do but oblige this young lady? I forgot about my shot and charged over to the woman at quite a rate of knots. I got nearer … and nearer … and then realised that there was *another* unusual feature about her. She wasn't a pouting young stunner at all. She was a mannequin.

'Oh, you bastards!' I said, as everybody roared laughing at me.

One afternoon, Bob Hope wandered over and told me, 'Come and see the Shed.'

'Uh, OK,' I said, a bit flummoxed. I followed him in my hire car up a mountain and through a pair of huge gates manned by security guards. And the property before my astonished eyes could not have looked less like a shed.

Bob's home was the most astonishing house I've ever seen. It was a modernist mansion designed to look like a volcano. From its balconies, it had unbelievable views of the Coachella Valley. There was an indoor and outdoor swimming pool, a waterfall and a par-three golf hole. Bob and I shot some pool and talked about golf and comedy. *Paradise*.

Bob invited me up to the, ahem, Shed two or three times. One day, I was talking to his wife, Dolores, in their kitchen when Glen Campbell walked in. 'Hey, Rhinestone!' said Dolores. 'What? You want to hear it?' asked Glen, and sang us his big hit, 'Rhinestone Cowboy'. And I wondered, yet again, if I was dreaming.

Bob put on a cabaret for the participants in the tournament and asked me to do a short set. I told a few gags about Ronald Reagan, who'd just become the US president. I was halfway through one when Bob walked on the stage. 'Hey, *I'm* the only guy allowed to make jokes about our president!' He grinned at me.

Bob Hope was a lovely, generous man and he was absolutely charming with me every time I met him over the years. He shagged anything that moved, mind you, but it can't have done him any harm because he lived to be one hundred. And, in any case, what a way to go, eh?

That trip to America was magical. I met Andy Williams in Palm Springs and he invited me to enter his own golf tournament in San Diego two weeks later. On the way, I stopped off in Los Angeles and stayed with Tom Jones in the Beverly Hills mansion that he had just bought from Dean Martin. He introduced me to Dean in the house. Nice feller.

I won that Andy Williams pro-am, and bumped into Bing Crosby while I was there. He asked me to play in his tournament in a week's time. I accepted. *Of course.* A couple of other people gave me similar invites. I said yes to them all. I called home to break the news to Pauline that I would be in America for a few more weeks yet …

'No, Jimmy,' she told me, nicely but firmly. 'You *won't*. I think it's time you came home now, don't you?'

She was right, of course. So, I did. But I flew back to Heathrow with a couple of golfing trophies and a lifetime of happy memories. What an unbelievable trip it had been.

I was probably slightly inspired by Bob Hope and his tournament when I launched my own Jimmy Tarbuck Golf Classic in Marbella in 1982. It was quite a small event at first, but it's been running, first in Spain and then later in Portugal, for forty-three years now. Not bad, eh? It's raised a lot of cash for charity. And I'm very proud of that.

I also got invited one year to be a marshal at the Ryder Cup, between Europe and the USA, at The Belfry in Warwickshire. This was an honour. One of my duties was spotting where wayward balls landed. As I was patrolling one of the fairways, I saw a ball land in a nearby lake with a splash.

It was one of the American players. He walked down to join me with his caddy. 'Where did the ball go in?' the caddy demanded.

'It was about here,' I indicated.

'No way!' the caddy demurred. 'It was more like there.' And he pointed at a spot that was conveniently a further twenty yards down the fairway.

'No, it was definitely here,' I repeated.

'How can you be so damn sure?'

I was losing patience with this guy. 'Because I walked across the lake, looked down into the water to check, and walked back,' I told him. And the US golfer burst out laughing.

'That'll do me,' he nodded.

* * *

In my lost but happy years when I did little but play golf, I wasn't on the telly all that much except for *Winner Takes All, International Pro-Celebrity Golf* and the occasional Royal Variety Performance. But one show that I *did* continue going on, whenever they asked me, was *Parkinson*.

The usual story: in the Liverpool dressing room, hoping to get a game.

My favourite pastime and my favourite feller: at the footie with Kenny Lynch.

Out on the course with, among others, Bing Crosby and US pro Johnny Miller.

If I got a racehorse, what should I call it? Tatty Head, of course...

With my old mucker Tom Jones on his TV show, 1971.

Now THAT'S what you call a night out: with Bruce, Cilla and Frankie Vaughan in 1973.

And a smarter evening out with the missus.

Elton John, Denny Lane, Kenny Lynch, me, Bill Shankly, George Best, Bobby Moore, Joe Bugner... all human life is here.

In Liverpool red with James, in the happy days before some sod took him to see Chelsea.

Still struggling to get a game: with Bob Paisley and the 1977 European Cup-winning Liverpool squad.

Bestie, Bobby Campbell and Bobby Moore: a dream team indeed.

Alan Ball, me and Bobby Moore at my 40th birthday bash. Please tell me what we came as, because I'm buggered if I can remember.

Three men, two microphones, one racket: with Kipper Lynch and Frankie Vaughan.

I was truly honoured to be awarded an OBE in 1994.

The Saint and Tarby: with
Ian St John in Portugal.

With the beautiful Pauline, who has
been my side ever since we met.

'Oh, look! It's Liza's dad!'

What life is all about: a great
night with friends and family.

We meet again: The Queen and I after a Royal Variety Performance in Liverpool, 2007. She was a wonderful lady.

Now here are four bricks! Cliff Richard, Tommy Steele, Des O'Connor and I unveil the London Palladium Wall of Fame, 2008.

Coming home: back at the Palladium for the unforgettable Barry Manilow shows, 2024.

I'd first met Michael Parkinson via a mutual friend: a golf-club pro up in Leeds called Marshall Bellow. Michael and I got to know each other, got on well and became firm friends. I used to go on his Saturday night BBC chat show both because of that, and because I thought he was the best interviewer I'd ever seen.

I liked *Parkinson* because you could go on and just take the piss out of everything. Like hosting a game show, it suited me: it was basically just talking and bantering. I always found chatting to Michael extremely enjoyable. It was never a chore.

My first appearance had come back in 1976. I was sporting a beard at the time – what can I say? It was the seventies – and Michael jokingly remarked on it. I had an answer ready for him.

'I've only grown it because I'm appearing in a film,' I said. 'It's *The Britt Ekland Story*.'

There was a titter from the audience.

'I play an armpit,' I added. There was a bigger laugh. But I'd hadn't finished.

'It could have been worse …' I added, with a wink. The audience roared. Apparently, the BBC got complaints that I was talking about ladies' private parts on primetime TV. To which I could honestly reply, 'What? I never said a single word about them …'

My first *Parkinson* show went down well, and the same happened every time I went on.* I guess it reminded people

---

* I did a great *Parkinson* with Ringo Starr. I hadn't seen Ringo for years but he hadn't changed a bit. He was still one of the lads, just like he'd been at Butlin's.

I was still around. That chat show *made* some stars and it was really good for me, too, at a time when I wasn't working as hard as I should have been.

I went on the last edition of *Parkinson* in 1982 before Michael left to join the new TV-am breakfast show. I gave him a giant bottle of Champagne and a Biggles-type flying helmet to say he could have a rocky journey ahead (which, as it happened, was just how TV-am worked out). My fellow guests were Spike Milligan, Kenneth Williams and Billy Connolly.

I think that was the first time I met Billy. We became mates. Three years later, I went with Parky to see his *An Audience With ...* special. He was inspired. Hilarious. I've never liked comics who eff-and-blind onstage but somehow, with Billy, you don't mind the swearing. It's all part of what he does, and he does it brilliantly.

I went out with Billy for a few beers one night. He crashed out at my place. James was about fourteen at the time, and woke up with a start at 3am because someone had turned on his bedroom light. He looked over to see a tall, pissed, hairy Scotsman, in just his pants, swaying in the corner of his room, saying, 'Ah, fuck!' It was Billy, searching for a toilet.

As everyone knows, Michael Parkinson loved cricket, especially his beloved Yorkshire. He was not a golf fan. He even started something called the Anti-Golf Society because he got so bored of his mates talking about it all the time. Eventually, he gave up, figured 'If you can't beat 'em, join 'em,' and started playing. He wasn't much of a golfer.

Very early in 1982, I played a round with Michael. I murdered him, as usual, and he invited me back to his house in Bray afterwards. We were sitting in his garden having a drink. He suddenly fixed me with a stare.

'Can I tell you something?' he asked.

'Yes.'

'You're not a bad golfer. You're a very good golfer. You'd get in any county team.'

'Thanks,' I said, chuffed.

'But you're not a *great* golfer,' Parky continued. 'And you never will be. You're a great comedian. A great entertainer. *That* is what earns you a living, and what brings you fame and fortune. *Not* golf. Leave the golf. Go back to what you're best at, Jimmy.'

I listened, and I listened hard. I took heed of Michael's words because, in my heart, I knew that he was right. It was very wise advice – and it came at an extremely timely moment. Because I was about to get a tremendous offer.

CHAPTER 13

This isn't right. We haven't rehearsed this.

There's a funny thing about show business. It's so unpredictable. You work hard, you do your best, but you never really know what's going to happen next. You go in and out of favour. Series come and go. And sometimes, just sometimes, an incredible break falls into your lap from nowhere.

At the start of 1982, the *Sun* newspaper ran a story about *The Generation Game*. Bruce Forsyth had left the BBC's Saturday evening game show in 1978 and it had been hosted by Larry Grayson since then. Larry had just announced that he was also leaving the programme and the *Sun* said it knew who was going to replace him.

Me.

One of the paper's showbiz hacks, Charlie Catchpole, wrote that the Beeb bosses had hired me to take over on

The Generation Game. He claimed that I'd insisted on a huge salary to do so, and that the BBC had 'succumbed to Tarbuck's demands for money'.

Now, there was one problem with this story: it was absolute bollocks. The BBC hadn't been in touch with me about *The Generation Game*. I hadn't spoken to them, had any meetings, nor made any 'demands for money'. It was pure tabloid trash, from start to finish. Yet it worked in my favour.

London Weekend Television had now taken over the commissioning of ITV's weekend shows from ATV. My old Palladium producer, David Bell, was by now the head of light entertainment at LWT. David read the pile of tosh in the *Sun* and called Peter Prichard in a panic.

'Am I too late?' he asked him. 'I don't want to lose Jimmy.'

Now, a lesser artist manager might have said: 'Oh, there's no truth in it. It's all a load of rubbish.' But Peter Prichard *wasn't* a lesser artist manager. So, he said something far cleverer.

'Well, I'm going to the BBC this afternoon to tie it all up,' he said. 'They've offered Jimmy a fortune. But I can come and see you on the way, if you like?'

'Yes, please,' said David Bell. 'I don't care about the money. We'll beat whatever they've offered. Because I have a new show that I want Jimmy to present.'

Peter went into LWT and negotiated me the best deal of my career: a very generous, five-year rolling contract to host a new programme that was right up my street. Because LWT were about to bring back the kind of show that had recently vanished from British telly: an all-singing, all-dancing variety show, live from a top London theatre.

A show, in fact, almost exactly like *Sunday Night at the London Palladium*.

Except that it wasn't to be at the Palladium. Not initially, at least. It was to be broadcast live every Sunday night from its sister venue, Her Majesty's Theatre, on Haymarket. And as David Bell told me all about it, I realised one thing: it was the show of my dreams. Again. Just like the Palladium had been. I owe so much to Peter Prichard for getting me that gig.

We started work on prepping *Live from Her Majesty's*. First of all, though, I took time out to attend a special event. Britain had sent a task force which had successfully repelled the Argentinian invasion of the Falkland Islands in 1982, and I was invited to appear at a big concert at the London Coliseum to celebrate that victory.

It was a star-studded event in the presence of Prince Charles, who is now our king but back then was still the Prince of Wales. The climax of the evening was a rousing sing-song of 'Land of Hope and Glory' led by Dame Vera Lynn. Also on the bill was a very good pal of mine: Les Dawson.

Now, Les was a fantastic lad but he liked a bevvy and, after he'd downed a few, he didn't care what he said to anybody. This was clear after the show as the entertainers all lined up to be presented to the Prince of Wales. Charles worked his way down the line until he came to Les ... who had a very abrupt question for him.

'Is it you?' he asked. 'Have you got the money?'

'Sorry?' said Charles. 'What?'

'Are you the one who's paying us for tonight?' asked Les.

Charles looked bemused and patted his pockets. 'Um, sorry, no,' he replied.

'Huh!' snorted Les. 'Anyway, the Argies are getting their own back.'

'Pardon?'

'They're taking the keys off all the cans of corned beef.'

Charles gave a half-smile and a slight eye-roll and continued walking down the line shaking hands. But Les hadn't finished yet.

'You miserable bugger!' he called after him. 'When you're the King, how are they gonna get those ears on the postage stamps?'

Mind you, I'm sure Charles got the joke. I've met him many times over the years and he's a delightful feller. I was once invited to lunch at Highgrove House. I was admiring his gorgeous gardens and he said, 'If you ever want to bring your family to see them, please do.' So I went back with Pauline and he showed us around.

'This is nice,' I told him. '*I* could live here!'

I've seen enough of Charles to know he's a good man with a good sense of humour. And he's somebody you'd want by your side in a battle. Look how he's rolled up his sleeves, gone into bat and fought cancer, now he's the King. His mum was a hard act to follow, but he's doing it extremely well.

* * *

I was back onstage and on the telly, suited and booted, as the compere when the first *Live from Her Majesty's* show went out live on ITV on Sunday, 16 January 1983. It felt great to be back doing what I loved. We had a cracking debut show. Lulu headlined; she was a mate back then, and she still is now.

We had some fantastic female singers in that first run. Dionne Warwick was on the next week and then the terrific Gladys Knight & the Pips, Elaine Paige and Cilla. But it was a real variety show so we mixed it up: Bob Monkhouse headlined one week, and we also had fun stuff like Chas & Dave. *Gorblimey.*

The last show of that first series was at the end of February. Little and Large came on. It was nice to see that pair doing well because I'd known them since we were both on the northern club circuit in the early sixties. A smooth crooner, Jack Jones, was our headline act. But then somebody else made a surprise appearance.

I'd known Eamonn Andrews ever since I'd met Bob Hope and Bing Crosby on his chat show back in 1967. By now, Eamonn was presenting *This Is Your Life*, and whenever I ran into him, I'd joke that he'd never get me on there. 'You'll never catch me, mate,' I'd laugh. 'No chance!'

How wrong can you be?

Jack Jones had just finished his set at Her Majesty's and we were all lined up onstage for the curtain call. Suddenly, there came a few bars of unexpected, but very well-known, music: *da, da-da-DA!* And there, approaching from one side of the stage, was Eamonn, a big grin on his face, carrying that famous big red book.

I hadn't had the slightest suspicion. I'd been done up like a kipper. 'No, no – I said you'd never get me!' I blurted out. 'It's not fair!'

They put me in a car and whisked me to a studio. The audience was already in place. Pauline was waiting with the kids. And what followed was a bit of a blur, really. It was all my yesterdays, and all very emotional. A show with me at its centre but where I hadn't got a clue what was going to happen.

The researchers had done their job. They brought on some old mates from Liverpool, which blew me away. Tex Williams was there, whom I'd worked on the Christmas post with as a lad. They tracked down the Dunkeld Arms football team. The goalie, Chunky Ellis, was still chunky.

There were tons of showbiz mates – Cilla, Kenny, Henry Cooper, Max Bygraves, Dickie Henderson, Tom Jones – and a few guests who were a surprise. They brought on some actor from Liverpool who'd worked with me at Butlin's. I hardly knew the feller but I did enjoy his account of a fist-fight at the camp (I can remember a few of those!).

I was flattered that three legendary golfers took the trouble to appear: Tony Jacklin, Gary Player, and the great Henry Cotton. Tony and Gary reminisced about us all playing the Lancôme pro-am tournament in Paris, and me making a prank phone call to Tony's room pretending to be a French journalist. *Sacre bleu!* I used to love doing stuff like that.

It was great to see them all, and quite overwhelming, but, of course, the two people I'd most have liked to be in the studio were no longer around: my beloved mum and dad. But our Norma and Kenneth came along, as did Pauline's mum, Frances. Frances was my mum for the night.

The three ex-Liverpool players I'd gone to Butlin's with, Bobby Campbell, Jimmy Melia and Johnny Morrissey, laughed about shoving me onstage for my unwanted first ever comedy gig. The whole current Liverpool FC squad came on – Rush, Dalglish, the lot. And the producers saved a big surprise for the end.

On walked a sixty-one-year-old Billy Liddell. *There he was*: my first childhood hero, the man who'd turned me on to football and on to Liverpool, and who, in my opinion, is *still* the greatest player ever to pull on the red shirt. I couldn't help myself: I genuflected. It was that feeling again: *being in the presence of greatness.*

What a night it was. I felt a weird mix of moved, elated and drained at the end of it. My *This Is Your Life* must have been a good one, because the show normally ran for thirty minutes and they took the rare step of extending my episode to an hour. I must admit, in a strange way, I was quietly proud of that.

* * *

There's a peculiar thing about being in the public eye for as long as I have. People think they know you. They see you on the telly and read about you in the papers, and assume they know everything about you. Even when some of the things they have been fed as facts are totally wrong.

In the spring of 1983, Peter Prichard asked me if I'd like to co-host an event with Bob Monkhouse. I always liked working with Bob, who was a comic genius, so I said yes. A general election was coming up and the event was a Young Conservatives' campaign rally at Wembley Conference Centre. This suited Bob as he was a Tory supporter and a very politically minded person. I wasn't. In fact, I had no interest in politics whatsoever.

As a teenager, when my dad brought a newspaper home, I read it backwards. I'd start with the football news at the back, hoping there'd be something about Liverpool FC.* I'd hardly read the general news at the front and, when I grew old enough, I didn't bother voting in elections. I got a few rollockings from Dad about this.

'People have fought to earn us the right to vote, Jimmy!' he'd say. 'You have a vote. You have to use it.' Yet Dad didn't really talk politics at home and nor did any of my family. I certainly didn't. I didn't have the slightest interest.

I remember Dad asking me to give him a lift to vote in one general election. I borrowed our Norma's car and drove him down the polling station. I was about to go out so I asked him to be quick. Dad came back out looking pleased with himself and told me the name of the feller he'd voted for.

'He's a good Labour man,' Dad said.

'Eh? Are you sure?' I asked, and pointed at a poster over the road. It was the same bloke, beaming away, over the words: YOUR LIBERAL PARTY CANDIDATE. Dad had only gone and voted for the wrong candidate. Well, he went potty.

---

* Can I be honest? I still do.

'It's your bloody fault, our Jimmy!' he moaned. 'Rushing me!' I swear he wanted to go back in and ask them to let him have another go.

I was roaring laughing. 'He'll phone you up, Dad!' I said. 'You'll be the only vote he gets. Who votes bloody *Liberal* in Liverpool?'

When I was coming up as a comic, I played Labour Clubs *and* Conservative Clubs. It was all the same to me. And when I'd got famous, I'd met, and done a few events with, the famous Bessie Braddock, the most socialist-leaning Liverpool Labour MP you can imagine. She was lovely and always very nice with me.

When Margaret Thatcher came to power in 1979, I wasn't fussed either way. I didn't pay it any great notice. If you'd pushed me to give an opinion, I'd have said I thought they were all as bad as each other. So, in 1983, when I got asked to play the Wembley event with Bob Monkhouse, I thought nothing of it.

I enjoyed doing the gig because Bob was great to work with. That night, he brought along a bag full of jokes and told me to pick out any that I liked. They were all brilliant gags and I rooted through and picked all the best one-liners out. They went down well. But then … something happened.

That Conservative rally became a big news story because of all the famous faces there: the snooker player Steve Davis, Lynsey De Paul, Michael Winner. Kenny Everett came out wearing huge fake hands and said, 'Let's bomb Russia! Kick Michael Foot's stick away!' And, once I'd done it, I started getting called a dyed-in-the-wool Tory.

Kenny later said he'd only taken the gig for the money, he'd been taking the piss, and he wished he'd never done it. I certainly felt the same. Because once everyone assumed I was a Conservative supporter, I started getting grief and hostility for it. Especially whenever I went back to Liverpool.

Liverpool is a very Labour city and it suffered badly in the early Thatcher years. Maggie wasn't a good person for a Scouser to be associated with. I'd only met her once, and I wasn't in the Tory party. But I started to get viewed as some kind of class traitor.

I'd be walking through Liverpool and some feller would yell across the street at me, 'Eh, Tarby, you Tory bastard!' And I'd answer him back.

'How do *you* know?' I'd say. 'I'll tell you what: I haven't voted in the last three elections.'

'Well, that's a bloody disgrace, as well!'

'You think what you want to think,' I'd say.

It wasn't all that many people and it wasn't all that often. I still had a lot more pals in Liverpool than I had enemies. If I was with friends, they wouldn't let anyone give me a hard time. But receiving negative, smartarse comments gave a new, unwelcome edge to visiting my home city.

It got worse after I was photographed with Mrs Thatcher again. I used to be captain of the Variety Club Golfing Society, and we played charity games and raised the money to buy a minibus for disabled kids. We got invited to 10 Downing Street for a photocall to hand the keys of the bus over.

That wasn't the first time I went to Number 10. I'd been to an event before when Harold Wilson – a Labour PM – was in charge. I found it fascinating. Alongside the photos of all the former PMs was a painting of Lord Nelson and the Duke of Wellington together. It appealed to the little boy in me who'd liked history at school.

At the minibus event, there were a load of kids there and they gave them all big cream cakes. I was standing talking at the reception when one lad, who looked about twelve, came up behind me. 'Jimmy Tarbuck?' he asked. I turned around. 'Yes?' And he hit me smack in the face with a cream cake. *Bosh!*

The little bugger! It looked like a cartoon. I was stood there, with my mouth hanging open, scraping the cream out of my eyes. And when I did, the first thing I saw was Mrs Thatcher standing bang in front of me, smiling.

'Excuse me, Prime Minister,' I apologised, as a blob of cream fell off my nose onto her nice carpet.

'Oh, not at all,' she replied, in her famous immaculate tones. 'It suits you. But you may wish to use a bathroom. Somebody will show you where they are.'

What was Maggie Thatcher like? If I'm honest, she was very nice to me. Just the same as Harold Wilson was. Just the same as Bessie Braddock. Well, that's what politicians do, isn't it? They're nice to people. And I appreciated that. But that didn't mean that I'd vote for them.

Of course, the pictures of that Number 10 bash made their way into the papers, and there I was: stood smiling next to Maggie again. The photos firmed up the negative opinions of people who already had it in for me. And it made going home to the 'pool even trickier.

If I'm honest, I stopped going to Liverpool for a while. I'd invite our Kenneth, our Norma and other family members down to Coombe instead. I hated having to do that, and being made to feel like a traitor in the city I'd grown up in and I loved. But it was just the easiest option, for a bit.

It felt unfair to be wrongly labelled a 'Tory bastard' ... but I was a big boy. I could handle it. It upset me more if it got to my family. Our Liza had just been accepted to study at the very prestigious RADA, the Royal Academy of Dramatic Art.* It was a fantastic achievement on her part, and I couldn't have been more chuffed for her.

Liza never said much about it to me, but I know that a few of her fellow students at RADA made a point of telling her they didn't like her dad, or what they imagined my politics were. To Liza's credit, she didn't let them beat her down. She stood her ground and she defended me. And good for her.

'Jimmy Tarbuck is a big Conservative Party supporter.' It's not true but it stuck to me. Even my Wikipedia page apparently says that. *Well, what can I do?* It's just one of those things. It was a long time ago and I'm glad to say it's finished now. When I go back to Liverpool, I don't get abuse any more.

---

* Liza thought of applying under a different surname, so if she got in, nobody could say it was nepotism. She didn't, in the end. But I'll say this: I've never opened a single door for Liza. Everything that lass has achieved is through her own talent and drive.

People are friendly again when they see me now: 'Alright, Tarby?' And I'm friendly back. I think they know that I'm a Scouser through and through, and they can see that my love for Liverpool FC has never dimmed. In fact, if anybody in Liverpool gives me grief now, I'll guarantee you one thing about them:

They're an Evertonian.

* * *

The second series of *Live from Her Majesty's* began in the spring of 1984. We were getting good Sunday night ITV viewing figures and attracting big stars from both sides of the Atlantic. Neil Sedaka flew over to appear, as did Engelbert Humperdinck, who used to be close mates with Tom Jones until they had a big falling-out. God knows why.

The producers tried to mix up established stars and new talent and they did a good job. So we'd have big names like Danny La Rue, or legendary bluesman B.B. King, appearing with new faces such as Shakin' Stevens. That's always been the secret of a great variety show: make sure there's something for everyone.

But, sadly, that particular series of *Live from Her Majesty's* will always be remembered for only one thing: the tragic events of the night of Sunday, 15 April 1984.

We had a good bill that evening. My mate Les Dennis was on with his comedy partner in those days, Dustin Gee. We had the deep-voiced American actor and singer Howard Keel. The headliner was Donny Osmond, who just a few years

earlier had been one of the biggest teen-heartthrob pop singers in the world.

And Tommy Cooper was on. I never tired of watching
Tommy. There was nobody like him. As I've said, he could
make you laugh without saying a word. You only had to look
at him and his big soppy grin under that ridiculous fez and
you'd be off. He'd shake his shoulders and, hardly moving his
lips, say, 'Juz like that!' and you'd be roaring.

Everybody in the game loved Tommy. He was what
you'd call a comic's comic: we all went to see him as often as
we could. If you were lucky enough to be on the same bill,
you never missed him. I reckon if you'd asked a hundred comedians to name their favourite comedian, they'd have virtually
all said: 'Tommy Cooper'.

That night, Tommy arrived with his son, Thomas. He
didn't look too well. He was pale and a bit frail. The producers rigged him up a temporary dressing room at the back of
the stage, behind a curtain, so he wouldn't have to go up the
stairs to the regular ones. Her Majesty's has a deep stage so it
was easy to do.

Yet once Tommy started doing his act, he looked fine.
He was as charismatic and larger-than-life as ever. He came
bouncing on with a model of a giant packet of Tunes cough
sweets on top of his bonce. 'I've had this tune running around
my head all day ...' he began. Everyone fell about.

Tommy took it off, stuck his trusty fez on and did a few
more gags. I was laughing in the wings. Then he switched
to magic. He produced a toy dove from a hanky, claiming

it was real, and placed it in a box. 'It will disappear from the box before your very eyes!' he claimed. The box exploded. Tommy looked hurt. 'Who did that?' he asked the audience.

Tommy's female assistant appeared from the side of the stage with a long, shiny, orange Ali Baba-style cloak and helped him slip into it. That was my cue to move from my vantage point in the wings and hide immediately behind him on the other side of the stage curtains. Because I was heavily involved in the next bit of the act.

We'd rehearsed a sketch where I passed items to Tommy through his legs under the curtain. He then produced them with a flourish as if they'd been inside his robe all the time. We had loads of props: a paint pot, a plant, whatever. The punchline was that I'd then walk out with a stepladder, moaning that it was too big to fit through his legs.

As I waited, I heard Tommy tell his assistant, 'Thank you, love!' in his inimitable gruff rasp as she fastened him into the robe. I prepared to pass him the first prop. But I never got the chance.

Tommy slumped to the stage. He didn't fall, as such: it was like he'd suddenly sat down. He sank onto his bottom and was just sitting upright in front of the curtain, not saying anything. He was a brilliant physical comedian, of course, so the audience thought it was part of the act. They were roaring.

David Bell, who was producing the show, was standing next to me behind the curtain. 'Oh, Tommy's put a new bit in,' he said.

'No, this isn't right,' I said. 'We haven't rehearsed this.'

'But you know Tommy,' David answered. 'He's always doing stuff like this.'

'Not this time,' I said. 'Look at him! He's not moving.'

We could see the curve of Tommy's back against the curtain. He was breathing heavily. He made a weird noise, almost like a snore, and toppled backwards. Now he was lying on his back on the stage. The audience were still laughing. *I wasn't.*

'Get the adverts on!' I told David.

'I can't! They're not due for six minutes.'

'Get the adverts on. *Now!*'

David quickly spoke to the director. The live TV broadcast abruptly cut to an ad break. No one was expecting it, so there were blank screens up and down the country for a few seconds as regional directors scrambled to get the adverts rolling.

Everybody came to help. Peter Prichard, my manager, was there, and we all managed to ease Tommy behind the stage curtain. By now, he was unconscious and motionless. The St John's Ambulance men ran over with a low trolley. Tommy was such a big guy that four or five men were struggling to lift him onto it.

Tommy's son, Thomas, appeared. 'Dad! Dad!' he said. He was standing next to me. 'Is he going to be OK?' he asked.

'He'll be alright, son,' I said. I looked down at Tommy. He didn't *look* alright. It was a horrible, horrible moment. But also I knew that I was in the middle of presenting a live TV show to millions of people who had no idea what was happening.

And the show must go on.

The double act, Les Dennis and Dustin Gee, were due on next. I collared them. 'Boys, can you do your bit in front of the curtain?' I asked.

Good old Les agreed straight away. 'Yes, of course, Jimmy,' he nodded. His mate wasn't so sure.

'No, I don't think I can …' Dustin began.

'Well, if you won't do it, *I'll* go on with Les instead!' I snapped at him. That threw him. They went on as soon as we came back from the ads. They did OK, but Les later told me that as they ran through their act, he could hear the medics pounding on Tommy's chest behind the curtain, trying to revive him.

I went to the wings to speak to Howard Keel, who was on next. 'Will you be able to sing in that little space?' I asked him, pointing in front of the curtain. Howard was a true pro. His reply has always stayed with me.

'Jimmy, I'll sing in the fucking aisle if it helps Tommy,' he told me.

Donny Osmond came over, all concerned, and asked if Tommy was OK. I knew we'd have to clear the stage before Donny came on because he had dancing girls doing a big spectacular number. The St John's Ambulance men got Tommy onto the trolley and raced him to an ambulance.

Nobody really knew what was happening. I didn't know, although I feared the worst. The audience were totally in the dark. But they knew something was seriously wrong at the end of the show. Because we all lined up at the front of the stage for the curtain call and Tommy wasn't there.

The ambulance had set off for the nearby Westminster Hospital with blue lights flashing and its sirens wailing. It was all in vain. Tommy had suffered a massive heart attack. He was pronounced dead on arrival at the hospital. He was only sixty-three.

LWT used to follow *Live from Her Majesty's* with the *ITN News*. ITN had heard what had happened and raced a news crew down to the theatre. Tommy's collapse was the lead story, and their reporter collared me as soon as we got off air. I went straight from hosting a variety show to talking live on the news about the loss of a dear friend.

I can't remember a word I said to them. I was in shock. We all were. How do you begin to make sense of something like that?

A week or so later, I went to Tommy's funeral at Mortlake Crematorium. The great and the good of the showbiz world were all there. Well, of course they were: everybody loved Tommy. There was sadness and laughter. We had readings and eulogies, and the feller who'd had a pop at me at the Water Rats, Charlie Chester, decided to stand by the coffin and recite a little poem he'd written:

> *Here lies a funny man,*
> *He wore a funny hat,*
> *And he wore it … just like that.*

Dear me. Bruce Forsyth was standing next to me. Bruce whispered: 'Jimmy, promise me something. If I go before you, don't let that man anywhere near my funeral.'

'I won't!' I whispered back. 'Please do the same for me.'

I will never forget that terrible, terrible night at Her Majesty's. Tommy Cooper wasn't just a tremendous comedian. He was a tremendous man. A big man in every way. We haven't seen his like again. And, you know what? We never will. R.I.P.

CHAPTER 14

You nearly took my bloody head off!

It took a long time to get over the shock of Tommy Cooper dying onstage. It's not the kind of thing you forget and move on from quickly. It played on my mind for quite a while and, after I'd finished recording the latest series of *Winner Takes All*, Pauline and I did what we often did and went to recharge our batteries in the sunshine.

It had been all change for us in Marbella. We had sold the little holiday home we had bought back in the seventies and got a bigger place. The problem was that it wasn't in the best part of town and kept getting burgled. So we sold that and had another house built up in the hills, overlooking the resort.

I'd also moved my Jimmy Tarbuck Golf Classic from Spain to a beautiful course I had played at in neighbouring Portugal. Partly because of that, Pauline and I spent a lot of time in Portugal and had a few holidays there. It was still cheap in those days, so we got ourselves a nice holiday home there as well.

Back in England, I became slowly aware that – much in the way I'd got grief from people wrongly assuming I was a Conservative supporter – I was getting criticised by some folk who'd decided they didn't like what I did. This time, though, it wasn't abuse from a few random blokes in the street. It was fellow performers.

The mid-eighties saw the rise in Britain of what was loosely called 'alternative comedy'.* Personally, I'm not sure that a lot of them *were* comedians. They were a bunch of upper-class toffs who came out of university and decided that they knew more about comedy, and what was funny, than people who'd been in the game for thirty years or more.

As far as I recall, it was guys like Ben Elton, Rik Mayall and Adrian Edmondson. They fancied themselves as the new cutting-edge of comedy and they were suddenly getting TV shows left, right and centre. And during those shows, they'd occasionally take pops and have digs at established stars such as Bruce, Kenny Lynch … and me.

They were trying to make a name for themselves. I understood that. I'd done it myself. When I'd broken through in the sixties, I'd been the shock of the new as well. I'd been a young, thrusting comic, the 'fifth Beatle', surrounded by comedians much older than myself. But I'd behaved in a very different way from these know-it-alls.

Unlike this new wave, I hadn't taken pot shots at the generation of comics who'd come before me. I hadn't started

---

* Maybe it should have been called an alternative *to* comedy.

sneering at Max Miller or Arthur Askey, or taking the piss out of Max Wall or Ken Dodd. And I'll tell you why. I didn't look down on those fellers. I admired them and respected them, and I wanted to watch them and learn from them.

The newcomers having a go at me didn't bother me too much. I never even met most of them. One double act came on one of my live Sunday-night theatre shows. I walked into the make-up room and they both jumped up and said, 'Hello, Mr Tarbuck!' I knew they'd had a dig at me on a telly show, and it had upset our Liza, so I ignored them.

Ben Elton had a few pops at me now and again, then years later he interviewed me on a TV show about different kinds of comedy. I answered everything he asked me and he was perfectly civil face to face. That was normally the way it worked. And, in any case, some of that new breed of comics were great when I met them.

I got on great with Mel Smith, and Dawn French was polite and charming. I thought she was brilliant. Pauline and I went to see her show. She came onstage in a tracksuit and said, 'I feel just like Harry Secombe.' That proper tickled me. And she was fantastic in *The Vicar of Dibley*. I have to say, I liked her a lot more than I did her ex-husband.*

Ultimately, being slagged off by those comics didn't do me any real harm. Alternative comedy was a bit of a fad and it didn't last very long. It certainly hasn't prevented me from

---

* Let's just say that I can't believe that Lenny Henry has got a knighthood when proper comedy giants such as Ronnie Corbett, Ronnie Barker and Eric Morecambe never did.

having a sixty-five-year career ... unlike most of those fellers criticising me, who aren't even around any more. That's what it boils down to, really: *Where are they now?*

And I always had my music career to fall back on, ho ho! I'd kept on releasing the odd record, just for fun, really. I'd even co-recorded an album with Kenny Lynch, *Having a Party.* We certainly had one while we were making it – it was a right laugh! – but it had stayed glued to record shops' shelves. As usual.

Then, in 1985, I put out a new single, 'Again'. It was a lovely song and I even contributed to the lyric. 'I want to see you again,' it went, 'to reach out and touch you'. It was a cracking tune and, for once, I wasn't the only person who thought so. Because – are you ready for this? – it got into the charts.

OK, it was only the Top 75, and it never got any higher than number 68, but even so, it was in the pop charts! I was a pop star! *Sort of.* People who heard it really liked it. It was an emotional song about missing someone and it started to get played at funerals. Which led to a bizarre thing happening.

A few fans wrote me letters saying that they'd recently lost loved ones, and asking me to go along and sing the song at their burial services. I did, a couple of times, but it felt very weird. I found it rather embarrassing: I didn't know the deceased, or anybody else at the funerals. I felt like an interloper. So, I didn't do any more.

The next series of *Live from Her Majesty's* rolled around. I was still loving doing it. A variety show is only as good as its guests and the producers were pulling in some crackers. I can remember we had some classy chanteuses on that series. Dusty Springfield was a living legend by now, and it was always a joy to work with Cilla.

I hadn't met Gloria Gaynor before but she was very friendly when she came on. She did her famous signature tune: 'I Will Survive'. Fantastic song! I already knew a lot of those disco hits, and liked them, because that was the stuff that I used to hear on my nights in Tramp.

Mind you, I was cutting down on those by now. Which made Pauline a lot happier …

* * *

Looking back, the mid-eighties was a very happy time for me. Everything was going well. My career was just where I wanted it to be: I was enjoying hosting variety shows on the telly again. Golf wasn't dominating my life any more but I still had enough time to play plenty of rounds and run my Classic in Portugal.

Everything was great with the family. Cheryl had gone off after school and studied at the Chelsea School of Art. I remember the day she came home all excited and told us she'd got a 2:1. 'Who scored?' I asked her. She had started working as an illustrator for books, magazines and on packaging.

Liza was just graduating from RADA, was living up in north London and had already started going to auditions. She was about to get her first big break: a lead role in *Watching*, an ITV sitcom set on Merseyside. Liza was to star as Pamela in that show for the next seven years.

James had just left school rather abruptly and was casting around for what to do next. My lad tried out drama school and art college and had put on his first club night by the time he was eighteen! He had loads of energy and ideas: I suppose a bit like me, at that age. I never worried about James. I always knew he'd do OK.

I also had time to indulge my other great passion in life: cars. I've always been mad for them and I've had so many in my time. For a while, I had a Volvo P1800, which used to get called 'The Saint's Car'. Why? Because it was what Roger Moore used to drive when he played Simon Templar in the TV crime show, *The Saint*.

Please indulge me while I remember the others. I had a maroon Aston Martin, and a white Jaguar E-type which, believe it or not, I won at Coombe Hill Golf Club. I even went out and bought a personalised numberplate: COM 1C. Which I guess is the kind of thing you do when you're young and foolish.

But my favourite car, *ever*, was my Rolls-Royce. I bought it second-hand from Tom Jones when he got a new one. I was so chuffed with it that I drove it all the way to Liverpool to show it off. We went around Pauline's mum's house. 'Do you want to see my new car?' I asked her, proudly. She came outside to have a look.

'Oh, it's lovely, Jimmy,' she said. 'What is it? A Rover?'

In 1986, I went on my favourite ever episode of *International Pro-Celebrity Golf*. The god that was Arnold Palmer and I only went and beat Gary Player and Sean

Connery 5 and 4.* James Bond was not happy! The game was over in no time. 'You've buggered up the show!' said the producer. They filled in the rest of the time with the two golf superstars doing exhibition shots. It was superb to watch. Gary was a genius in the bunker.

That same year, it was all change for the live Sunday night variety show. Andrew Lloyd Webber's *The Phantom of the Opera* had taken over at Her Majesty's, so we decamped down the road to the Piccadilly Theatre. It has a beautiful old Art Deco auditorium so this was no hardship.

One of the first guests on *Live at the Piccadilly* was Lena Zavaroni. She had a lovely voice but she seemed a sad little mite. Lena had been a child star and, like a lot of them, she had found it hard to cope. She suffered from depression and anorexia for most of her life and was to die in her mid-thirties. Poor lass.

I loved having Frank Carson, the Northern Irish comic, on the show. Frank was a mate, a good lad, and just a brilliant comedian. If ever we had a slot to fill on the theatre show, I'd tell Alec Fyne or David Bell: 'Just get Frank on.'

'But he was on six weeks ago,' they'd say.

'I don't care if he was on six minutes ago,' I'd reply. 'People will still laugh.' And they did: he could tell the same bloody jokes he'd told the previous time and the audience would *still* be falling about. Frank was right: it *was* the way he told 'em.

---

* If you're not a golf fan, that means we were playing nine holes and Arnold and I won every one of the first five. A whitewash!

We didn't half have some brilliant female singers on, yet again, as well. Shirley Bassey had a great pair of lungs, as ever, not to mention that sense of humour. And what an amazing voice Patti LaBelle has got! There was a performer you didn't forget in a hurry.

I'd left *Winner Takes All* by now, and Yorkshire TV gave me a new game show to replace it: *Tarby's Frame Game*. It was a game where the contestants were given two words and had to find a 'middle' word that connected them. If I said 'water' and 'outing', the answer would be 'works': 'waterworks' and 'works outing'. Do you see?

It was a nice idea but *Tarby's Frame Game* never really took off. It's hard to say why but it just hadn't got the appeal, the magic, of *Winner Takes All*. Well, that's telly for you: some shows work and some shows don't. We did three series and then it was dropped.

Far more exciting, for me, was the fact that LWT's Sunday night theatre show was moving again. In 1987, it transferred from the Piccadilly to the motherlode, the place where it had all started for me, almost a quarter of a century earlier: the London Palladium.

And I'll tell you this, there's only one way to describe how it felt when I started hosting *Live from the Palladium*: it felt like coming home.

When they'd brought *Sunday Night at the London Palladium* back four years earlier, it hadn't worked. They hadn't spent enough money on the show and it had looked like a cheap imitation. LWT didn't make the same mistake this time. They made sure it was as lavish, as extravagant and as glamorous as ever. And well done them.

We did the first couple of shows in the spring of 1987. Tom Jones did a brilliant headline appearance to kick the series off and the following week we had Kim Wilde. Kim was nice, but it was impossible not to reflect that my very first compering job, nearly thirty years earlier, had been introducing her old feller, Marty, on Larry Parnes's rock and roll tour.

Ah, well. That's one of the secrets, and the golden rules, of show-business success. *You stick around.*

* * *

You can say what you like about me – and, believe me, people have! – but one thing no one can deny is that I'm consistent. I've always had the same interests through my life and up there with golf as my great sporting love is football. As long as I was able, I was always dead keen to get a game. *Always.*

By 1987, I was in my late forties and knocking on a bit but that didn't stop me saying yes when I got a great offer. I was asked to pick, manage and play for a celebrity team in a seven-a-side charity match at Wembley before the FA Cup final between Spurs and Coventry City. The opposing player-manager? David Frost.

I liked David. He was a good man and, I thought, a very honest and fair feller. He mixed with kings and queens, with presidents and prime ministers, and was at home with all of them. Whenever he interviewed politicians, he never spared them, whichever party they might belong to.

David was also very good at introducing new talent on his various telly shows. Not many people know (as Michael Caine would say) that David got the Two Ronnies together. It was him that invited Ronnie Corbett and Ronnie Barker to appear, with John Cleese, in the famous sketch about class on *The Frost Report*. It got them known.

The Wembley game was to be Tarby's Sky Blues vs Tottenham Frostspur. I didn't feel like I was betraying Liverpool FC because it was nice to be supporting Coventry temporarily. It brought back happy memories of doing all those shows in Coventry, in my early years, with Frankie Vaughan and Anita Harris.

I put a decent team together. Or so I thought. Bobby Moore wasn't a bad start, and I had Steve Davis, Steve Cram the athlete, Lloyd Honeyghan the boxer, Nick Owen the newsreader and Michael Le Vell from *Coronation Street*. It turned out a couple of them couldn't play for toffee. But who cared? It was only a bit of fun.

That doesn't mean it wasn't competitive. It got quite tasty out there. Frosty's team won 2–1. Why? Daley Thompson was playing for them! Daley had been winning Olympic gold medals just three years earlier. He was as fit as a butcher's dog and scored both of their goals. One was a volley Kevin Keegan would have been proud of.

I must admit, I *wasn't* as fit as a butcher's dog. I was carrying a bit of weight (in fact, I was heavier in those days than I am today) and Jimmy Greaves, who was doing the TV commentary, noticed that I was blowing a bit. 'Ah, there's

Tarbuck!' he laughed. 'Live at the Palladium, knackered at Wembley ...'

In the autumn, we picked up *Live from the Palladium* with a classic mix of the old and the new: David Essex, my old muckers Cannon and Ball, and the Pet Shop Boys. The following week, we had The Shadows. It was great to see Hank and Bruce again and reminisce about life on the road (and pushing Joe Lee's coach down it).

The Shads were on with Victor Borge. Victor was wonderful. He was an elderly Danish musician and comic with a brilliant deadpan style. He was famous for his 'phonetic punctuation'. He'd read something out, making weird noises with his mouth for each full stop, comma or exclamation mark. It sounds daft but it was hilarious.

Victor was nearly eighty but he was still a brilliant classical pianist. He walked out at the Palladium, took the crowd's applause, and sat at his grand piano. 'I have two pianos,' he announced, lugubriously. Everyone looked baffled. 'The other one's at home,' he added. It was all in the timing. Everybody roared.

That was Victor's impish sense of humour. At the end of the show, as we all stood on the revolving stage, he took my handkerchief from my top jacket pocket and said, 'That was fun, young sir.' He had a hanky sticking out of his own pocket, so I took that one.

'Here's your handkerchief back,' he said, as we walked backstage.

'I don't want it,' I replied. 'Can I keep yours, instead?'

'You really want it?' He smiled.

'Yes, please, Mr Borge, I do.' I nodded. Because I wanted a souvenir of Victor Borge. He was lovely and very funny.

The following week we had two A-list male singers on. Joe Cocker was superb. He was a proper blues singer, a real man's man, and a no-nonsense northerner to chat to. I was so impressed with Joe that I went to see him at the Albert Hall soon afterwards. What a performer. There was no messing with Joe.

Barry White was a different kettle of fish. He made amazing records that everyone loved … especially women. Your wife, your daughter and your gran all loved Barry. But for a sex symbol, he was an enormous feller. Unbelievable voice but, hand on heart, I've never seen anyone sweat so much.

That series was a real mix-and-match of talent. One week we had the Welsh comic Max Boyce – *I was there!* – that fantastic singer Elkie Brooks, and David Copperfield, the American magician. Copperfield was a very good-looking, clever feller, and did amazing tricks, but my God, did he love himself. He had feathers up his arse.

He came back on for an encore, impossibly handsome and immaculately dressed, and I said, 'Bloody hell, he looks just like Tommy Cooper!' Well, the Palladium roared.

David Copperfield looked perplexed. 'Hey, Jim, I didn't get that?' he said.

'It was just a silly throwaway remark,' I told him.

'Oh. OK.'

For the last show in the series, one of my heroes from my first Palladium stint, Roy Orbison, came back and was on alongside Tammy Wynette. Tammy was sweet to talk to but I sensed a sadness about her, if you know what I mean. There was a real loneliness in her singing. Maybe that was what made her so good.

* * *

As my five-year contract with them was coming to an end, LWT were keeping me busy. In addition to *Live from the Palladium*, in the spring of 1988 they gave me a new late-night show to present. It went out on Saturday nights and it was called *After Ten with Tarbuck*.

The format of the programme was part variety show, part talk show. I enjoyed doing the chat-show host bit; I didn't find it hard at all. I turned to my contacts book to get a few of my best pals on. Tom Jones made sure the first episode was a ratings winner, and Bruce and Shirley Bassey both made appearances.

I interviewed a lot of sportspeople. It's funny: in my life, I've met some of the very biggest names in show business, but when I get overawed, it's nearly always around sportsmen. Billy Liddell overawed me. So did Bobby Moore. I think it's because I knew they could do great things that I would never be able to.

I was thrilled to chat to Barry McGuigan, the world featherweight boxing champion, and Ian Botham, a true cricket legend. Saint and Greavsie – Ian St John and Jimmy Greaves – had been footballing heroes, at Liverpool and Spurs, but now they were more like a comic double act. It worked because they were funny guys and genuinely close friends.

And I was about to have another of my own occasional close encounters with football. In the spring of 1988, David Frost called me up again.

'Jimmy, it's the FA Cup final again in three weeks—' he began.

'I know it is!' I interrupted him. I was looking forward to it because Liverpool were in the final. They had already won the league and were going for the double. They were to play London's new footballing upstarts, Wimbledon.

'Well, we've been asked if we can do another match before the final,' David continued. 'If we do, it will raise £100,000 for children's charities. Can you do it?'

'Of course!' I said. I put the phone down, picked it up again straight away, and phoned Bobby Moore. I explained the situation. 'Count me in,' said Mooro. *Yes!*

Bobby told me later that five minutes after I'd rung him, Frosty had called. 'Can you play for my team on Cup Final day ...' he began.

'You're too late, David,' said Bobby. 'Jimmy has already asked me.'

'Oh,' said David Frost. 'Fuck it.'

Come the big day, there were 100,000 fans crammed into Wembley. There was quite an array of stars playing in our curtain-raiser: Rod Stewart, Eddy Grant, Jasper Carrott, plus ex-players such as Arsenal's Terry Neill. I gave my team a pep talk in the dressing room and we headed to the tunnel.

It was time to walk out onto the pitch. 'Lead us out, Bobby,' I said.

Bobby Moore shook his head. 'You're the skipper, Jimbo,' he said. '*You* do it.'

'I can't do that!' I protested. 'You're the World Cup-winning captain. It has to be you!' But Bobby was adamant that I had to lead the way.

The referee gave me and Frosty the nod and we walked out of the tunnel ahead of our teams. The sight that greeted us was breathtaking. Wimbledon didn't have that many fans so Wembley was a sea of Liverpool red: flags, scarves, banners. The noise was colossal. It was all too much to take in.

'Bobby, this is amazing,' I said, over my shoulder. 'Incredible. I know you've done this a hundred times before, and you're used to it, but I can't believe what I'm seeing. Wow! This is one of the best days of my life ...'

Bobby wasn't saying anything back.

I'd reached the centre circle by now. I stopped, turned around to my team, and saw ... nobody. Bobby Moore had kept the rest of the team back in the tunnel. I could see them, creased up with laughter. I'd walked out talking to myself. I must have looked like Simple Simon. *Bastards!*

But I had to admit: it was a good stitch-up.

Once the match started, the tackles were flying in. I was determined to win because, well, *we were Liverpool.* Towards the end of the game, we got awarded a penalty. Chris Quinten, who played Brian Tilsley in *Coronation Street*, picked up the ball.

'I'm taking this,' he announced.

'Are you 'eck as like!' I told him, and took the ball off him. I exerted captain's privilege. *The chance to take a penalty*

in front of tens of thousands of Liverpool fans, at Wembley, on
FA Cup final day? This is Tarby's, thank you very much!

David Frost was in goal for his team. Frosty wasn't a bad
goalie. He was brave and he didn't mind throwing himself
around and getting in where it hurt. But I had a plan.

I'd once been lucky enough to talk to my hero, Billy
Liddell, about taking penalties. Billy had said, 'Just make sure
you hit the target – and hit it hard.' So that was exactly what
I did. The ball flew past a startled David Frost's left shoulder
and into the top of the net like a rocket.

'Christ, Jimbo, you nearly took my bloody head off!'
Frosty told me later, back in the dressing room. 'And now
you're beaming all over your face. You enjoyed that, didn't
you?' And I certainly had. What a glorious experience.

The final itself didn't go quite so well. Wimbledon won
1–0 and our centre-forward, John Aldridge, missed a penalty.
Aldridge had scored eleven penalties that season already, and
never missed them. And I knew why he'd missed that one: the
Wimbledon goalie, Dave Beasant, had moved before he took
it. But the referee allowed the save.

Years and years later, I was playing golf with Dave Beasant
at a Variety Club charity event (Dave later became the club
captain) and I collared him as we walked down a fairway.

'Oi! You moved early when you saved that cup-final
penalty,' I told him.

'No, I didn't,' he replied.

'Yes, you did!'

And Dave Beasant grinned at me. 'Yeah, I did, actually.'

* * *

Autumn 1988 came around and it was time for what turned out to be the final series of *Live from the Palladium*. And, if you're going to go out, go out at the top. The producers pulled their fingers out and got us some fantastic bookings, from both the showbiz old guard and the bright new talents.

Dionne Warwick came on, as did Ronnie Corbett, Tom Jones and Cliff Richard. In the days when *EastEnders* was all about Den and Angie, Anita Dobson was huge news. We got Robert Palmer, Erasure, and two of the top pop stars of the day in Rick Astley and a fresh-faced, demure little Aussie lass named Kylie Minogue.

We had a young Steve Coogan. Way before he invented Alan Partridge, he was just a nervy impressionist doing David Coleman and Bob Geldof. The late, lovely Marti Caine did a turn, and Five Star got the kids screaming. Not as much as Bros, though. My ears are still ringing.

For the last show, we got a true international superstar. Barry Manilow was a force of nature and a terrific performer. We had a bit of banter and I got Barry to try telling a gag. When he did, the Palladium roared. He looked delighted. We got on really well but, as we said goodbye after the show, I didn't imagine I was likely ever to see him again.

I was wrong.

CHAPTER 15

On a cold day,
a tea leaf

It was a new decade and, looking back, I was probably heading into a new phase of my life. In February 1990 I turned fifty, which I suppose meant I was moving – reluctantly! – into middle age. And, just to emphasise the point, Cheryl married her partner, Oscar, and they had a gorgeous little lad called Louis. Just like that, I was a grandad.

I had time to enjoy the experience because, work-wise, I was ticking over at a slightly quieter level than I was used to. My LWT contract had expired so I wasn't regularly hosting a variety show or a game show. This was fine with me. I've never had a problem filling my downtime when I have family, golf and football to occupy me.

I was still appearing at Royal Variety Shows. In 1992, I did one at the Dominion Theatre in front of Prince Charles and Princess Diana. It had the Chinese State Circus and the cast of *Cats* (no, not together!) so it was pretty spectacular. And a month later, I did my first pantomime in a few years.

I put a knotted handkerchief on a stick over my shoulder and headed to Bromley to play the (very inappropriately named!) Idle Jim in *Dick Whittington*. My main co-star was the successful actor George Sewell, who was best known for playing a hard-bitten detective in an ITV cop series, *Special Branch*.

George and I got on well and I was soon to spend more time with him. In 1993, he was in the cast of a BBC comedy drama series, *The Detectives*, which was basically a spoof of police shows like *Special Branch* and *The Sweeney*. It starred Jasper Carrott and Robert Powell as two hapless cops who got everything wrong but still solved their cases.

I appeared in an episode as a gangster who loved playing golf (nobody say type-casting, OK?). I enjoyed it because we made it at St George's Hill golf course, not too far from me in Surrey. They closed the course off to the public while we were filming, so I managed to get a couple of rounds in.

I liked doing a straight acting role, even if it was in a comedy. I think I held my own and did OK. In fact, I enjoyed it so much that I even introduced a little improvisation.

I had a scene with Jasper and Robert where I had to slap Jasper in the face. I did it and then, just for good measure, I gave Robert a smack around the chops, as well: 'And one for you!' Robert looked a bit miffed, because it wasn't in the script, but Jasper thought it was hilarious. He liked it so much that he kept it in.

If you remember, I was talking earlier about how up-and-down it can be when you're in the public eye. You might be having a relatively quiet time, and then – *BAM!* Something happens to put you right back in the spotlight. That happened to me in 1994 when I was awarded an OBE in the New Year's honours list.

I certainly hadn't expected it. It came totally out of the blue. I was elated, thrilled, but at the same time, a little voice inside me was asking: *Why me?* It felt such a huge thing for a tatty 'ead from Liverpool. I was touched to be given such a tremendous honour.*

The OBE ceremony was held at Buckingham Palace. I was told that I could only take two guests but I managed to sneak Pauline, Cheryl and Liza in. The Queen was otherwise engaged on the day, so I was presented with my medal by Prince Charles.

'I'm terribly sorry that my mother can't be here,' he told me.

'Sir, I'm honoured to be here with you,' I replied. And so I was.

My OBE was a massive deal for me, and so was what happened next. Which was that I got honoured in a similar way, but this time by the show-business world. LWT got in touch and told me they wanted to give me a special one-off show: *An Audience with Jimmy Tarbuck*.

---

* I felt the same in 2000 when I was granted the Freedom of the City of London. I haven't herded any sheep over Tower Bridge yet, but I'm not ruling it out.

Wow! This was very prestigious. They only give those kind of shows to people who have survived at the top of show business for a very long time. At the same time, if it doesn't sound big-headed, I didn't feel undeserving of it. Because that was exactly what I had done.

I felt delighted and very proud to be given my own *An Audience With* ... show. And then, as the big day neared, I felt another emotion entirely. I felt bloody nervous.

Why? Well, I was used to getting up onstage or hosting a television show. After all, I'd been doing it for more than thirty years. But this was something else. This was getting up on a stage, and hosting a television show, in front of an audience composed entirely of the great and good of the entertainment world. In front of my peers.

I invited my closest showbiz mates, of course, such as Bruce and Kenny and Ronnie, but I said that, otherwise, I didn't want to know who was going to be there. It would just have made me even more nervous. On the night, I stayed in my dressing room and didn't go to the studio to have a sneaky peek.

I always put my suit on just before I go on because I like the trouser creases to be sharp. I was just doing that when Peter Prichard came in to check on me.

'What's it like out there?' I asked him.

'Do you really want me to tell you?' he replied.

'No,' I answered, truthfully. So, I walked on the stage with very little idea who would be there. And I scanned the audience as they applauded my entrance. *Oh. My. God.*

Henry Cooper was there. Cilla. Frankie Vaughan. Sebastian Coe. Harry Secombe. Parky. Barbara Windsor. Des O'Connor. Nerys Hughes. John Inman. Les Dennis. Loads of footballers: Dalglish, Keegan, Rush, Bobby Campbell, Ron Atkinson, Lee Chapman (and his wife, Leslie Ash). It was an audience of everyone I knew, admired and loved.

No pressure then, Tarby! Here we go …

I laughed nervously – ho ho! – as they all carried on clapping. My eyes fixed on Cilla, who was sitting right on the front row. In fact, I think I said my first words directly to her, rather than to the whole audience:

'My bottle's gone already!'

Cilla laughed and came back with some quick remark, as usual. I did a lot of bantering with her throughout the show. It helped to put me at my ease. And, as I gradually relaxed and got used to where I was, and what I was doing, I started enjoying it. A lot.

I opened with a few gags, including one at dear old Des's expense. 'I went into a shop to buy the new Des O'Connor album,' I said. 'A lady served me. It was very embarrassing, so I bought a pack of condoms instead …'

They all roared. Even Des. In fact, especially Des.

The show's format was that it was mostly a Q & A with the audience. I didn't know any of the questions in advance and I didn't want to. I'd told Peter Prichard not to tell me. Why? Because I wanted to hear them, think on my feet and answer them spontaneously. It made it more natural.

Cilla reminisced about us hanging out in the Cavern in Liverpool and asked if I'd ever thought I'd get where I was now. 'Of course not!' I answered. 'It's been like a fairy tale.' Michael Parkinson asked who my first comic heroes were. I pointed at Harry Secombe, in the front row. 'He is a wonderful comedian,' I said. 'Wonderful.'

One of the greatest British footballers ever was in the audience. For anybody too young to remember him: George Best could do things with a football you could not believe. He looked fantastic. Even his name was perfect. George did the impossible of making even a diehard Liverpool fan like me fall in love with a Manchester United player.

I was good mates with George. We used to go drinking and have nights out in Tramp. If any sportsman had the right to be cocky and full of himself it was George, yet he was the most modest and unaffected of fellers. It's pretty well known that he liked a drink but he was always down-to-earth.

Bestie didn't pose me a question on my *An Audience With …* but I had one for him. I'd watched him in action on the football pitch *and* in Tramp, so I said, 'As a young man, you had the greatest talent of all of us. Are you still seeing any of them?' George just laughed. What else could he do?

Another football giant in the house was Terry Venables, who was then England manager. Venners was a fun guy, and good value on a night out. If we'd had a couple, I'd normally say to him, 'Go on, Terry, give us a song!' You didn't need to ask him twice. Usually a Sinatra number. He had a decent voice, as well.

Halfway through the show, Billy Connolly appeared on a video link live from Canada, where he was on tour. I was dead touched that Billy had bothered to do that. And he had a very specific question for me. 'Did your family seek psychiatric help after I visited your house yon time?' he asked.

A-ha! Billy was talking about the night he'd stumbled back to mine pissed, and woken us all up crashing about in the early hours trying to find a toilet. But I had an answer for him.

'I hate to bring this up, but I know for a fact that you peed out of the window,' I said.

The audience chuckled.

'Because what you didn't realise was that it had been snowing,' I added.

More laughter.

'And what I *didn't* like was it was in Pauline's handwriting.'

That got a roar. 'Ah, good on yer, Tarby!' said Billy.

One guest who came out of left field was Leslie Nielsen, the American comic actor and star of hilarious films like *Airplane!* and *The Naked Gun*. I'd never met Leslie. When I saw him in the audience, I thought, *What the bloody hell's he doing here?* It turned out that he was in London doing promo interviews and his PR had nabbed him a ticket.

Leslie was comedy gold. 'Can I say, I'm really honoured to be in the company of so many distinguished British celebrities,' he began. Then he fixed me with his famous quizzical stare. 'Mr Tuckbar, what is it that you do?' he inquired. The whole studio was in fits.

Leslie wasn't finished yet. 'In *The Naked Gun* movies, I do a lot of undercover work,' he continued. 'Let me ask you: if you had to go undercover in a nudist colony, what kind of disguise would you use?'

'On a good day, a fig leaf,' I quipped back. 'On a cold day, a tea leaf!'

Another of the guests was Keith Floyd, the celebrity chef. Let me tell you, that man liked a bevvy! And then some. And he didn't mess about with his question to me.

'Jimmy, you've been giving us all this nonsense about sport but, in fact, you're quite fat,' Keith kindly informed me. 'Which indicates to me that you're a bit of a trencherman. So, if I cooked for you, what would you like me to cook? What's your favourite meal?'

'My favourite meal? Fish and chips,' I answered, honestly, while thinking: *Quite fat?! Cheeky bugger!* There again, Keith probably only said it because he was quite pissed. But I'd still have loved him to cook for me. Even if it might have made me a bit fatter.

I finished off the show with a musical number. Scattered around the audience were Hank Marvin, Rick Wakeman, Kenney Jones from The Who and Justin Hayward and John Lodge from The Moody Blues. They became my supergroup backing band as I belted out one of my favourite songs: Chuck Berry's 'Johnny B. Goode'.*

How did I feel after *An Audience with Jimmy Tarbuck?* Very like after my episode of *This Is Your Life*. Excited, elated, drained … and, mainly, very flattered and honoured that all of these famous, talented people had turned out just for me.

---

* Even today, I still often lead the crowds at my shows in a sing-along of 'Johnny B. Goode'. Just because I can.

It left me both proud and humbled. And that's not a bad way to be.

* * *

When the BBC had launched *International Pro-Celebrity Golf* back in 1975, it had felt like all my dreams come true: a show that allowed me to play, and talk about, golf on TV. It seemed like it might be about to happen again in 1996 when the Beeb gave me a new game show to present: *Full Swing*.

The idea was simple. Video games and virtual reality were getting massive in those days, and *Full Swing* stood celebrity contestants in front of a screen showing a real-life golf hole. They took aim and swung their club at an imaginary ball, and sensors at their feet measured the shot and showed them on the screen where it would have landed on the course.

It was a clever idea and it attracted plenty of willing participants. Ronnie Corbett, Kenny Lynch, Henry Cooper, Eric Sykes, Parky, Frank Carson, Tim Brooke-Taylor, Hale and Pace and even Floella Benjamin all trooped down to the studio and had a bash at a pretend ball. But despite all this star power, *Full Swing* wasn't a success.

Why not? It came down to the same reason that *Tarby's Frame Game* fell short. Some TV programmes work and some don't. The only way to find out if a show has wings is to try it out, and *Full Swing* just didn't capture the public's imagination. The ratings were poor and the BBC dropped it after one series.

By this stage of my career, not being contractually tied to one television company quite suited me. It allowed me to pick and choose which programmes appealed to me and which shows I'd like to go on. And one intriguing offer that came my way in 1998 took my fancy.

Caroline Aherne was a razor-sharp stand-up and a brilliant comic actress on shows like *The Fast Show* (and later, of course, *The Royle Family*). Her other gig was getting done up like an old lady to host her spoof chat show, *The Mrs Merton Show*. When I got an invite to go on, I just figured, *Why not?*

It wasn't without its risks, of course. Caroline was very much one of the new breed of comics who liked to take the piss out of, shall we say, more *senior* performers such as Tarby here. And I could tell she wasn't going to pull her punches with me as I stood waiting to go on and heard my introduction.

'He's the undisputed king of comedy,' Mrs Merton said. 'All other comics shudder when you say the name ... Jimmy Tarbuck!'

Ho ho! It's like that, is it? But I'm too long in the tooth to be fazed by a bit of mickey-taking. I strode out, joined my fellow guest, Richard Whiteley – an old chum from my *Winner Takes All* Yorkshire TV days – fixed my hostess with a friendly stare, and gave her one of the best ad libs I've ever come out with.

'Let's have a look at you, in person,' I said. 'It's wonderful. Parky with a perm!'

I turned to survey the audience. It was mostly elderly ladies: a sea of grey rinses (rather like my own shows nowadays!). 'Ah, they're just about my mettle, some of these,'

I said. 'They don't yell, they don't tell, and they're grateful!' They roared. And I was away.

Mrs Merton and I both had a twinkle in our eyes. She went on trying to gently send me up. We got to talking about my early days. 'Tell me, Tarby,' she asked me, 'did you ever consummate it with Cilla, round the back of the Cavern? It's a lovely image we'd all like to have in our heads.'

'Well, how about you and I getting it on later in the dressing room?' I shot back. 'You don't start flirting with me, or I'll tell them about you and The Ink Spots ...'

The show was a proper hoot. We were both falling about and the audience were roaring. Mrs Merton went back on the wind-up (not that she ever came off it): 'Do you like all the new comedians of today, or do you think they don't play enough golf?' she asked.

Good one! I listed some of the young comics that I liked at the time: Paul Merton, Harry Hill, Eddie Izzard, Frank Skinner. But I saved my highest praise for an oldie. 'Ken Dodd is still the best comic on the stage,' I said. 'Easily.'

'Does he do your accounts?' she inquired.

'No,' I replied. 'But when he went in for his open-heart surgery, they opened him up and found another forty grand ...'

Caroline turned the conversation to the Palladium. An old-timer sitting in the audience chipped in to tell us that he had been there many years ago to see Bing Crosby. 'Just in time,' he added. 'He kicked the bucket two weeks later.'

I turned to face the old feller. 'Bloody hell!' I said. 'I hope that's not an omen for tonight.'

I think it's fair to say that my appearance on *The Mrs Merton Show* was a success. It did me no harm at all, especially with the younger generation of television viewers.

Things were ticking over very nicely. I didn't have a regular programme of my own but I was being offered loads of shows to guest on. I'd mull them over with Peter Prichard. Sometimes I'd agree and others I'd say no. But when I got offered a chance to work with my own flesh and blood, it was a complete no-brainer.

Our Liza's TV career was going great guns. She'd taken the main part in a comedy play on Victoria Wood's show (now *there* was a funny woman) and spent a couple of years co-presenting *The Big Breakfast*. And, in 2001, she got offered the lead role in a BBC comedy-drama series, *Linda Green*.

Linda Green was about a woman in her thirties who was partying hard and enjoying her life. Not much of a stretch for our Liza! Her character worked in a car showroom by day and was a club singer by night, which gave Liza the chance to show that she's got a decent set of pipes. And I was invited to guest in one episode.

I played Liza/Linda's Uncle Vic ... or was I her dad? There were suspicions in the family: Vic was a bit of a rogue and had had a one-night stand with Linda's mum decades ago. It was a nice little story and I loved acting with my girl. Again, it was nice to show that I could pass muster as an actor, if I needed to.

Liza and I also formed a father-and-daughter team on a charity episode of *Who Wants to Be a Millionaire*? We were trying to raise money for the St John's Ambulance. I've got to be honest: Liza got more questions right than me. She's a smart, well-educated woman. I didn't pay attention in school. She did.

We were motoring along nicely and we'd won £16,000 for St John's when we got a tricky question. Liza said she thought she knew the answer but she wasn't 100 per cent sure.

'What do you think, Dad?' she asked.

'If you're not certain, let's play it safe,' I answered. 'That's a lot of money for them. We don't want to lose it.' We did the right thing and handed over sixteen grand to a great cause.

Now my work career was no longer so intensive, I was taking the opportunity to relax, socialise … and play golf (let's face it, those three activities have always been firmly intertwined in my life). In 2003, good old Eric Sykes turned eighty, and a few of us pals took him golfing at Coombe Hill for the day.

After the round, we were all in the showers before we headed over to the bar. Eric came out of the shower in his glasses and got a beer and a cigar on the go. He thanked us for giving him a great birthday and we all applauded him. Then he looked down at his body and addressed it.

'Hello, feet,' he began. 'You've carried me around for eighty years.'

We clapped his feet.

'Hello, legs,' he went on. 'And you've carried me around.'

We clapped his legs.

'And hello, willy. If *you* were still alive, it'd be your birthday, too …'

And we all roared. Good old Eric. R.I.P.

* * *

My own parts were all still in reasonable working order, give or take the odd bit of wear and tear.* But I still baulked at an unexpected offer that came my way from the BBC in 2006. Because, out of the blue, they asked me if I would appear on *Strictly Come Dancing*.

I was in Portugal with Pauline when Peter Prichard called me with the news. Initially, I scoffed at the offer. 'Come off it, Peter!' I said. 'Me, ballroom dancing on the telly? I'm sixty-six now. I'm too old. Forget it. Tell them no.'

But the producers were determined. Peter called me back the next day. 'They want to fly one of the professional dancers out to Portugal to talk to you,' he said. 'Are you willing to meet her?' Against my better judgement, I agreed. But I still thought it would be a waste of her time.

The next day, a lady called Flavia Cacace materialised at the door of our holiday home. Flavia was a beautiful, tiny little Italo-Englishwoman and a ball of energy and vitality. She was the UK Argentine Tango champion and she quickly set about persuading me that that going on *Strictly* was a good idea.

'Look, I'm flattered that you've flown out to see me,' I said. 'But I don't think it's for me.'

---

* Or so I thought.

'Ah, Jimmy, but you must do it!' Flavia urged me. 'We will have so much fun. And if you do what I teach you, and what I tell you, we can do really well.'

Flavia was very persuasive and she was also good fun. She was laughing a lot as we sat in the Portuguese sun. Her enthusiasm was infectious, and eventually I said, 'Oh, you know what? Bugger it – let's do it!' She clapped her hands. I was in.

Back in London, we went into rehearsals at BBC Television Centre. Flavia was a great coach. She talked about balance, posture and movement, and taught me all the steps. Flavia worked me hard but we did a lot of laughing. She built up my confidence. I thought I was doing OK.

The dance in the first week of the competition was the waltz. *Well*, I thought, *even I can do that!* I mean, it's just one-two-three, one-two-three, and that's it! Flavia carefully explained that, *no*, there's a bit more to it than that, and we rehearsed hard. By the day of the show, I felt ready.

My old pal Bruce was presenting *Strictly*, of course. He wished me luck and, well, I thought that we did OK. The judges weren't *too* hard on me – except for Craig Revel Horwood, but you expect that – but they put us in the bottom two. This was before they had introduced dance-offs, so we went straight into the public vote, against Nicholas Owen the newsreader.

And Flavia and I won.

'Blimey.' I laughed to Pauline when I got home. 'The viewers like my dancing. So, who knows? Maybe I'll win it!'

For our next dance, Flavia and I had the choice of doing a tango or a jive. And I grinned. *A jive? That's bang up my street!* That was how I'd first met Pauline in the Cavern, all those years ago. I could remember all that palaver: standing still and twirling the girl around me. I thought that we were as good as through to the next week.

But Flavia was a tango champion, of course, so she thought it might be worth us attempting that. She tried to lead me through the steps. 'I'll dance away from you,' she explained. 'Then I'll dance back to you. You put your hand on your hip, I slide my arm through your arm, and you bend and roll me across your back ...'

I shook my head. 'I can't do that, love,' I said. 'Sorry. I just can't do it.'

And, in truth, I was struggling. Flavia was cool but the rehearsals were demanding and intense. I was finding myself out of breath and having to stop and take rests. And when Peter Prichard dropped in to see how I was getting on, he didn't like what he saw.

'You don't look great, Jim,' he said. 'Let's get you to see a doctor.'

I protested, at first, but that was what we did. The doc sat me down, talked to me, and ran a few tests. And the results weren't good. 'I'm afraid your blood pressure is very high, Mr Tarbuck,' he said. 'I strongly advise that you don't continue in this competition.'

So, that was that for me trying to win *Strictly Come Dancing* at the age of sixty-six. Which, let's face it, was probably always a bit of a long shot. I was disappointed, for Flavia as much as for me: it didn't seem fair on her. I put a statement out to the press.

'I would like to thank my wonderful partner, Flavia, who's taught me so much and been patient in trying to turn this old carthorse into a proper dancer,' I said. 'I'll keep watching to see how my fellow contestants are shaping up now their hottest competition is out of the way!'

I also went on that week's show to explain to the viewers why I had to drop out, and I insisted on going to watch the grand finale and support the other contestants. Mark Ramprakash, the former England cricketer and a ridiculously handsome man to boot, won it.

I had to have treatment for my high blood pressure. The papers were following the story, of course, so some people were worried that I was going to have to go through heart surgery and a bypass operation. But it was nothing as serious as that, thank God. The doctors told me they just wanted to put in some stents.

OK, docs: whatever you say. I went in for the op and it wasn't a major procedure at all. I didn't even need a general anaesthetic. They just placed three metal stents in various veins and arteries in my body. And they're great. They brought my blood pressure down. Twenty years later, touch wood, they still seem to be working.

My main concern was how soon I could start work again. Which, as it turned out, was very quickly. I went on a Royal Variety Show in 2007, and another the following year. And I carried on happily doing bits and pieces: a show about comedy with Dawn French; an eightieth-birthday TV tribute to Bruce; the odd stand-up show.

In 2008, I co-hosted a one-off variety show, *For One Night Only*, with Emma Bunton from the Spice Girls. Emma was smashing and we became pals. I even did my first telly dance routine since *Strictly* as the pair of us duetted on 'Let's Face the Music and Dance'. 'Here we go: more comedy!' I warned as we got going. But I enjoyed it.

That show featured one of John Bishop's first television appearances. I clocked him – *oh, look, a new Liverpool comic* – but I didn't get a chance to talk to him for very long. I've since got to know him a lot better. John is a good lad, extremely funny, and very good-looking. *The bastard.*

I got interviewed on *Piers Morgan's Life Stories*. I knew Piers had had a go at a couple of comics, so I had a word with him beforehand. 'Ask me what you want,' I said. 'But if you mess with me, I'll have a go back. So, look out.' And he was nice as pie with me. I know Piers isn't everyone's cup of tea, but I get on with him. I think he's an OK feller.

And then, in November 2012, I was privileged to attend a very special occasion indeed.

I think I've done fifteen Royal Variety Performances in my life to date but, along with my first one in 1964, this was the most memorable. The 2012 show marked one hundred years since the first ever Royal Command Performance, for King George V, and to mark the occasion, it was staged in the Royal Albert Hall for the first time.

It was a suitably star-studded bill. David Walliams did most of the hosting and flew down to the stage on a zip wire. Bill Bailey did a funny comic turn with an orchestra of car horns. They had Girls Aloud, One Direction, Kylie Minogue and Robbie Williams, and the headliners were Rod Stewart and Neil Diamond.

The show was very special for me, as well, for a very good reason. I was invited on along with three other former Royal Command Performance hosts, who also happened to be three of my best friends in the world: Bruce Forsyth, Ronnie Corbett and Des O'Connor. We were all to do our own bits, and then come on together at the end.

I bounced on to do my set and beamed at the audience. 'All this night brings for me, ladies and gentlemen, are memories,' I said. 'Memories of my first royal show. And I did OK. The Queen turned around to Prince Albert and said, yes, we are amused ...'

As the crowd roared, I fixed on one woman chortling in the front row. 'It was a joke, luv!' I mock-chided her. 'I wasn't really on it, alright?'

Later, before our big joint entrance, we four pals were in a dressing room together. Bruce was fussing with his cufflinks. Des was resting his bones in a chair. Bradley Walsh, who was doing a bit of the hosting, popped in to say hello. He couldn't believe that Bruce, Ronnie and Des called me 'the boy'. Well, I *was* the youngest of us.

So, there we were, 317 years old between the four of us. Before we went on, I clapped my hands.

'Can I say something?' I asked.

'Oh, here we go.' Bruce grinned. 'The boy is talking. Or is it the boss?'

'Look, let's not rush this,' I said. 'When we walk out there, we're going to get a reception like we've never experienced before. And like we never will again. So let's *Take. Our. Time.* Let's soak it all up and make sure that we never forget it.'

And that was what we did. As soon as Bruce, Ronnie, Des and I appeared on the stage, the Albert Hall was on its feet. The applause was deafening. The ovation went on and on and on. And we just stood, taking it all in. *What a moment.* I'll never forget it. It brings goose bumps to my arms thinking about it even now.

My head was still spinning after the show when all the performers lined up in time-honoured fashion to be presented to the Queen. I'll tell you this: I admired and loved the Queen. I met her many times over the years and she was always charming, dignified and impeccable. She was a wonderful woman. We were lucky to have her for so long.

I was even invited to lunch at Buckingham Palace once. Prince Philip met Pauline and me when we arrived and was walking us through to see Her Majesty. As we passed a side-room, I spotted one of Pietro Annigoni's famous paintings of the Queen. I nipped in to have a closer look.

'Where the hell's he gone?' I heard Philip ask Pauline.

'He's looking at a painting,' she replied.

Philip came in to find me. 'Do you like that picture?' he asked, brusquely.

'Yes, I think it's wonderful,' I said.

He stared at me. 'Let's hope it's still there in the morning, then,' he snapped. *Cheeky bugger!* But that was Prince Philip for you.

At the big Albert Hall show, as the Queen worked her way down the line of performers, I was standing next to Ronnie Corbett. I bent down and murmured in his ear. 'Eh, Ronnie,' I whispered. 'Don't bow too low, or she won't see you.'

Ronnie was normally very correct and proper but, I'll tell you, he gave me a right old mouthful back. Luckily, the Queen was too far away to hear. She carried on walking down the line, thanking everybody … then, when she came to me, she stopped dead.

'How many of these have you done now, Mr Tarbuck?' she inquired.

Silly bugger here gave a smartarse reply. 'Four more than you, ma'am,' I said.

Her Majesty gave the slightest flicker of a smile. 'It certainly seemed like it tonight.' She nodded, and glided on. *Bosh!* What a mic-drop moment! You know what, I reckon it's a shame that the Queen never tried her hand at comedy. She might have been a natural.

I floated home from that anniversary Royal Command Performance on an absolute high. It felt almost as if my entire career had been leading to that night, and that unforgettable ovation. *You know what?* I thought to myself. *Life doesn't get any better than this.*

It's extraordinary how quickly, and how terribly, things can change.

CHAPTER 16

If it had been
ten Tiller Girls …

The knock on the door came early in the morning on Friday, 26 April 2013. I'm always an early riser so I was in the kitchen, in my dressing-gown, making a cup of tea. I was puzzled: *Eh? Who's this, then?* Pauline and I weren't expecting anyone, and we never really get surprise visitors these days. *Maybe it's the postman?*

What I didn't expect, when I opened the door, was to be confronted by fourteen men and women. *Fourteen.* Some in police uniform. The feller at the front produced a piece of paper and held it out.

'Mr Jimmy Tarbuck?' he asked. 'We have a warrant to search your property.'

What did I think? Can I be honest here? I thought I was being pranked. I thought it was a wind-up, like Cilla used to do on *Surprise Surprise*, or Jeremy Beadle and Noel Edmonds did on their shows. I think I may even have laughed. But the looks on their faces as they stared at me showed they weren't joking.

'You'd better come in,' I said. All fourteen of them followed me into the house and split off in different directions. Some went in the kitchen; some in the study; others vanished upstairs, where Pauline was as shocked to see them as I was. And the chief detective spoke to me again.

'Mr Tarbuck, you are under arrest on suspicion of historic child sex offences,' he said. 'You are not obliged to speak, but anything you say …'

My head was in a whirl as the copper continued reading my rights. *Huh? What the …? How could …?* But I hardly got a chance to collect my thoughts before one of the other policemen began to fire questions at me.

'Have you got a computer?' he asked.

'No.'

'No? You must have!'

'No,' I repeated. 'I don't have anything like that.* My wife has got one.'

'We'll take that then,' he said. 'Where is it?'

What I *should* have said to them was: 'Good luck taking Pauline's computer! All you'll find on that are searches for Marks & Spencer's closing times, and what's on at the Odeon in Kingston.' But I didn't. I didn't say anything. I was in too much of a daze.

---

* And I still don't. I must confess that the digital revolution has passed me by.

Pauline came downstairs: 'What's going on, Jimmy?' I told her the truth: 'I don't know, love. I haven't got a clue.' The police were buzzing in and out of doors. One of them came to me holding a picture in a frame. It was a photo of James and me when he was a lad. We had it out on display.

'Who's this boy?' he asked, abruptly.

I stared at the feller in amazement. 'It's my son.'

'Your son?' He looked as if he didn't believe me.

The police were in the house for two hours. They took away every work diary I had, going back years, and every video I owned: a whole load of Liverpool FC and golf videos, and a handful of recordings of my early days at the Palladium. I like to re-watch them, now and then, to remind myself what I did back then.

When they'd finished their search, the cops took me to a police station somewhere out near Heathrow airport. They repeated that I was arrested but immediately released me on bail. I was free to go home. Where I shook my head and thought, *What in the name of God is going on?*

I wasn't the only entertainer to be arrested around then, of course. There was a lot of it about. Everyone knew why. The previous year, months after he died, it had emerged that Jimmy Savile was one of the most prolific sex offenders in British history. Savile had exploited his position and celebrity to abuse hundreds of young women.

Young women ... and children.

I'd met Savile over the years. I'd never liked him. I never had a clue what he was up to, but he wasn't a pleasant man.

He always gave it the big 'I am': the king of the castle. You couldn't talk to him. Not properly. He'd just repeat his stupid catchphrases, over and over: 'Now then, now then, goodness gracious!' And I'd think, *Oh, piss off!*

When Savile's crimes emerged, I was horrified. The same as everyone was. I felt angry that he'd died: that he'd got away with it. He should have had to pay for all the wicked things he'd done. I mean, can you imagine what a time he'd have had of it in prison? And he'd have deserved it.

In the wake of Savile, the police had set up an investigation, Operation Yewtree, to look into similar allegations against show-business stars. A load more entertainers had been arrested: Gary Glitter, Dave Lee Travis, Freddie Starr, Rolf Harris, Jim Davidson.*

And now it was my turn.

I didn't know what to say. I didn't know what to *think*. All that I knew was that it was lies. Utter, utter lies and bollocks. I'd never touched a child in that way in my life. *Good God!* I never would. So where the hell had this come from? *What was it?*

I wasn't arrested in Operation Yewtree. The Met Police in London, who were running that, decided I didn't fall within its remit and passed me on to the local force where a complaint had been made against me, which was apparently North Yorkshire Police. And I had to go to get questioned by them.

---

* Glitter and Harris were convicted and imprisoned. Dave Lee Travis received a suspended sentence. Freddie Starr and Jim Davidson were cleared and not charged.

A few days later, I got a train up to Harrogate. With a lawyer by my side, I was interviewed by two female detectives from the North Yorkshire force. I finally learned what I was accused of. And it beggared belief.

The cops said they'd received a complaint from a member of the public. A man had said that forty-three years earlier, at Christmas 1970, I'd gone to a hospital in Harrogate to do a show for sick kids and give them presents. He said I'd taken him off in the hospital and molested him. And he was six years old at the time.

This. Was. Ridiculous.

I couldn't believe my ears. I felt like telling these coppers: '*You what?* The worst I've ever done to a young lad is make him go in goal when we play football!' But it wasn't a time for jokes. The detectives said they had to take the allegations seriously. They had to look into them. I returned to London shocked and bewildered.

The police didn't let it be known that I'd been arrested. Nobody was aware for a week or so. Then one of our lovely newspapers found out and splashed it all over their pages. And, suddenly, it was public knowledge:

Jimmy Tarbuck is accused of historic sex abuse.

When the news broke, Pauline and I had press and paparazzi on our doorstep for a day or two. They'd ring the bell and shout questions through the intercom. I remember the thing that bugged me most was the hassle for our neighbours. They couldn't get in and out for reporters blocking the road.

Let me tell you: it was a horrible time. How did I get through it? With the support of my family. Pauline was a rock, as she has been all through my life. And Cheryl, Liza and James were just as strong. They knew it was bollocks. They knew their dad, and that he'd never do anything like that.

Peter Prichard had total faith in me. 'It's a load of crap, Jim,' he said. 'The police are out to get people.' And my friends stood by me. Almost every one of my closest showbiz mates phoned to support me. 'It'll pass, Tarby,' they all said. 'Hang in there.' That meant everything to me.

As I've said, I've never been that close to Ken Dodd, but he said a funny thing. Doddy was being interviewed and got asked about me. 'It's crazy,' he said. 'If it had been ten Tiller Girls, I might have believed it. But Tarby and a six-year-old boy? *Really? Come on ...*'

But those allegations cast a shadow over everything. Over my life. I was due to do a stand-up tour and I cancelled it. I couldn't crack gags with this hanging over me. Before I'd got arrested, I'd been interviewed for an ITV tribute to Les Dawson. When the show was broadcast, I was cut out of it.

I'll be honest with you: I started leaving the house by the back door instead of the front, especially if journalists were around. But I didn't hide away. I still went to Coombe Hill and played golf. My pals there were amazing. Fantastic. They rallied around me. Golf helped to keep me sane.

And when I *did* go out, people were supportive. Everyone was so kind. If Pauline and I went to the shops, or the pictures, people would come up and greet me. I never once got abused in the street. I went to football and got an amazing reception. Everywhere I went, the public gave me sympathy and support.

Thank God they did.

I'd get updates from North Yorkshire Police. They told me the director of the show I'd appeared in at Harrogate hospital in 1970 had come forward. 'Jimmy and I shared a dressing room that day,' he'd explained. 'He never left my sight once. It's impossible he did anything like that ...'

And yet, after the news broke, four or five other people went to the police to accuse me of stuff. Not to put too fine a point on it, they were fantasists. I don't want to be cruel if I say they may have been in need of psychiatric help. But the police had to talk to them. Had to hear them out.

I'll give you an example. A woman came forward and said I'd molested her at BBC Television Centre in London in 1964. She said I'd been appearing on *Top of the Pops*. She'd been in the audience, and I'd taken her to my dressing room and done things to her with 'four of my road crew'.

Well, where do I start? There were a few holes in this story. I hardly had two bob to rub together in 1964, let alone 'four road crew'. I've never been on *Top of the Pops*: given the (non-)sales of my records, why the hell would they want me? Oh, yes, and in 1964, *Top of the Pops* wasn't made in London. They filmed it in Manchester.

The shadow hung over me for nearly a year. It was March 2014 when the North Yorkshire Police passed their 'evidence' to the Crown Prosecution Service. The CPS had a look at it and saw there was nothing there. They announced that there would be no charges and the case was dropped.

How did I feel when I was told? Mixed emotions. Relieved, of course ... yet 'relieved' isn't quite the right word. I always knew nothing would come of it, because it was all a load of rubbish. Mostly, I felt angry that my family and I had to go through so much grief and stress for a year. To endure such an ordeal.

I wasn't the last one to suffer. Less than six months later, poor Cliff Richard had to sit in Portugal and watch as the police ransacked his British home live on BBC News. I saw Cliff not long after that and he had the weight of the world on his shoulders. He is a truly decent man. How they treated him was a disgrace.

Then there was Jim Davidson. Jim had the same as me: got arrested, splashed all over the papers, then declared innocent. I know not everyone loves Jim, but I stand by him. He's always been great with me, and he flies all over the world entertaining our troops for nowt. He deserves a pat on the back for that.

Eighteen months after the false accusations were dropped, I went on the *Loose Women* TV programme. The ladies hosting the show asked about what had happened to me and how I'd coped with it. They were very sympathetic, as were the studio audience, and I was totally honest with them.

'I won't get emotional now ...' I said, but, of course, I did. 'The real thing that annoys me about it all is that *these people*' – by which, I meant the ones accusing us of terrible things –

'can remain anonymous.' I'll admit, I got pretty teary-eyed, saying it. One of the ladies gave me a hug.

I suppose I could have sued over what I went through. A few people told me I should have done. But, really, once it was over, I just wanted to put the nightmare behind me. I wanted to try to forget about it, and to move on. And, luckily, a very happy experience was on the horizon.

CHAPTER 17

My God, you've given the catalogue a bashing

I hadn't really done any work while the false sex allegations were hanging over me. I hadn't been able to and, if I'm honest, I hadn't particularly wanted to. But the first job that came along when it was all over … well, it was a proper belter.

ITV had just brought back *Sunday Night at the London Palladium* again (you can't keep a good show down!). They were using a different host every week, rotating young stars such as Stephen Mulhern, Jack Whitehall, Jimmy Carr and Rob Brydon. Bradley Walsh was presenting one of the shows. And Bradley asked me to go on.

Wow! If I'm honest, I guess I probably imagined I'd trod the boards of the Palladium for the last time, especially during the terrible time when I'd been living under a cloud. And as comebacks go, this was pretty high-profile. Was I up for it? Well, I hope that one good thing about old Tarby is that I've never been one to shirk a challenge.

And it was the Palladium. 'Yes, please!' I told Bradley. I was in.

The show was on the night of 12 October 2014. It was more than fifty years – *my God!* – since I'd made my first Palladium appearance. So, so many memories were flooding through my mind as I stood waiting nervously in the wings. And I heard Bradley Walsh give me quite the introduction.

'Well, folks, in 1967, when I was seven years of age, my mum and dad would let me watch *Sunday Night at the London Palladium*,' he told the audience. 'There was a young man hosting the show, and I thought, *That's what I want to do.* Ladies and gentlemen, please welcome home one of my all-time heroes. It's Mr Jimmy Tarbuck.'

I stepped out onto the stage. And if any part of me had feared that the public might have turned against me during my dark time, it was quickly forgotten. The standing ovation hit me like a tidal wave. People weren't just out of their seats: they were clapping with their hands over their heads. I felt like I couldn't move. I was rooted to the spot.

Let me tell you: that was a moment that restored – no, *confirmed* – my faith in human nature. So, how did I repay that faith? In the only way that I know how: by gently taking the piss out of them.

'I salute the ladies tonight because you've all got dressed up to come to the Palladium,' I began. 'My God, you've given the catalogue a bashing ...'

It was a wonderful, wonderful night. It stands out even among so many that I've had on that unique stage.

* * *

I loved getting back in the game and doing that Palladium show, but it couldn't help but be tinged with sadness. Just six weeks before I went on, dear old Peter Prichard had died. Peter was an incredible manager who, by then, had looked after me for close on fifty years.

I spoke at his funeral and said that Peter was a fabulous character who'd always, and I mean *always*, had jaw-dropping stories. He'd once danced with Ginger Rogers – at her insistence – and, even more weirdly, had a fight with Mario Lanza. One of his obituaries called him the last of the old-school showbiz managers. It was spot-on.

Nothing ever threw Peter, although Rock Hudson came close. Peter was once asked to look after the superstar American actor at a showbiz party in London. At the end of the night, he'd driven him back to his hotel. Rock had leaned in towards Peter for a thank-you hug … and French-kissed him. That story got a laugh when I told it at the service.

Since Peter passed, I've been managed by a feller called Alan Field, who has also spent decades looking after The Searchers, a band that I used to go and watch in the Cavern as a lad. I'll tell you: showbiz is a small world. And, sometimes, it goes full circle.

Right at the start of this book (it seems a long time ago now!), I talked about how my lad, James, called me the last of the dinosaurs. Well, one problem about walking the earth for as long as I have is that you have to wave goodbye to so many of your friends and peers. And one of my oldest, closest chums of all passed in 2015.

Cilla hadn't been too well for a while. She'd been suffering from arthritis and starting to struggle with her eyesight. One of her aunties in Liverpool, her mum's sister, had been in a lot of pain at the end of her life. That had stayed with Cilla, and she'd once told me, 'I'd rather die young than be like that.' But the way she passed was extremely sad.

Cilla was only seventy-two when she slipped and banged her head at her holiday home in Spain. The autopsy found that she'd had a stroke. Her funeral was at St Mary's Church in Woolton, which I knew from when I was a kid. And most of Liverpool and half of the showbiz world turned out.

I gave a reading at the service, as did Christopher Biggins. Cliff Richard sang and Paul O'Grady did a eulogy. 'The Long and Winding Road' by The Beatles was played as Cilla's coffin was carried out. We all stood around the grave and threw roses and soil on it as it got lowered into the ground.

Tom Jones had flown in on a private jet from Slovakia, where he'd played a show the night before. 'Cilla was a great girl, Jimmy, wasn't she?' Tom asked me as we slowly, sadly, made our way from the graveside.

And I simply replied, 'Yes.'

Because she really, really was.

* * *

Now I'd made my comeback at the Palladium, I was keen to do any more shows there that I possibly could. And I got a terrific opportunity at the end of 2015. Because Des O'Connor's agent got in touch and asked if I would do a joint-headline show with Des to raise money for the Royal Variety Charity.

And Des and I had a great time. We laughed our way through the rehearsals and arrived at a format for the show that worked for both of us. We went on as a pair at the start of the night, then I did a stand-up set. After an interval, Des did his songs and jokes, and we got together again at the end.

It was a lovely night. We got a lot of laughs.* Over the years, I've rarely been reviewed in the *Guardian*: it's not my world. But the critic they sent down that evening wrote: 'There were two proper stars on the Palladium stage.' He even added: 'I was thrilled to see this little piece of theatre history.' And I guess, in a way, it was.

The evening went so well that Des and I did a whole load more shows together, up and down the country, over the next year or two. They were always a joy. I'd known Des for so long that we were totally relaxed in each other's company. We had some grand times hanging out backstage, shooting the breeze and reminiscing.

Des was a giggler. I loved making him laugh onstage. I'd tell him: 'There's a pensioner at the stage door. She said to tell you that the lad's fifty-seven now, can you send her some money?' And Des would just stand there, giggling. After the show, he'd chastise me: 'You've got to stop saying those things, Tarby!'

As if.

* * *

---

* And that was just Des's singing, ho ho!

Bruce Forsyth had not been well. In the summer of 2017, he had a fall, which meant that a TV tribute to Max Miller I was about to film with him had to be put on ice. Instead, he was at home, next door to Wentworth golf course, resting up and recuperating. Kenny Lynch and I went round to visit him.

Bruce was frail. He was eighty-nine by now and mostly restricted to his bedroom. We couldn't go and sit out in the July sunshine. But he was out of bed, sat in a chair in a track-suit and trainers, and telling me and Kenny about the exercises he was doing to get fit and mobile again. He was as sharp and as quick-witted as ever.

His wife, Wilnelia, brought us in sandwiches, cakes and a pot of tea and left us to it. And I can't say I blame her. Because Bruce, Kipper and I were like three superannuated school-boys as we sat together howling with laughter at some of the memories we'd built up over our sixty-year friendship.

We reminisced about people we'd known, TV shows we'd made, rounds of golf we'd played and holidays we'd taken together. We talked fondly of friends we'd lost: Harry Secombe, Eric Sykes, Les Dawson, Bob Monkhouse, Ronnie Corbett. But the mood wasn't sombre. Far from it. We were roaring. The afternoon flew by.

I'll forever treasure my final memories of Bruce. Because, within a month, he was no longer with us.

And then, a few months later, in 2018, we had to lay Ken Dodd to rest. Doddy had a good innings. He was ninety when he died in Knotty Ash in the same house he'd been born in. Thousands of folk lined the route of his funeral cortege as it drove from his home to Liverpool Cathedral, where the Bishop of Liverpool conducted the service.

I spoke at his funeral. It was an honour. I looked out at the faces of some of the biggest comics of my generation and I said, 'Ken Dodd was *not* a good comedian.' Pause. 'He was a *great* comedian.' I went on to say that Doddy was the funniest man I'd ever seen on a British stage.

And I stand by that today.

* * *

You know what? I've loved writing this book. I don't want the last chapter to read like one long obituary column. But it's just a fact of life that when you've been around as long as me, when you're *the last of the dinosaurs*, you end up going to a lot of funerals. But life's not all gloom and misery. Far from it. There's always good stuff going on.

In 2018, the London Palladium underwent some much-needed renovation. There were builders knocking around for weeks as they touched up the outside of the theatre. And when it was finished, that October, they unveiled a wonderful new feature at the venue: the Palladium Wall of Fame.

Located right next to the stage door where I used to run the gauntlet of screaming fans in the sixties, it's a beautiful stainless-steel installation of portraits of the biggest and best-known names who have graced the famous stage over the decades. It's a Who's Who of show business captured for posterity.

I was invited to unveil the Wall of Fame with a few fellow survivors from my showbiz generation: Cliff Richard, Des

O'Connor and Tommy Steele. Frankie Vaughan's widow, Stella, represented him. And, as we posed by the wall for photographers ('Hey, this way, Tarby!'), my eyes wandered upwards to the greats towering over us.

There were those who'd come before me: Arthur Askey, Vera Lynn, Max Miller, Tommy Trinder. So many of my peers, sadly no longer with us: Bruce, Cilla, Ronnie Corbett, Ronnie Barker, Max Bygraves, Frankie Vaughan, Norman Wisdom. Even a few who are, happily, still going strong, including Tom Jones and Shirley Bassey.

Yet among all those British celebrities were some of the biggest names in American show business, who had been drawn across the Atlantic by the Palladium: Bob Hope, Bing Crosby, Sammy Davis Jr, all of whom I'd been lucky enough to meet. Miss Judy Garland, whom I'd escorted onstage on that unforgettable night.

And up near the top, in between Gracie Fields and Tommy Steele, was a grinning, gap-toothed young Liverpool comic who, in 1963, had driven through the night, had a bloody awful rehearsal, leaned against the theatre wall in despair and then, come the show, gone onstage and knocked 'em dead. And who had never looked back since.

I gazed up at myself and I felt very, very proud.

I was back at the Palladium that year for another Royal Variety Performance, in front of the Duke and Duchess of Sussex, Prince Harry and Meghan Markle, who was pregnant with their first child, Archie. I got to talk to the great blind Italian opera singer, Andrea Bocelli.

At the show, I made a cameo appearance with the host, Greg Davies, and they showed a short film I'd recorded about Brinsworth House. It's a lovely old thirty-six-bedroom building in Twickenham which is owned and managed by the Royal Variety Charity as a retirement home for people who've worked in the entertainment industry.

It's a wonderful place, and a wonderful cause, and I've made a few visits to Brinsworth House over the years. I'll never forget going there with Bruce Forsyth. We went into a sitting room to meet some of the residents. Bruce walked over to an elderly lady in a wheelchair and leaned down to speak to her.

'Hello, my love!' he said. 'Do you know who I am?'

She stared at him balefully. 'No, I don't,' she replied. 'But if you ask nurse, she'll tell you ...'

* * *

It's always a heartbreak when a dear friend dies. By now, I've lost so many showbiz pals: it pains me to think just how many. And, just before Christmas 2019, I had to say goodbye to my closest mate of them all, the fantastic feller who was like a brother to me: Kenny Lynch.

Kipper had been very ill with prostate cancer. I think I knew he was probably on the way out when I went to see him in his cottage in Nettlebed in Oxfordshire. His partner, Julie, showed me through to their bedroom. Kenny was lying in bed and looking very weak. 'I didn't want you to see me like this, Jimmy,' he told me.

I sat down and we chatted for an hour or two. Kipper had some lovely pictures on the wall. There was a beautiful painting of Arnold Palmer on the course at a British Open. Kenny gestured towards it. 'Tarby, I bet you'd like that?' he asked.

'Of course! I'd love it,' I replied.

'Well, when I go, I want you to have it,' Kenny said.

'There's no need to talk like that, Kipper!' I told him. But Kenny knew his time was up. A few weeks later, he was dead.

I gave the eulogy at his funeral in Bray. Tom Jones and I were among the coffin-bearers and Michael Parkinson, Jim Davidson, Bobby Davro and Jess Conrad came along. The priest called me up to speak first and, as I stood next to Kenny's coffin, I couldn't help but make a gag about his legendarily awful timekeeping.

'Good morning, everybody,' I began. 'We are gathered here today for a reason – because we loved this feller. Well, he is here with us now and he is looking down on us.'

And I gestured towards the coffin.

'There he lies,' I said. 'The *late* Kenny Lynch.'

Well, we were in a church, a sacred place, but the folk in the pews roared. They'd all been kept waiting by Kipper at one time or another. The painting of Arnold Palmer that he gave me is in my sitting room at home now, and every time I look at it, I think not just of Arnold but of the brother and lifelong friend who gave it to me: Kenny Lynch.

I miss him every single day.

* * *

Life can be a bugger. Sometimes, it plays the cruellest tricks on you. In February 2020, I turned eighty. *Eighty! How the bloody hell had that happened?* I celebrated at home with Pauline, Cheryl, Liza, James and all of my grandkids: Cheryl's two, Louis and Tattia, and James's three, Vito, Saffina and Rico. We had a smashing time.

And then, the very next day, I was told that I had prostate cancer. Just the same as Kenny had had.

They broke the news at the Royal Marsden Hospital in Kensington. I'd been in for tests a few days earlier. They'd given me an MRI scan. As I was lying down waiting to go into the machine, a nurse asked me: 'What's your musical request for while you're in there?'

'Pardon?'

'We can play music in the scanner,' she explained. 'What would you like?'

'I don't care, as long as it's not, "So Long, It's Been Good to Know You",* I said. We had a chuckle about that.

And now I was back at the Marsden to get the results. And they weren't good. A doctor invited me into his room, sat me down, and gave it to me straight. 'Mr Tarbuck, I'm afraid you have prostate cancer,' he said.

Well, it was a shock. I'm not going to pretend otherwise. But the doc went on to say that my prognosis wasn't at all bad. 'We have caught it early,' he explained. 'It hasn't spread.

---

* It's a song that was originally called 'Dusty Old Dust', by Woody Guthrie. A Liverpool folk band called The Spinners used to play it in the Cavern when I was a lad.

We can give you treatment that has a very, very good chance of getting rid of it.'

And that was what they did. Over the following few months, I had injections and I took tablets. And I spread the word about the disease. I went on *Good Morning Britain* and urged the nation's men to get themselves down to the doctor's for a prostate check. And I told their missuses to make sure they did it.

'I have prostate cancer,' I announced on live TV. 'But I'm gonna try and beat it. And all the men, out there watching … wives, get your husband to go for the tests. After [you pass] fifty, just have a test. Let them have a look at you. You'll be relieved, and you'll be with your families for a few extra years.

'Men are shy,' I continued. 'But boys, go! Even if it *is* embarrassing. Especially when the feller said to me, "We're gonna give you a thumbs up." And I said, "I hope not!"' Kate Garraway had a good guffaw at that one.

And my treatment worked. It's still working. I go for check-ups every now and then. A doctor told me recently that, even if the cancer comes back, it won't necessarily be the cause of my death. I'll die *with* it, not *from* it. And I replied, 'OK, I'll buy that. Put me down for one of those, please!'

Once I was clear of the cancer in 2020, I started working again, and I got some exciting news. My manager, Alan Field, told me that the Palladium had been in touch asking about me maybe doing another joint show or two with Des O'Connor. 'Would Des be up for it?' he wondered.

'I'm sure he will!' I replied. 'But let me ask him.' I put the phone down and then I called Des straight away. His wife, Jodie, picked up. 'Hello, love,' I said. 'Can I speak to Des, please?'

'I wish you could, Jimmy,' she replied. 'But he had a fall at home last week, so he's been in hospital. And he died in his sleep last night.'

And, just like that, another one was gone.

* * *

I might be in my eighties now but I still try to keep busy. I still like to try new things when I can, especially in work. And, at the end of 2021, I got a cracking gig when I was invited to perform on a cruise ship sailing from Southampton to the Canary Islands.

I was on the *Queen Mary 2* with my old mucker Lulu and Russell Watson, the opera singer. I told a few gags and stories in the onboard Royal Court Theatre as we sailed for twelve days, calling at Lanzarote, Tenerife and Cadiz, as well as a couple of stops in Portugal. We caught some winter sun and had a great laugh. Nice work if you can get it!

As you grow older, the time you spend with old friends becomes more precious. Back in England, in September 2022 I attended a tribute lunch to Michael Parkinson at Lord's cricket ground. Parky was always as mad on cricket as I am on golf, so this honour must have meant a lot to him. Well, I *know* it did.

And if spending time with old friends is precious, so is meeting new ones. Especially if you've always admired them.

I walked into the function room, said hello to Parky, and a feller came up to me. It was Barry Humphries.

'Hello, Jimmy,' Barry greeted me. 'How nice to meet you at last. My God, what a career you've had!'

'Thank you,' I said. 'And it's wonderful to meet *you*. I'll never forget seeing you when I first moved to London from Liverpool, in 1964. You'd just started being Edna Everage – you were chucking gladioli off the stage. And I was crying with laughter.'

'Christ, that was nearly sixty years ago!' He laughed. He was a smashing guy and we got on like a house on fire. I had such a good time that lovely afternoon at Lord's, having a drink and swapping gags and stories with Parky and Barry Humphries.

And yet, in less than a year, they were both dead.

I saw Michael just a week before he died, in August 2023. I spent an hour or two at his home in Bray with him. Then I thought he was looking a bit tired, so I told him, 'I'll be off now. I'll let you get some rest.'

'OK,' said Parky. 'Thanks for coming. Lunch next week?'

'I'd love to,' I said. 'You arrange it and I'll be there.' But, sadly, it wasn't to be.

I went on *Good Morning Britain* to pay tribute to Michael. I said what a fine journalist he was and that he was, for me, the greatest television interviewer ever. 'Simply the best,' I reflected. 'He listened, and he could be serious, and he had serious people on his shows.' I added that he was a modest man and delightful company.

I expressed my gratitude to Parky for having me on his show so many times and helping to give me a boost and turn my career around. In fact, I got quite emotional as I tried to explain what he'd meant to me. 'He was a giant of our industry,' I said. 'I'm getting choked now. He was a giant, and he was a giant friend to me.' And so he was.

I lost somebody even closer to me in the same year. Norma, my sister, died. Norma had lasted well – she was nearly ninety – and yet, somehow, it still came as a shock. She'd stayed up in Liverpool, living her life and raising her two lads, but I'd seen her as often as I could. We'd always stayed close.

Norma was the last person left in my life who'd been there with me, and for me, from the day I was born. I went up and spoke at her funeral: just personal things, and memories. Norma had told me that she wanted to be buried next to Mum and Dad. So, I took care of that. She's gone … but she'll always be my big sister.

I was still upset about Norma when I had a mishap: a local driving accident in Coombe. A feller was coming the other way. I swerved to avoid him and bashed into a couple of parked cars. *Oops!* I should have stopped, of course, but I didn't. Why? My head was all over the place. Grief does that to you.

I wrote a letter to the court apologising and pleading guilty to driving without due care and attention. I got a fine, which was fair enough. And, you know what? That was my first court case since I'd half-inched Terry-Thomas's cigarette holder in Liverpool in 1960. So I don't think you could call me a habitual criminal …

* * *

There's an old showbiz saying about leaving people with a smile on their faces. And that is exactly what I want to do. This is a life story called *Laughter Is the Best Medicine* and I don't want to finish it off bringing everyone down by talking about death and losing loved ones. I want to finish it on a high.

And, luckily, I can. Because I've been fortunate enough to have a couple of great late career, and *life*, events recently.

Early in 2024, my manager, Alan Field, called me with some extraordinary news that I could hardly believe. Barry Manilow, the American superstar and one of the greatest light entertainers of all time, was doing a farewell tour. He was coming to England, and would be doing one night in Manchester and fourteen at the London Palladium.

What did this have to do with me? Well, as it happened, quite a lot. Because, Alan told me down the phone, Barry wanted me to support him.

Me? Yes, me. Incredible as it seemed, Barry still remembered me introducing him and us bantering on the stage during that last episode of *Live at the Palladium* in 1988. And now, more than a third of a century on, he wanted a comic to tell a few gags and warm up for him on his final tour, and wondered if I'd like to do it.

Well, it was the most unexpected work offer I'd received since Terry Miller phoned in 1963 to tell me I'd been asked on *Sunday Night at the London Palladium*! But it didn't take a second to work out my answer. It was a complete no-brainer. 'Yes, of course,' I said to Alan. 'Tell him that I'd *love* to do it. It would be an honour.'

And it was. It was great. It looked a funny bill: Barry Manilow and Jimmy Tarbuck. I'll be honest, it seemed a bit odd even to me. But it worked. Barry is of a similar vintage to me so a lot of our fans are roughly the same age. And the other thing they have in common is they're up for a great night out.

Barry Manilow shows are joyful experiences. He's a true showman, very razzle-dazzle and glam, and he gives his fans a great, uplifting show. They arrive in a fantastic mood, knowing they're about to have a brilliant time, so they're in the right state of mind for a comic to make them roar.

And that was what I did. Barry and I started off with one night at the Co-op Live, a huge new arena venue in Manchester. It holds more than 20,000 people. I'll be honest with you: at the risk of sounding coarse, I was seriously considering going on in brown trousers. At the age of eighty-four, it was the biggest crowd I'd ever played to. And it was a thrill.

Then it was time for the Palladium. From 23 May, we did two weeks, taking us up to the end of the first week in June. Barry's fans were the loudest, most excited, most dolled-up and exuberant audiences I'd seen in my six decades of treading that legendary stage. And they were fantastic. Every show was a delight.

And every night I did what I've done each time I've played the Palladium. I put my suit on, walked down the corridor, and checked myself in the floor-to-ceiling mirror just before you reach the stage. The same check that I've been doing, on and off, since 1963:

Are my trouser creases sharp? *Yep.*

Is my tie straight? *Yep.*

Are my flies done up? *Yep.*

OK, then – it's showtime!

And every performer does the same thing. Every entertainer who's ever trod the Palladium boards has done it, from Frank Sinatra to Bob Hope to Bing Crosby to Ella Fitzgerald to Nat King Cole to Vera Lynn to Arthur Askey to Ken Dodd to The Beatles to Bob Dylan to Shirley Bassey to Tom Jones to Cilla. *I mean, the stories that mirror could tell …*

The shows were terrific and Barry was unbelievable. Nearly every night, I stayed until the end of his set. Why would I leave? It was life-affirming! Barry couldn't go on at one show because he had a bad throat. The theatre told everyone to hold on to their tickets and we did a matinee for them instead. He was a pro. A gent. A toff.

One night, just before the end of our run, I came off after my set, with the crowd still cheering, and walked back down the corridor. Barry was coming towards me, looking like at least two million dollars. He gave me his dazzling Vegas smile.

'James, did you kill them?' he asked.

'Yes, I killed them.'

'Awesome!' he beamed. 'Did you do anything special tonight?'

'Yes,' I said. 'I did three of your songs.'

'Three of my …?' Barry's grin faded, just for a second. A couple of the members of his band were hanging out near us in the corridor. He called them over.

'Hey, guys, has Jimmy been singing my songs?' he asked. Unseen to him, I winked at one of them.

'Yes, boss,' the feller said, totally straight-faced. 'Nearly all of them ...'

'What? You ...?' Barry stared at me. I stared back ... and burst out laughing. His band members began roaring as well. And then Barry joined in.

'OK, you got me there,' he admitted. 'Good one!'

What an experience those Barry Manilow shows were. I'd never have imagined I'd be lucky enough to get offered them, but I'll tell you this for nothing: they made a very old man very, very happy.

EPILOGUE

PAULINE! WHERE'S THE CRISPS?

The dates with Barry Manilow whetted my appetite for doing live shows again. Now that I'm not on the telly so regularly these days, I have more time and scope for setting a few weeks aside and going out on the road. And so, in 2025, at eighty-five years young, I carried on with a UK tour I'd begun the year before.

I gave the tour the same name as my one-off telly special, back in the nineties: *An Evening with Jimmy Tarbuck*. There was a good reason for that. Some people have come to my shows and supported me throughout my career. I wanted to give them the chance to ask me questions, and for me to have the opportunity to answer them.

They were nice, laid-back shows, a few hundred people a night in some lovely theatres up and down the country. And, you know what? I had the time of my life on that tour. In a way, it reminded me – not that I've ever forgotten – why it is that I do what I do, and why I love doing it so much. It took me right back to the basics.

Let me tell you, going out on tour at eighty-five is very different from doing it at twenty-five. In what way? Well, I know what I'm doing so much better. I've got a lifetime of stage experience to draw on. I'm not running on adrenaline and nervous energy any more. I can pace myself. And, in a way, it allows me to enjoy it even more.

I took the chance to tell some cracking jokes. Some nights, I walked out and told the audience about advice that Peter Ustinov once gave me about how long a show should last. 'He told me, "Never do any longer than it takes you to make love,"' I explained. 'So, thank you and goodnight!'

I did a few gentle wind-ups of the audience. They all expect it. They'd feel let down if I didn't. A lot of fans have grown old with me, so I'd look mock-shocked as I gazed out at a sea of bald heads, grey hair and blue rinses. 'Here we go!' I'd say. 'Yet another crowd sponsored by Saga: Sex Annually, Generally August.'

Or I might pick on some harmless old-timer sitting down the front with his missus. 'Did you ever meet Elvis?' I'd ask.

'No.'

'Don't worry, it won't be long now.'

As well as telling gags, I reminisced about highlights from my life. I talked about going to school with Lennon and him telling gags about me having half-crowns jangling in my pockets. I told them about Mum telling me, 'Wash your knees!' before Dad took me to the Empire, Liverpool, to see Laurel and Hardy.

I remembered my first ever stand-up set, when I got unwillingly shoved up onstage at Butlin's in 1958. I chatted about watching Larry Parnes discover Billy Fury, compering Marty Wilde and Cliff Richard tours in my teens and, later, meeting Sinatra in Miami and Tom Jones introducing me to Elvis in Vegas.

The crowds laughed as I recalled Tommy Cooper asking the Queen for her FA Cup final tickets, and Les Dawson asking Charles how they'd fit his ears on the postage stamps. I showed old bits of film: me bursting through Tarby's Wall on my first night hosting at the Palladium, and nearly taking David Frost's head off with my penalty at Wembley.

When people put their hands up to ask questions, they wanted to know about hanging out with Cilla in the Cavern, or coaxing Judy Garland onstage at the Palladium, or just who my favourite ever Liverpool players are. I was happy to tell them. After the shows, I hung out and signed things. I had a lovely time and I think they did, too.

It wasn't only the shows that I enjoyed. I liked being back on the road and roaming up and down the land. I went back to the magnificent old City Varieties Theatre in Leeds and chuckled to myself as I recalled, as a lad, cheekily introducing a stripper and getting a smack in the chops for my pains.

And *I met people.* That's what I've always liked doing. I went to Keswick, right up in the Lake District, a beautiful part of the country that I've always adored. Before my show, I went for a stroll on my own along the prom and bumped into a group of elderly ladies walking small dogs.

They all greeted me: 'Ooh, hello, Jimmy!'

'Hello, ladies,' I replied. 'If you don't mind me asking, why do you all have such tiny dogs?'

'We daren't have big ones,' one woman said. 'They pull us over.' And I had a giggle to myself, imagining a row of old dears all getting dragged into a lake. Meeting folk like that made the tour a joy.

I had to postpone a couple of dates for minor health issues but, as I write, my *Evening with Jimmy Tarbuck* tour is still going on, I'm glad to say. When it started, I was telling all and sundry it would be my final tour. Now that it's nearly finished, I'm not so sure. I've loved it so much … and performing live has always been my life. It's a lot to give up.

So, is it my farewell tour, my last goodbye, or will I be the comeback kid yet again? All I can tell you for now is … *watch this space.*

* * *

Writing this book over the last few months has brought home to me how much I've done in my life. I've certainly crammed a lot in. Sometimes, I find it all hard to believe as I think back over my past. Did all those things *really* happen to me? And, as they clearly did … *why me?*

I guess one reason I've had the life I've had is I've always been confident. I've always believed in myself. I don't know exactly where I got that self-confidence from, but I'll tell you this: I'm so glad that I've had it. Because it's taken me places that, otherwise, I might never have got to.

Without it, I might never have got down to London and to the Palladium. I might never have got to make people laugh not only in this country but in the United States, Hong Kong and Australia. It showed me that laughter is the best medicine not only where I come from, but all over the world.

And there's another important reason that I've been lucky enough to have the life I've had. And her name is Pauline.

Pauline has been a rock to me for sixty-six years now. She's held our family together and raised three fantastic kids. The great thing about Pauline is that, unlike me, she's never been bothered, or starry-eyed, about show business. She can take it or leave it. Pauline is still exactly the same cool, level-headed girl from The Dingle that I met at the Cavern.

And thank God for that.

Nowadays, Pauline and I have a great day-to-day life together in Coombe. We see our kids and our grandkids all the time. They're all doing great. Our Cheryl is a successful art director and interior designer. She's styled on TV ads and movies, worked for magazines and written kids' stories for BBC TV and radio. You name it, Cheryl's done it.

So has our Liza. She's always busy. Each weekend, Pauline and I sit down with a cuppa to listen to her Saturday evening show on Radio 2. It makes me roar whenever I hear Liza give the nation her impersonation of me, at home, yelling:

'PAULINE! WHERE'S THE CRISPS?'

I'll admit, it's not a bad impression. Pauline agrees. And she should know.

James has worked in fashion, film, TV, music management and more besides. He runs what they call a 'creative content production studio' (look, don't ask me!) and is very good at it. James, his wife Sacha and their three kids live on a beautiful island just off Mozambique. But they're over a lot so we still see plenty of them.

There's just one way that James has proved a profound disappointment to me. I always hoped he'd be a Liverpool nut like me, but when he was a lad, some of his chums took him to Chelsea and his head got turned. *Ah, well.* James makes up for that by being a far better golfer than I ever was.

I still play a lot of golf. Why wouldn't I? I've still got that fantastic course right over my garden fence. I hit balls most days. I can't hit them *as far* as I used to, but that's OK. I still love it. I play nine holes with Pauline and she regularly beats me. Well, there's no shame in that. She's a very good player.

James helps me put on an annual charity tournament at Coombe Hill and I still run my Jimmy Tarbuck Classic in Portugal. Over the last twenty-plus years, we've raised more than two million pounds for the Refúgio Aboim Ascensão children's home for disabled kids in Faro. And I'm very proud of that.

What else do I do nowadays? Well, I speak to the showbiz mates I have left as much as I can. There are still a few other dinosaurs prowling around! Tom Jones calls me up, more days than not, to see how I'm doing and tell me what he's up to. He always invites me to his shows. Tom's a true pal, and he always will be.

I'm still mad about Liverpool FC. I never miss a game on TV. I love us being champions again – up where we belong! We've had great managers over the years: Bill Shankly, Bob Paisley, Joe Fagan, Kenny Dalglish. And, for me, the current boss, Arne Slot, and the feller before him, Jürgen Klopp, are right up there with them.

I've had a fantastic life. It's been wonderful. Would I like to do it all again? *Yes, please!* I wish I was just starting out today. I've had the most unbelievable luck – Lucky Jim? You can say that again! – but I believe that luck rides with you. That luck comes from the heart: from being sincere. And I sincerely say, to the British people:

Thank you.

IMAGE CREDITS

All from Jimmy Tarbuck's private collection except for the below.

Plate Section 1
P. 1 bottom © Barry Farrell
P. 2 middle left © Trinity Mirror / Mirrorpix, middle right © Rodney R. Green, bottom © Mirrorpix
P. 3 top © Daily Herald Archive, middle right © PA Images, middle left and bottom © Mirrorpix
P. 4 all © Trinity Mirror/Mirrorpix
P. 5 top left © Pic Photos Ltd, top right and bottom © ITV/ Shutterstock
P. 6 top © J.E. Harvey, middle © Popperfoto
P. 7 top left © Popperfoto, top right © Mirrorpix

Plate Section 2
P. 1 top and middle © TV Times
P. 2 top and bottom left © ANL/Shutterstock
P. 3 middle right © Harry Ormersher/Popperfoto
P. 4 bottom © ITV/Shutterstock
P. 5 bottom © Keith Hailey/Popperfoto
P. 6 bottom © PA Images
P. 7 middle left © Richard Young/Shutterstock, middle right © Mike Floyd/Daily Mail/Shutterstock
P. 8 top © Ken McKay/ITV/Shutterstock, middle © Dave Benett, bottom left © PA Images, bottom right © WENN Rights Ltd